The
DEACONS
HANDBOOK

Library of Congress Catalog Card No. 80-66860
ISBN 0-934874-01-8

Printed in the U.S.A.

The DEACONS HANDBOOK

A MANUAL OF STEWARDSHIP

By
Gerard Berghoef
Lester De Koster

Christian's Library Press
Grand Rapids, Michigan

First Printing - October, 1980.
Second Printing - February, 1981.

THE AUTHORS

Mr. Gerard Berghoef is a native of
the Netherlands, who emigrated to
the United States early in the 1950s.
He is presently a furniture manufac-
turing executive, and has served the
Christian Reformed Church as an
elder for twelve years.

Dr. Lester DeKoster is a native of
Michigan, and has been professor of
speech and director of the library for
Calvin College and Seminary, Grand
Rapids, Michigan. He retired in
1980 as Editor of *The Banner*,
official weekly publication of the
Christian Reformed Church.

The authors have previously published *The Elders Handbook,* A
Practical Guide for Church Leaders.

The authors are grateful to
our wives, Audrey Berghoef and Ruth DeKoster
for wise counsel and persistent support, and to
Pastor Verlyn Verbrugge, Southern Heights
Christian Reformed Church, Kalamazoo,
Michigan, for insightful criticism and advice.

"Let your loins be girded and your lamps burning, and be like men who are waiting for their master to come home for the marriage feast, so that they may open to him at once when he comes and knocks. Blessed are those servants whom the master finds awake when he comes; truly, I say to you, and he will come and serve them. If he comes in the second watch, or in the third, and finds them so, blessed are those servants!

"Peter said, 'Lord, are you telling this parable for us or for all?' And the Lord said, 'Who then is the faithful and wise steward, whom his master will set over his household, to give them their portion of food at the proper time? Blessed is the servant whom his master when he comes will find so doing.'" (Luke 12:35-38; 41-43)

TABLE OF CONTENTS

PREFACE

"As each has received a gift, employ it for one another, as good stewards of God's varied grace: whoever speaks, as one who utters the oracles of God; whoever renders service, as one who renders it by the strength which God supplies; in order that in everything God may be glorified through Jesus Christ. To him belong glory and dominion for ever and ever. Amen" (I Peter 4:10-11)

Life, time, talent, and all that each of us has are gifts of God.

The right stewardship of all these gifts is what life is for.

The textbook to right stewardship is the Bible.

The school for instruction in the Bible is the Church.

The executive agent for good stewardship in the Church is the Deacon.

This *Handbook* is an effort to serve the Deacon in his service of the Church.

We use the term "diaconate" for deacons as a body, and the term "diakonia" as descriptive of the work that deacons do.

"It is required of stewards," St. Paul writes, "that they be found trustworthy" (I Cor. 4:2). The aim of this *Handbook* is to challenge deacons to large dimensions of trustworthy service in their important office.

· May the Lord to that end bless it through His Spirit!

                                                              The Authors

INTRODUCTION

"From the fig tree, learn its lesson..." (Matt. 24:32)

DIAKONIA: FROM LEAVES TO FRUIT

The parable of the fig tree is a parable for deacons. The truth it etches upon our conscience is a diaconal truth.

Here is the story, as told by St. Matthew:

"In the morning, as he was returning to the city, he was hungry. And seeing a fig tree by the wayside he went to it, and found nothing on it but leaves only" (Matt. 21:18).

Trees bear leaves for themselves.

Trees bear fruit for others.

Diakonia hangs upon these two correlative truths: leaves for self, fruit for others!

A congregation well furnished with plant, facilities, and staff is the richly leafed tree. How well that congregation, through its diaconate, cares for its own needy and for the poor within its reach is one key measure of the fruit which this tree bears.

Returning to Jerusalem from Bethany, the Lord was hungry. He looked to the flourishing tree for sustenance. So now He looks to the Church for fruit.

How does the Lord look to His own Body, the Church, for fruit now? He looks with the eyes of the needy, both within and without the congregation. He puts it unmistakably: "I was hungry...I was thirsty...I was a stranger...I was naked...I was sick...I was in prison" (Matt. 25:35-36). God, who possesses everything and needs nothing for Himself, appears in the person of our neighbor so that we can serve Him with the fruit of our faith. For the congregation as a Body this implies serving Him through the diaconate.

No matter how flourishing the tree, the measure of its worth to the Lord lies in its bearing fruit for the hungry, the thirsty, the stranger, the naked, the sick, the victims of injustice, and the forlorn. Such fruit-bearing is blessed: "Come, O blessed of my Father, inherit the kingdom prepared for you from the foundation of the world..." (Matt.

13

25:34). The active diaconate is a double blessing for and to the Body it serves: 1) the needy are supplied, and 2) the Body accumulates blessing in heaven.

But the Body which neglects fruit-bearing is judged: "Depart from me, you cursed, into the eternal fire prepared for the devil and his angels; for I was hungry and you gave me no food, I was thirsty and you gave me no drink, I was a stranger and you did not welcome me, naked and you did not clothe me, sick and in prison and you did not visit me" (Matt. 25:41-43). And this is precisely the fate of the fruitless fig tree: "And he said to it, 'May no fruit ever come upon you again' " (Matt. 21:19).

Because it bore no fruit, the tree had no claim to its leaves. And St. Mark records that as Jesus and His disciples passed by the cursed fig tree the next day, "they saw the fig tree withered away to its roots" (Mark 11:20). St. Matthew reports that the withering begins even as the curse is made (Matt. 21:19). Glorious foliage is no substitute for the fruit of good works.

A great challenge, and grave burden, open to the diaconate in this parable. As agents of fruit-bearing, deacons are duty bound to stimulate congregational obedience to the Biblical demands for cheerful giving (II Cor. 9:7). And the conscientious diaconate cannot rest until a respectable ratio is maintained between the luxury of the Body's leaves and the distribution of the Body's fruits.

One thing more: St. Mark reports that it was not, in fact, "the season for figs" when the Lord sought fruit from the well-leafed tree (Mark 11:13).

What does this mean for us?

Commentators explain that the fig tree bears fruit before being fully leafed out; that is, the presence of leaves implies the presence of fruit. Given the leaf, the fruit should be there, or the leaf is a fraud. So, too, for the Church. Given an impressive plant or elegant services, the Body should produce an equally rich harvest of fruit, presented to the Lord as He waits in the persons of the needy.

But St. Mark means to teach more than horticulture.

The Lord expects fruit in an un-natural season, too. He expects, then, the super-natural! Fruit beyond the natural capacity of the tree to furnish!

So, too, with His Body the Church.

Self-service is natural to us. The introverted Church, proud of its facilities—or the introverted Church proud of its lack of facilities, the

14

sin is the same—determines for itself how the Lord is best served. Leaves luxuriate.

But what the Church is unequal to, naturally, becomes possible supernaturally through the power of its Head and the presence of His Spirit.

When leaf-bearing turns into fruit-bearing, it is because the Lord's Spirit has come to apply the Lord's Word to the hearts, minds, and consciences of the Body. The deacon who is disturbed by the difficulty of coaxing fruit out of believers must turn again and again to the pulpit for more powerful preaching of the Word, and to prayer for more abundant yielding to the Spirit. Then by this super-natural strength he must seek to draw out and distribute the fruits of such indwelling love!

A challenging task!

A rewarding task!

We invite you to study its working-out together with us in the pages that follow.

PART I

STEWARDSHIP

Chapter 1.

THE FUNDAMENTALS OF STEWARDSHIP

The practice of stewardship is the supreme challenge of the Christian life. The Bible makes stewardship the key to Christian behavior.

A. *THE STEWARD*

Who is a steward?

What is a steward?

Eliezer was steward over the vast household of Abraham. That is to say, Eliezer was in charge of all that Abraham had (Gen. 24:1).

Joseph was steward of the household of Potiphar, officer of Pharoah, who "put him in charge of all that he had" (Gen. 39:4).

The steward owns nothing and governs everything. To him the master commits control of all that he possesses. Of all, that is, of the master's material goods. This high and responsible office, mentioned in the first book of the Bible, appears still in the parables of Jesus: "There was a rich man who had a steward..." (Luke 16:1); "And when evening came, the owner of the vineyard said to his steward..." (Matt. 20:8).

"It is required of stewards," St. Paul writes of his own calling, "that they be found trustworthy" (I Cor. 4:2).

And St. Peter applies the concept of stewardship to the Christian life, saying: "As each has received a gift, employ it for one another, as good stewards of God's varied grace: whoever speaks, as one who utters oracles of God; whoever renders service, as one who renders it by the strength which God supplies; in order that in everything God may be glorified through Jesus Christ" (I Pet. 4:10-11).

The parables of the talents (Matt. 25:14-30) and of the pounds (Luke 19:11-27) show that the steward will be required to render account of all that has been placed under his stewardship.

God makes man steward of His world. Who is man, asks the Psalmist? And answers: "Thou hast made him little less than God, and dost crown him with glory and honor. Thou hast given him dominion over the works of thy hands; thou hast put all things under his feet..." (Ps. 8:5-6).

God makes man the master of His temporal household. Like all stewards, man is not the owner. He is the overseer. For three score years and ten, more or less as the case may be, each of us is steward over those talents and those pounds alloted us by divine Providence.

And at the end comes the accounting: "Now after a long time the master of those servants came and settled accounts with them..." (Matt. 25:19); "When he returned, having received the kingly power, he commanded these servants to whom he had given the money, to be called to him, that he might know what they had gained by trading..." (Luke 19:15).

As each has managed his stewardship, so will he be judged: "Well done, good servant," or, "But as for these enemies of mine, who did not want me to reign over them, bring them here and slay them before me" (Luke 19:17, 27).

The quality of stewardship depends upon obedience to the master's will. The steward who does not obey the master's law rejects the master's authority and serves another.

Our stewardship is the test: do we mean to serve God or Mammon, the Lord or the Devil?

Stewardship is, we repeat, key to the Christian life—and death, and judgment.

B. *BASIC PRINCIPLES OF STEWARDSHIP*

The fundamentals of stewardship as revealed in the Scriptures are briefly stated:

1. All things are made and sustained by God: "In the beginning God created the heavens and the earth" (Gen. 1:1). "The earth is the Lord's and the fulness thereof, the world and those who dwell therein..." (Ps. 24:1). "Behold," says Moses, "to the Lord your God belong heaven and the heaven of heavens, the earth with all that is in it..." (Deut. 10:14). All is God's, including man himself. This is the first and most basic fundamental of stewardship. It is a truth of revelation that the deacon must never forget!

2. God also gives and sustains human life, as He sets man within

His world: "Then the Lord God formed man of dust from the ground, and breathed into his nostrils the breath of life; and man became a living soul" (Gen. 2:7). "In his hand is the life of every living thing and the breath of a mankind" (Job 12:10). God gives us life, and time, and a world in which to live it! Still all is from Him. Deacons, remember!

3. God decides when to terminate the life He gives: "Thou turnest man back to the dust, and sayest, 'Turn back, O children of men!' " (Ps. 90:3). And God sustains all the moments between birth and death: "My times are in thy hand" (Ps. 31:15).

4. God determines upon the distribution of goods received by each during his lifetime: "The Lord makes poor and makes rich; he brings low, he also exalts" (I Sam. 2:7). What each of us has to steward, what each receives as talent or pound, is wholly from God! This sobering truth deacons may not easily teach themselves. They will find it no easier to teach others. Everyone believes that whatever he has was acquired by the sweat of his own brow or the shrewdness of his own wit. But this is not what the Scripture teaches: "Beware lest you say in your heart, 'My power and the might of my hand have gotten me this wealth.' You shall remember the Lord your God, for it is he who gives you power to get wealth" (Deut. 8:17). There are no self-made men; there are only God-made men! All that we have is His gift! "The blessing of Jehovah, it maketh rich..." (Prov. 10:22). The steward must first of all know whose goods they are which he administers, and recognize that whatever he has in his hands comes to him from the Master. Not to know this is to risk idolatry, as the Prophet says of Israel: "And she did not know that it was I who gave her the grain, the wine, and the oil, and who lavished upon her silver and gold which they used for Baal" (Hos. 2:8). It is pagan to think that things come by chance. It is self-idolatry to think that possessions come by our own earning. It is Christian to know that all we have comes as a gift of God. This knowledge, too, is basic to right understanding of stewardship. Indeed, if we owned that which we are called to steward, we would no longer be stewards but masters!

5. Because He is creator, owner, and master of all, God alone sets the requirements for stewardship of His goods and world. Between Himself and those who would be His faithful stewards, God makes covenant: "Listen to my voice, and do all that I command you. So shall you be my people, and I will be your God" (Jer. 11:4).

6. The revealed law governing stewardship comes to expression in the Ten Commandments. The meaning of the Commandments is expound-

21

ed by the Prophets. It is repeated by Jesus Christ, and applied by the Apostles. The whole Bible is the book of this covenant: "...do all that I command you. So shall you be my people, and I will be your God." Our Lord sums up the law and the prophets in a sentence: "So whatever you wish that men would do to you, do so to them; for this is the law and the prophets" (Matt. 7:12).

7. To every steward there open two ways: "Enter by the narrow gate; for the gate is wide and the way is easy, that leads to destruction, and those who enter by it are many. For the gate is narrow and the way is hard, that leads to life, and those who find it are few" (Matt. 7:13-14).

8. And finally, both ways come to judgment: "And I saw the dead, great and small, standing before the throne, and books were opened. Also another book was opened, which is the book of life. And the dead were judged by what was written in the books, by what they had done" (Rev. 20:12). The Bible opens with the days of creation and ends with the day of judgment. And between them lies, for every one, the period of stewardship, when God makes each of us responsible for the use of His gifts according to His directions.

These are the fundamentals of the doctrine of stewardship. They explain why stewardship is key to the Christian life.

C. SUMMARY

Let us summarize briefly, now, the basics of stewardship:

1. God creates, sustains, and thus owns all things, man included. Not only in the beginning, but always. Every child born into the world receives life from God.

2. God brings us to life within His vast and beautiful and challenging world, and permits us to use and enjoy all that He sustains.

3. He intends, however, that His will shall govern our wills and His desires control our desires. He reveals His will in the inspired Scriptures. As we walk in His world, His law shall be lamp to our feet and light upon our path (Ps. 119:105).

4. Our use of God's property, whether as faithful or rebellious stewards, is, therefore, what life is all about.

5. Our obedience, or disobedience, to God's will revealed in His Word becomes the basis for the Last Judgment, prelude to heaven or hell.

D. *DIFFICULTIES: CREATION*

The basic tenets of stewardship can give rise to problems and objections which deacons may meet. We discuss some of them here:

1. The doctrine of creation is, of course, confronted by the theory of evolution. This theory is now advocated with far less assurance than once it was, but it still sets the secular trend. The deacon cannot hope to demonstrate the truth of creationism before he acts upon the truth of stewardship. Without engaging in endless dispute, the deacon wisely proceeds upon faith in the Scriptures. God is creator. Man, too, is His creation, not only the first man, but each and every person born into the world. Whether or not the Biblical account permits an interpretation which allows for long periods of time in the process of creation, the crux of the issue is that *God made all that is,* that He made man in His own Image, and that man, made perfect, chose to disobey and fall into sin. All this is revelation. All else is speculation. Far better to take the Word at what it says than lose the truth and clarity of Genesis in a haze of shifting "science".

2. Do not be misled, either, by secular depreciations of the earth as but a tiny speck of dust lost in an immense universe. Remember that Genesis teaches that God spoke the universe into being. When the infinite and majestic God speaks, He says *something*! Small wonder that the glories of the starry skies stretch far beyond our comprehension. Are you surprised that galaxies and universes and mysteries happen when God speaks! Leave it to those of no faith to belittle man in comparison with the stars made expressly for man's delight. Recall that of all created things, only man is made in God's Image: "...for God made man in His own image" (Gen. 9:6). And about the stars God says: "Lift up your eyes on high and see: who created these? He who brings out their host by number, calling them all by name; by the greatness of his might, and because he is strong in power not one is missing" (Is. 40:26). And, the Prophet goes on to say, far from demeaning us, let the wonder of the heavens excite our confidence in their Creator, for He is "the everlasting God, the creator of the ends of the earth. He does not faint or grow weary...He gives power to the faint, and to him who has no might he increases strength..." (Is. 40:28-29). The unending extent of space, the throbbing energy, the sparkling fire, the utter mystery—all these are not to demean us, but to awaken us to whose Image we bear and upon whose strength we can depend.

3. In making His universe, God lays down patterns of behavior to

it. We call these patterns "natural law". Do not let natural law intrude between you and the active presence of God all about us. "My Father is working," our Lord says, "and I am working" (John 5:17). We call this working "natural law". God, not meteorology, sends the weather. God gives the leaves, awakens the sun, rides on the storm: "...to the snow he says, 'Fall on the earth'; and to the shower and the rain, 'Be strong'...By the breath of God ice is given, and the broad waters are frozen fast. He loads the thick cloud with moisture; the clouds scatter his lightning. They turn round and round by his guidance, to accomplish all that he commands them on the face of the habitable world" (Job 37:6, 10-12).

The doctrine of stewardship is impressed upon us by a vivid sense of God's immanent activity in all that we often take for granted or account as natural behavior.

E. *DIFFICULTIES: LIFE*

1. None chooses to be born. That is a decision made before birth. We did not ask for life. God gives it to us. Medicine employs all that is now known of "natural law" to prolong life against disease, but God numbers our days: "the number of his months is with thee, and thou hast appointed his bounds that he cannot pass" (Job. 14:5). The time for the tests of stewardship is not ours to measure, nor enlarge: "And which of you by being anxious can add one cubit to his span of life?" (Matt. 6:27). The hoarding of goods which competes with stewardship roots in anxiety about the morrow, an anxiety our Lord rejects because our tomorrows are in God's hand.

2. The time and place of our birth, our family, race, talents, looks— all these are by God's design. Some are born to wealth; others see the light of day in the clutch of destitution. Where and how life is given is God's choice, our lot. Neither envy of the rich nor scorn for the poor befits our heritage, for where we were born was not of our choosing— and envy or scorn falls upon Him who made us.

F. *DIFFICULTIES: FREEDOM*

1. God holds us responsible for our stewardship because He has made us free. But freedom cannot be harmonized with "natural law". We are not patterned, as are the stars and the atoms, by a divine activity so consistent that we speak of it as "law". God respects the

liberty of His Image-bearer. God does not invade the human spirit. Demons take possession if they can; God stands "at the door and knocks" (Rev. 3:20). With infinite delicacy, the Creator respects the integrity of the man He has made. But this cannot be explained. A freedom explained is not freedom, for explanation involves cause and effect. Freedom has no cause; it is a divine gift.

2. But the atoms of our bodies obey natural law. This is the foundation of medicine. Yet the self inter-twined with the flesh of the body is free. And because free, therefore responsible for the stewardship it exercises. This we do not explain; this we affirm: every command in the Scriptures assumes freedom.

3. The mystery of freedom is further complicated by the "mystery of iniquity" (II Thess. 2:7). How sin entered God's good creation is told us in Genesis (chapter 3). But explanation for sin there is none: "the mystery of iniquity." But as sinner, man lost an aspect of his freedom. No longer, after the defection of Adam, could man obey the laws of stewardship simply through his own choice: "As it is written, 'None is righteous, no, not one; no one understands, no one seeks for God. All have turned aside, together they have gone wrong; no one does good, not even one' " (Rom. 3:10-12).

4. What fallen man, then, could not do for himself—properly use God's goods—Jesus Christ makes possible for us, dying for our sins that in Him we might have newness of life (Rom. 6:4), a newness manifest in stewardship—that is, in what the Bible calls good works: "For we are his workmanship, created in Christ Jesus for good works, which God prepared beforehand, that we should walk in them" (Eph. 2:10). Stewardship, freely chosen in accord with God's law, is possible in Christ Jesus. Not that our works save us (Rom. 3:28), but rather that we are saved for good works—that is, for stewardship.

G. DIFFICULTIES: GETTING THE WORD

1. How shall the law go forth? How shall mankind hear the demand for stewardship?

Through the Church. As explained in our *Elders Handbook,* God lays upon the Church the responsibility for educating in stewardship: "Go therefore and make disciples of all nations, baptizing them in the name of the Father and of the Son and of the Holy Spirit, teaching them to observe all that I have commanded you..." (Matt. 28:19-20). Observe from this passage, commonly called The Great Commission:

a. The mandate is given to the Apostles, founders of the New Testament Church.

b. Through them the Church is required to disciple all nations; a disciple being one who follows the teaching of a master. Believers are to be Christ's disciples, taken into the Church by baptism.

c. The Church is commanded to teach disciples to do all that the Lord has commanded; that is, teach all believers His application and interpretation of the law and the prophets—in other words, the governing principles of stewardship.

d. The primary task of the Church, then, if to proclaim the Word which generates new birth, and to teach the Word which governs the life of stewardship.

Obviously, the work of the deacon will be most successfully accomplished whenever and wherever the Church most obediently is...the Church!

H. *DIFFICULTIES: WHAT LIFE IS ALL ABOUT*

The meaning of life is the subject of endless speculation and confusion among those who fail to seek life's purpose from the Giver of life. Those looking for light on life from words other than the Word of God can find countless books, articles, lectures, study groups, exotic religions, gurus and "masters" crying out to confuse them. But only God knows why He gives us life, and time to use life, and all His gifts, along with the talents to employ them aright. And God tells....

In the Scriptures, and,

Through the Church, which He sustains for the purpose of teaching mankind from the Bible what life is, indeed, all about.

Life and time are God's primary gifts. To live is to have time. To have time is to live. Time enshrines what we do with life. There is no doing over. Past is past!

What our doing pours into the mold of time: this is what life is all about.

Whom our doing serves, God or mammon, the Lord's Word or the devil's lie: this is the crucial choice for which time gives life opportunity: "...choose this day whom you will serve..." (Josh. 24:15). Time always registers today. Today is always opportunity, and obligation, for choice: "But exhort one another every day, as long as it is called 'today,' that none of you may be hardened by the deceitfulness of sin" (Heb. 3:13). Jesus said, "We must work the works of him who sent me, while it is day; night comes, when no one can work" (John 9:4).

To live is to be confronted by choice. Choice emerges in doing. Time crystallizes deed, in testimony to the presence or absence of saving faith, in anticipation of the judgment.

Life is the God-given power to use the God-given gift of time in obedience to the Giver. Faith is the God-given power to obey the Word of the Lord instead of the interests of self or the words of unbelief: "choose this day..," for it is always "today" until the night comes!

I. *DIFFICULTIES: JUDGMENT*

If salvation is by faith, the free gift of God, why then the final judgment: "For God will bring every deed into judgment, with every secret thing, whether good or evil" (Eccles. 12:14). "And the dead were judged by what was written in the books, by what they had done" (Rev. 20:12). "For he will render to every man according to his works..." (Rom. 2:6).

How can this be if salvation is not by works but by faith: "For by grace you have been saved through faith; and this is not your own doing, it is the gift of God—not because of works, lest any man should boast" (Eph. 2:8-9)?

Every believer knows, in the depths of his heart, that he can no more earn heaven than climb the sky to reach it. We are not really surprised that the Bible rejects the notion that salvation is the reward of good works.

For what, then, are believers to be judged? It is undeniable that judgment upon our works does await us. Texts affirming that, like those already quoted, could be multiplied.

An answer to this difficulty is suggested by the miracles of Jesus. He made the blind to see, the deaf to hear, the lame to walk. He even made the dead alive again.

Why all this? Sometimes to validate the Lord's call for belief in Him (John 20:30-31), but also for another reason: to restore these crippled organs to use! That even the dead-made-alive could put the gift of life to use once more.

What once stood in the way of normal life was removed. The sick, and the deformed, and the demon-possessed were liberated by a Word from the Lord.

So the believer is today liberated by the same Word, through faith, from what stands in the way of a new life of obedience.

Take note of these things about the Lord's miracles:

1. The miracle is not an end in itself. Often it is followed by the Lord's own parting admonition: go, do! A handicap is gone. A life is restored. What then? How will the new freedom be used? The question then—the question now!

2. The Lord's healing usually came in response to faith: "Thy faith hath made thee whole" (Matt. 9:22). "And Jesus said to him, 'If you can! All things are possible to him who believes'" (Mark 9:23). Faith is commonly the road that miracles walk. Faith is the vehicle on which miracles ride. No less today than when Jesus walked the earth.

3. Faith is the means to wholeness. Faith accepts newness of life. Faith enters upon liberation in Christ Jesus. And the new life, given through faith, reveals its presence in good works: "...by works was faith made perfect" (Jas. 2:22). The purpose of healing finds its goal in the obedient use of the body made new.

The miraculous restoration of life through faith, of liberation by faith, goes on now in every believer. Life dead in sin is raised by the Word to newness in obedience. Eyes blind to the presence of God in creation (Ps. 19:1), and to the presence of Christ in the needy, see once again. Ears deaf to the Word and to the cries of the oppressed now hear and inspire response. Limbs lamed by self-indulgence now are extended to serve the neighbor. All this as evidence that faith, true and saving faith, is indeed present; none of these if faith be dead: "So faith by itself, if it has no works, is dead" (Jas. 2:17).

The final judgment, being focused upon works, is passed upon the presence or absence of faith. By faith are we saved, as revealed by our works. By unfaith are we lost, as revealed by our works: "And the dead were judged...by what they had done," just because "by grace you have been saved through faith...."

This teaching of Scripture must inspire the deacon to ever-renewed effort to stimulate the emergence of faith into the doing of good works by everyone.

Chapter 2.

WHAT MAY I KEEP FOR MYSELF?

How much of my goods, time, interests, talents do I owe the needy?

Or, how much of all that God gives me may I keep for, and use on, myself?

How does a deacon answer such questions?

First, by putting them to the Scriptures. Second, by setting the Scriptural answers into his own time and place.

A. *THE SCRIPTURES*

The Bible never gives a dollar and cents answer to questions like these. The Bible functions through conscience (see Chapter 15, B). And to sensitize conscience, the Bible does suggest an investor's guide which the pulpit should be urged to apply frequently to the congregation, and which the prudent deacon will apply to himself and assist others in applying to themselves.

Yes, an investor's guide!

It is simply this: give away to the needy all the goods, time, talent, effort which you want to invest in heaven. Give to the needy whatever you want to reap beyond the grave. Keep for yourself whatever you don't want to see again in any form after your eyelids close for the last time.

The Bible serves conscience as an investor's manual. The prudent investor takes heed. The involved deacon helps the potential investor do so.

This is what the Lord teaches through His remarks to what is commonly called the rich young ruler: "Go, sell what you have, and give to the poor, and you will have treasure in heaven..." (Mark 10:21). The Lord thus confirms the inspired teaching of Proverbs: "He who is kind to the poor lends to the Lord, and he will repay him for his deed" (Prov. 19:17).

St. Paul compares heavenly investment with sowing seed which comes to fruition in eternity: "He who sows sparingly will also reap sparingly, and he who sows bountifully will also reap bountifully" (II Cor. 9:6). A stingy planting guarantees a poor harvest.

Deacons must take the significance of this language of sowing and reaping very seriously. God does. The Spirit inspires the Apostle to say very plainly: "Do not be deceived; God is not mocked, for whatever a man sows, that he will also reap" (Gal. 6:7).

Lending to the Lord via giving to the poor is secure investment. It survives even death itself. It is, moreover, gilt-edged and blue-chip: "Give and it will be given to you; good measure, pressed down, shaken together, running over, will be put in your lap. For the measure you give will be the measure you get back," says the Lord Jesus (Luke 6:38). Again: "And he said to them, 'Take heed what you hear; the measure you give will be the measure you get, and still more will be given you'" (Mark 4:24).

This is why St. Paul molds the conscience in these words: "It is more blessed to give than to receive" (Acts 20:35), a saying he attributes to Jesus.

It is in this light that deacons must understand the warnings in the Bible against riches (see for details Chapter 16, B, The Mystery of Wealth). Conscience must view wealth, and the pursuit of wealth, with a very wary eye. The Lord calls him a "fool" whose heart is set solely upon personal gain, and He tells a now familiar parable to illustrate the warning. A rich man tears down barns too small for his holdings. He builds bigger storehouses and says to his soul, "Soul, you have ample goods laid up for many years; take your ease, eat, drink, be merry!" But God confronts this short-sighted investor with the fact of death: "Fool! This night your soul is required of you; and the things you have prepared, whose will they be?" They will not be fruit-bearing investments for the fool. Having kept all for himself, his riches pass upon his death into the hands of others: "So is he who lays up treasure for himself, and is not rich toward God," Jesus says (Luke 12:16-21). And we know, now, how one becomes "rich toward God," and that is by giving to the poor.

"How hard it will be," Jesus says, "for those who have riches to enter the kingdom of God," that is, how hard for the rich to obey God's commandments—for only they are truly citizens of a kingdom who obey its laws in obedience to its king. Indeed, the Lord goes on to say, "It is easier for a camel to go through the eye of a needle than for a rich man to enter the kingdom of God" (Mark 10:23,25).

"Come now, you rich," St. James writes, "weep and howl for the miseries that are coming upon you" (Jas. 5:1). The day of accounting is coming. Those who have made no investments beyond that judgment day do well to "weep and howl," and quickly amend their selfish ways.

Are warnings like these sounded from your pulpit? Urgently and often?

Or does someone try to blunt their edge by saying that salvation is only by grace?

Beware of this fatal mistake!

Of course, salvation is God's gift, out of His sheer grace—this is the teaching of the whole Bible. And grace *is* free! So the Scriptures everywhere declare. But those who have truly received this free grace at once are made investors in heaven through deeds of love: "What does it profit, my brethren, if a man says he has faith but has not works? Can his faith save him? If a brother or sister is ill-clad and in lack of daily food, and one of you says to them, 'Go in peace, be warmed and filled,' without giving them the things needed for the body, what does it profit? So faith by itself, if it has no works, is dead" (Jas. 2:14-17).

Grace, received through faith, does not ease conscience of the obligation to invest in heaven by gifts to the needy. Grace simply makes such investment possible, against the pull of self-interest and the excuses of selfishness.

What, then, shall I give the needy out of all the gifts of life, time, concern, talents, and goods which God has given me?

The deacon's answer must be clear and courageous: give whatever you want to invest beyond the grave. Keep whatever you, after a few brief years, never hope to see again.

This is the clear teaching of the Scriptures, God's investment manual.

B. *PRACTICAL APPLICATION*

Efforts by the diaconate and by the pulpit ministry to apply the Bible's warnings against seeking and keeping wealth exclusively for self will run into opposition. The deacon functions, by divine appointment, where the love of money and the love of God meet, and clash. The deacon is likely to feel the tensions of that conflict.

It will be pointed out, perhaps, that in fact the Bible mentions with divine approval certain very rich men. Abraham, the father of the

31

faithful (Rom. 4:16), was rich: "Now Abram was very rich in cattle, in silver, and in gold" (Gen. 13:2). So was Joseph of Arimathea, whose riches gave him access to Pilate, the Roman governor of Israel (Matt. 27:57-58).

And while it is true that the rich young ruler was asked to "sell all you have, and give to the poor" (Mark 10:21), it is also true that wealthy Zacchaeus was blessed upon the confession that only "the half of my goods I give to the poor" (Luke 19:8-10).

What practical instruction for conscience may be derived from these and similar Biblical examples?

We suggest these lessons:

1. The rich who win God's favor in this life, and the next, are generous to the needy. Job was rich, and received God's final blessing after many trials; he speaks for all the Biblical wealthy who enjoyed God's favor: "I delivered the poor who cried, and the fatherless who had none to help him. The blessing of him who was about to perish came upon me, and I caused the widow's heart to sing for joy. I put on righteousness, and it clothed me; my justice was like a robe and a turban. I was eyes to the blind, and feet to the lame. I was a father to the poor, and I searched out the cause of him whom I did not know. I broke the fangs of the unrighteous, and made him drop his prey from his teeth" (Job 29:12-17).

2. The rich who received God's blessing in the Scriptures made double use of their wealth:

    a. They ministered directly to the needy, and

    b. They used the power entrusted them by their God-given wealth to rescue the defenceless from the clutches of the unrighteous ("I broke the fangs of the unrighteous, and made him drop his prey from his teeth," says Job). So used, the riches kept after generous giving to the needy ("the half of my goods I give to the poor") attain the purpose for which God gives them.

3. It is not money in itself, which is a good gift from God, but the *love* of money which is evil. The aged St. Paul sums up to Timothy the verdict of his own experience in these inspired words: "For the love of money is the root of all evils; it is through this craving that some have wandered away from the faith and pierced their hearts with many pangs" (I Tim. 6:10). Paul thus repeats the teaching of our Lord in the parable of the sower: "As for what was sown among thorns, this is he who hears the word, but the cares of the world and the delight in riches choke the word, and it proves unfruitful" (Matt. 13:22). Wealth and

power generously given by God to the "successful" may bear no fruit in help to the needy and upholding their cause against oppression. Why not? Because the love which should focus on the poor is turned inward to focus upon the possession of wealth and the enjoyments it seems to provide. Such love of money is condemned.

4. Joseph of Arimathea was able to ask the body of Jesus from Pontius Pilate. No doubt he found Pilate's door open to him because he was rich. Not everyone had immediate access to Pilate's office. Wealth opens doors. What is at stake, then, is whether these doors are opened in the service of Jesus or of self. This antithesis the rich man really knows. Is his influence, for example, in local politics, or national politics, exerted for the common good or for his own? Is the influential word he might speak silenced by self-interest, or is it spoken from the rooftops for benefit of justice? God gives wealth to whom He will. Wealth not only can provide goods to supply the wants of the needy, but it is also power. The Bible does not require that every believer give all his money away. Why not? Because God has uses for the power of wealth committed to justice and right. It is the task of the Church, stimulated by the deacon, to alert the conscience of the rich to this supreme obligation imposed by God's gift of their wealth.

5. There remains, though, the nagging question: what, then, may anyone keep for, and spend upon, himself? The answer, which must finally be measured by each for himself, in the light of Word and of conscience as schooled by the Church is this: *I may keep and use whatever I truly need for my calling.* God allots each human a task in the world. Whatever gift is required for effectively doing that task, as in God's service, is ours for the keeping. Indeed, charity to the needy is God's way of providing them with the essentials of life requisite to their own callings. No one can decide for another precisely what he may keep for himself. The Church through pulpit and diaconate can, and must, school conscience all it can from the Word upon this vitally important question. And God will, at the Last Day, pass judgment upon how much His gifts were in fact used in His service.

6. It is easy to understand, from our own experience, why the Bible warns so soberly, and so frequently, and so vividly against the "deceitfulness of riches." How easily we are beguiled into thinking that our wealth is all our own. That *we* have *earned* "every penny" of it. That those who have less must be lazy or spendthrift. That God signals our special virtue by giving us special blessings. All the while the Word is warning against just such self-deception.

7. In short, God's gifts of life, time, talent, possessions, skills are realized as blessings when used to sustain us in *our* callings, *and* to support the needy in *their* callings, *and* to get justice done among men to the fullest extent of our ability and power. But these gifts become a curse when exclusively ab-used for our own selfish designs.

8. "It is appointed to man once to die, and after that the judgment" (Heb. 9:27). It is with an eye upon this solemn guarantee that the deacon *must*, however difficult it may be, share with the pulpit in doing what they can to alert every member of the congregation to the obligations imposed upon each by whatever of God's gifts he receives. The warning given by God to the prophet Ezekiel passes on, now, to the Church, and also to the deacon as officer of the Church: "Son of man, I have made you a watchman for the house of Israel; whenever you hear a word from my mouth, you shall give them warning from me. If I say to the wicked, 'You shall surely die,' and you give him no warning, nor speak to warn the wicked from his wicked way, in order to save his life, that wicked man shall die in his iniquity; but his blood I will require at your hand. But if you warn the wicked, and he does not turn from his wickedness, or from his wicked way, he shall die in his iniquity; but you will have saved your life. Again, if a righteous man turns from his righteousness and commits iniquity, and I lay a stumbling block before him, he shall die; because you have not warned him, he shall die for his sin, and his righteous deeds which he has done shall not be remembered; but his blood I will require at your hand. Nevertheless if you warn the righteous man not to sin, and he does not sin, he shall surely live, because he took warning; and you will have saved your life" (Ezek. 3:17-21).

Deaconing is a sober business.

Pray quickly and fervently and often that God will qualify you for doing it well.

Chapter 3.

WHY GIVE?

The deacon must be prepared to answer the question: why should Christians give?

Deacons do well to pose this question among themselves, to better prepare themselves for answering it when put by others.

The Bible clearly teaches that giving is not optional. Much of this *Handbook* is about the obligation laid upon Christians to give.

Why?

A. *LOVE GIVES*

Because giving is the natural expression of love. "God is love..." (I John 4:16). And, "God so loved the world that he gave his only Son..." (John 3:16). Love gives. The Son Himself equates love with giving: "Greater love has no man than this, that a man lay down (give) his life for his friends" (John 15:13). Love compels giving. Love and giving imply each other. Indeed love *is* giving. So much so that refusal to give betrays absence of love: "If any one has the world's goods and sees his brother in need, yet closes his heart to him, how does God's love abide in him?" (I John 3:17).

St. Paul defines willingness to give as evidence of love: "So give proof, before the church, of your love..." This after he has boasted of the love shown through liberality by the churches of Macedonia, "who gave according to their means, as I can testify, and beyond their means, of their own free will..." (II Cor. 8:24, 3).

Giving, then, flows from love. To love is to give. Not to give is not to love.

B. *LOVE IS MANDATORY*

"Walk in love, as Christ loved us and gave himself up for us..." (Eph. 5:2).

"And this commandment we have from him, that he who loves God should love his brother also" (I John 4:21).

"You shall love the Lord your God with all your heart, and with all your soul, and with all your mind. This is the great and first commandment. And a second is like it, You shall love your neighbor as yourself. On these two commandments depend all the law and the prophets" (Matt. 22:37-40).

Love is mandatory!

But what shall we give to God to show our love?

Obedience.

And what shall we give to our neighbors to show our love?

A generous share of the gifts God has made to us.

C. *LOVE IS THE TEST OF TRUE DISCIPLESHIP*

"By this shall all men know that you are my disciples, if you have love for one another" (John 13:35).

"This is my commandment, that you love one another as I have loved you" (John 15:12).

The true disciple loves.

The unloving lay false claim to discipleship.

D. *LOVE MEANS KEEPING THE COMMANDMENTS*

"If you love me, you will keep my commandments" (John 14:15).

"He who has my commandments and keeps them, he it is who loves me" (John 14:21). "If a man loves me, he will keep my word" (John 14:23). "For this is the love of God, that we keep his commandments" (I John 5:3).

Note very carefully: the Bible does not permit us to confuse true love with warm feelings. Emotional "love" roams around inside us. What God calls love overflows into deeds done for others, according to the commandments of God.

The confusion of feeling with love is not a minor mistake. It appears also in the substitution of "sharing faith" for sharing goods. We are quite willing to share our faith with others, something which costs us nothing. But what love requires is sharing goods which cost us a great deal of effort to obtain.

E. *THE PRESENCE OF SAVING FAITH IS CONFIRMED BY LOVE*

"For in Christ Jesus neither circumcision nor uncircumcision is of any avail, but faith working through love" (Gal. 5:6).

"If I have all faith, so as to remove mountains, but have not love, I am nothing" (I Cor. 13:2).

"For as the body apart from the spirit is dead, so faith without works is dead" (Jas. 2:26).

"God is love, and he who abides in love abides in God, and God abides in him" (I John 4:16). Because, "he who loves is born of God," while "he who does not love does not know God; for God is love" (I John 4:7-8).

True believers are obliged "to stir up one another to love and good works" (Heb. 10:24).

A saving faith is manifest in a passionate love. And such a love is manifest in good works.

F. *IN SUMMARY*

The teaching of the Scriptures is very plain:

1. To love is to give: "God so loved the world that he gave..." (John 3:16). For such evidence of love God Himself generously provides us with the gifts we are to share. He first provides what love obliges us to give.

2. Love is not optional. That is, giving and sharing are mandatory.

3. Giving thus becomes the indelible test of true discipleship.

4. But love is not warmth of feeling or fired-up emotions. Love is obedience to the commandment to share.

5. The believer's claim to saving faith is confirmed by love, that is by generous giving of all that the believer has to share.

Chapter 4.

WHY GIVE MONEY AND GOODS?

The deacon must expect to encounter this question: why should my giving through the Church take the form of material things?

Would it not be more "Christian" to share spiritual things? To give away my faith rather than my money? Or, is it not more obedient to support "faith ministries" than to give money to the poor, who may not merit help or are likely to squander it away? Again, is it not the sole duty of the Church to evangelize, rather than become socially activist?

These are serious questions, even if it may be suspected that they sometimes root in a preference, as noted above, for sharing faith, which cost us nothing, over sharing goods which we think were hard-earned.

The deacon preparing to answer these queries does well to recall the Lord's healing of ten lepers on the border of Samaria and Galilee. All ten had "lifted up their voices and said, 'Jesus, Master, have mercy on us'." And the Lord did. He healed them all. And then what happened? Only one paused to return thanks for his healing, and that one was a Samaritan: "Then said Jesus, 'Were there not ten cleansed? Where are the nine? Was no one found to return and give praise to God except this foreigner?' " (Luke 17:11-19).

Was the Lord unaware *before* the miracle that only one of the lepers would be grateful? Not at all. It is written of Him that, "he knew all men and needed no one to bear witness of man; for he himself knew what was in man" (John 2:25). Jesus gave healing to all ten lepers, knowing full well that only one would be grateful. Lacking the endless resources of God, man must be prudent in his giving. But we must never forget that the Bible knows nothing about "the deserving poor" when it requires sharing goods with them. Rather, all who would be "sons of your Father who is in heaven" are admonished to follow His example: "for he makes his sun rise on the evil and on the good, and sends rain on the just and on the unjust" (Matt. 5:45).

The Christian gives money and goods because he is so required by the Scriptures, as the texts quoted throughout this *Handbook* abundantly demonstrate. For just such material obedience the Lord gives us the goods He expects us to share.

There is no Biblical license for substituting "sharing faith" for sharing money and material possessions. This is the burden of the prophets: "Is not this the fast that I choose: to loose the bonds of wickedness, to undo the thongs of the yoke, to let the oppressed go free, and to break every yoke? Is it not to share your bread with the hungry, and to bring the homeless poor into your house; when you see the naked, to cover him, and not to hide yourself from your own flesh?" (Is. 58:6-7). And words of the Prophet are repeated by our Lord: "Give to him who begs of you, and do not refuse him who would borrow from you" (Matt. 5:42).

The scene of the Last Judgment so vividly sketched by the Christ in Matthew 25 (vv. 31-46) makes unmistakable that evidence of love must appear in the form of very material gifts to the poor: food, drink, warmth, clothing, the touch of tender care.

True love gives in terms of need. Where the need is material, the gift must be material. Where the need is justice, the gift must be the battle to achieve that. Where the need is time, comfort, use of talent or skill, the gift must fit it.

God gives faith. He who receives faith will give generously of the goods and talents which God has given him.

40

Chapter 5.

WHY GIVE
TO AND THROUGH THE CHURCH?

Let it be said very plainly, and at once: a body without hands, or eyes and ears, is not wholly a body.

Deacons are seeing eyes, hearing ears, and serving hands of the congregation, that is, of any congregation which is determined to be a true manifestation of the *Body* of Jesus Christ. The presence and activity of the diaconate declares to the congregation, and to the community: here *is* the visible, concrete, unmistakable Body of the Lord, redeemed by Him for good works (Eph. 2:10)!

This, then is the summary answer to the question: why give to, and through, the Church? To demonstrate that you are, and know that you are, member of a Body—and that a body lacking hands, or hands lacking gifts, is less than the Lord's Body is called to be.

The Church, visible in each local congregation, is the Body through which the Lord Jesus Christ chooses to act in your community. And the diaconate is that Body's hands outstretched to serve, that Body's eyes alert to signs of distress, and that Body's ears ever open to even the silent cries of despair.

As the Lord's Body, the Church provides Him with lips to proclaim His Word, thus bearing courageous witness to His Truth through her pulpit ministry. As the Lord's Body, the Church provides Him with seeing eye and hearing ear and serving hand through the diaconate. And as the Lord's Body, the Church elects an eldership to oversee obedience to His will (see our *Elders Handbook).*

All this was self-evident to the New Testament Church, but because ours is an era of individualism, of doing one's own thing in one's own way, deacons must be fully prepared to answer the query: why should I give through you?

To that end, we offer the following perspectives:

A. *PRACTICAL PERSPECTIVE*

1. From a purely business point of view, the diaconate assures the congregation of a systematic, disciplined, orderly approach to meeting the overall financial and material necessities requisite to its existence and function.

2. An active diaconate assures the congregation that each individual member's material and financial needs, even when unknown to most others, are systematically discovered and met. This is important because:

a. Very real needs could be otherwise overlooked, especially when these are hidden behind a facade of, "Oh, everything's fine."

b. The diaconate brings together resources—in money and in talent—which individual members of the Body could not always provide, nor so well focus.

c. The diaconate remembers routine services, perhaps on schedule week after week, which individual members might well neglect.

d. Knowledge of the active presence of a diaconate relieves the conscience of individual members who wonder, otherwise, if there be needy and if their wants are being supplied—and who quite honestly confess that if such services depended upon themselves, many needs would go unnoticed or unmet.

e. Each member knows that his own contribution, however small, becomes a part of the whole program of diakonia. *Each* thus shares in the service of *all* who need service. Through her deacons, in short, the congregation does indeed act...like a Body!

3. In a practical way, too, the pulpit ministry can hardly lay on the conscience of the individual what the congregation as a Body neglects to pursue, namely the relief of the needy. Diaconal services do not entirely supplant individual diakonia. Rather they model it, and involve the skills and talents of the whole for the benefit of those who can use them. There will be good works of all kinds left to do for those who have an eye and ear for wanting to do them.

4. Practically, too, congregational diakonia has virtually no overhead. Neither deacons nor members accept reward for their services—this side of the grave. The church building provides most of the facilities. The full value of each gift, therefore, makes its way to the recipients. This is less likely to be true of charities set up independently of the Church and run as private ventures, however well-inten-

tioned. The diaconal dollar, or gift in kind, or focusing of skill or talent, is carefully stewarded charity.

B. *WITNESS PERSPECTIVE*

Diaconal service is the Lord's prescribed form of witness: "Let your light so shine before men, that they may see your good works and give glory to your Father who is in heaven" (Matt. 5:16). St. Paul advises the Church to be "children of God without blemish in the midst of a crooked and perverse generation, among whom you shine as lights in the world..." (Phil. 2:15). And St. Peter writes: "Maintain good conduct among the Gentiles, so that in case they speak against you as wrong-doers, they may see your good deeds and glorify God on the day of visitation" (I Pet. 2:12).

Consider, from this perspective:

1. Diaconal service boosts, as it were, the Church to a hilltop position. The Lord declares that, "A city set on a hill cannot be hid." How, then, does the Church become visible? This we have already noticed: by diaconal good works, which glorify the Lord's Father in heaven. These are the deeds which testify that the congregation has heard and understands, as a Body, her Lord's instruction: "Not everyone who says to me, 'Lord, Lord,' will enter the kingdom of heaven, but he who does the will of my Father who is in heaven" (Matt. 7:21).

2. Diaconal service bears evangelical witness to the world by displaying the fruits of faith: "So, every sound tree bears good fruit," and "By their fruits will they be known" (Matt. 7:17, 16).

3. Diaconal service bears witness to the congregation itself that she has heard and understands her Lord's commands, and dwells, there-fore, in the warmth of His love: "If you keep my commandments, you will abide in my love, just as I have kept my Father's commandments and abide in his love" (John 15:10). And, indeed, a congregation that serves unitedly through the diaconate grows into more virile unity in the process. Muscles used grow stronger.

4. Diaconal good works bear witness to the congregation's aware-ness that here is a very special and unique form of unity, that of a Body whose hands are busy through an office instituted by God for just this purpose.

5. The Body's deed witness is correlative to its pulpit's word witness. The Bible nowhere suggests that either one may be

substituted for the other. The Word witnesses to the Truth that self-sacrifice lies at the heart of Christianity. The deed, done by the Body and for the Body through the diaconate, as well as individually, witnesses to the fact that the Word has been heard and believed. Both forms of witness speak for the Lord to the world.

C. *THEOLOGICAL PERSPECTIVE*

There are theological perspectives on giving through the diaconate, like these:

1. The office of the deacon is the New Testament form of the office of the Levite, as is explained in Chapter 9. St. Paul carefully specifies divinely inspired requirements for deacons (I Tim. 3:8-13). Sectarians may neglect the diaconate, but a Church which has no deacons lacks one of the essentials of her being.

2. The deacon replaces the so-called "Christian communism" practiced by the fledgling Church. This is sometimes overlooked by liberation theologians. The early enthusiasm reflected by the initial believers' "having all things in common" quickly broke down. The "Hellenists" (Greek speaking believers, perhaps immigrant Jews) murmured that "their widows were neglected in the daily distribution" from the common fund (Acts 6:1), showing that the communal sharing reported earlier (Acts 2:44, and 4:32) lapsed early. And the diaconate, not a holding all things in common, soon becomes the normative model provided to the Church by the New Testament. Deacons, not communism, respond to needs within—and without—the Body. The office of deacon declares that systematic diakonia, rather than enforced Communist equality, is the Church's inspired answer to disparities in wealth and talent. This, in our times especially, is a fundamental theological lesson for the Church—and the deacons in particular—to learn and remember, and practice.

3. The diaconate is the Protestant substitute for the Catholic religious order. Through the deacons, as well as by using skills alongside them, the Church member shares of his gifts in talent and goods with the needy.

4. Giving through the diaconate avoids all ostentation, and is thus obedient to the Lord's command: "Thus, when you give alms, sound no trumpet before you, as the hypocrites do in the synagogues and in the streets, that they may be praised by men. Truly, I say to you, they have their reward. But when you give alms, do not let your left hand

know what your right hand is doing, so that your alms may be in secret; and your Father who sees in secret will reward you" (Matt. 6:2-4). Through the deacons, the largest gift merges with the smallest, exactly as the Head of the Body requires. God knows. That is enough.

5. It may well be that those who are surprised, on the Judgment Day, by the extent of their service to the needy, in fact performed that service through the deacons: "Lord, when did we see thee hungry and feed thee, or thirsty and give thee drink? And when did we see thee a stranger and welcome thee, or naked and clothe thee? And when did we we see thee sick or in prison and visit thee?" (Matt. 25:37-39). A striking surprise awaits those who serve through the Body by her deacons.

6. St. Paul teaches explicitly that God deliberately distributes gifts in difference and variety so that members of the Body (and of the human race) will be drawn to each other by need of each other's goods and talents (I Cor. 12, the whole chapter). This mutual sharing by divine design is facilitated in and for the Church by an alert and active diaconate.

D. *CONCLUSION*

The import, we believe, of all the above is clear: the diaconate is a key office in the Church. Giving to, and through the deacons is primary giving, first-claim giving, not grudging or after-thought charity. Just as membership in the Lord's Body has a basic priority in all of life, so sharing by way of the Body's hands has a basic priority in congregational membership. The priestly office of each believer, like the priestly office of Christ, is fulfilled in self-sacrificial devotion to the internal and external needs of the Church and her parish.

Chapter 6.

HOW MUCH? (FROM MITES TO MILLIONS)

Has the Church no Word from the Lord as to exactly how much the believer owes God? That is to say, owes the Church as representative of God?

Yes, it has that.

The believer, because he is a true believer, knows very well that he owes God everything: "...for the world and all that is in it is mine" (Ps. 50:12). God has first claim by right of ownership to everything each of us calls his own.

To ask with the Psalmist, "What shall I render unto the Lord for all his benefits toward me?" (Ps. 116:12) can only be completely answered by the acknowledgment: all, Lord, is thine!

Moreover, God gives in order that His obedient children may give: "And God is able to provide you with every blessing in abundance, so that you may always have enough of everything and may provide in abundance for every good work" (II Cor. 9:8).

Can we come no closer than this to some measure of "how much" we owe the Lord?

The most ancient measure of what the believer owes to God is the tithe, one-tenth of what God gives to us. The Israelites were obliged to give the Levites one-tenth of the produce of their soil, of their orchards, of their flocks. And every third year a tithe—probably a second tithe—was to be shared with the stranger and the poor (Lev. 27:30-33; Deut. 12:5-18).

In addition, the Lord required "offerings" of His people, of two basic types: 1) offerings for sin, and 2) thank offerings. The prophet Malachi charges Israel with robbing God by neglecting both tithes *and* offerings: "Will man rob God? Yet you are robbing me. But you say, 'How are we robbing thee?' In your tithes and offerings. You are cursed with a curse, for you are robbing me; the whole nation of you. Bring the full tithes into the storehouse, that there may be food in my house; and thereby put me to the test, says the Lord of hosts, if I will not open the windows of heaven for you and pour down for you an overflowing blessing" (Mal. 3:8-10).

There is no suggestion in the Scriptures that the Lord's demand upon the Old Testament Church is abated for the New. Nor is there any suggestion that what we give elsewhere can be "credited," so to speak, against the tithe owed the Church. Indeed, St. Paul sets a higher standard, it may well be, especially for those who are richly blessed: "Upon the first day of the week let every one of you lay by him in store, as God hath prospered him..." (I Cor. 16:2). The more generous God, the more generous we!

Is God pleased, then, with our liberality? Indeed: "...for God loves a cheerful giver" (II Cor. 9:7).

There is, however, one more thing to be added on the matter of "how much" do we owe the Lord and His Church?

It is taught us by the familiar story recounted in both St. Mark and St. Luke: "And he sat down opposite the (temple) treasury, and watched the multitude putting money into the treasury. Many rich people put in large sums. And a poor widow came, and put in two copper coins, which make a penny. And he called his disciples to him, and said to them, 'Truly, I say to you, this poor widow has put in more than all those who are contributing to the treasury. For they all contributed out of their abundance; but she out of her poverty has put in everything she had, her whole living'" (Mark 12:41-44; Luke 21:1-4).

By making such a point of calling His disciples, who represent the Church, to Him, the Lord intends that we should take careful note of what He has to say. And what does He have to say?

It is this: God measures the amount of what we give by comparison with the amount we keep for ourselves. The widow gave most because she kept back nothing. The others gave less because they kept back more.

This is not pleasant truth to hear. Especially not for those who think themselves very generous because their gifts are substantial, and who expect that the Church and the Lord will think the same.

There must be no mistake about this: the Lord does love the cheerful giver. The Lord does expect those whom He has richly blessed to be richly generous. And the Lord does accept each gift as investment in heaven. All this is true. Let those who are generous always be appreciated.

But when we are asking "how much" do I owe the Lord's work in the Church and for the neighbor, then we come finally to the Lord's own measure of how much it is that we really give, say in comparison with one another. And then His teaching is clear: he gives most, in the sight of heaven, who keeps back least by comparison. He gives least, in the sight of heaven, who keeps back most by comparison.

This follows, when we come to think about it, from the fact that all we have is God's to begin with. What we give, He gave us to share; what we keep is still His, not shared.

The King James Version speaks of the poor widow's gift as "two mites," the smallest Hebrew coins. From mites to millions may loom differently in the sight of God than in ours—and the giver's! This is important for deacons—and others—to remember.

Remember, too, that the Bible takes very seriously a dividing-line we tend to ignore, namely the dividing-line marked by death. In terms of giving, death marks the watershed of reward. Generosity which is publicly acknowledged this side of the grave already has its reward. Generosity done without fanfare this side of the grave is rewarded in heaven: "Thus, when you give alms, sound no trumpet before you, as the hypocrites do in the synagogues and in the streets, that they may be praised by men. Truly, I say to you, they have their reward. But when you give alms, do not let your left hand know what your right hand is doing, so that your alms may be in secret; and your Father who sees in secret will reward you" (Matt. 6:2-4). When God comes in judgment, on the Last Day, He will reward: "Behold, the Lord God comes with might, and his arm rules for him; behold, his reward is with him, and his recompense before him" (Is. 40:10).

For this reason the Apostle can say, "And let us not grow weary in well-doing, for in due season we shall reap, if we do not lose heart" (Gal. 6:9).

In times of discouragement, let deacons take heart from the knowledge that quietly and all about us diaconal service is being rendered, seen now by the untiring eye of God to be rewarded when it is no longer *today*: "For truly I say to you, whoever gives you a cup of water to drink because you bear the name of Christ, will by no means lose his reward" (Mark 9:41). Reward-bearing service is out of the reach of no one. But reward-seeking notoriety risks having all the praise it will receive from men rather than from God.

The Lord's warning is unmistakable: "Beware of practicing your piety before men in order to be seen by them; for then you will have no reward from your Father who is in heaven" (Matt. 6:1).

49

PART II

THE DEACON: BACKGROUND

Chapter 7.

THE OFFICES OF THE CHURCH

The Church is the Body of her Lord Jesus Christ, and is knit by the Holy Spirit into a living unity with Him. She therefore displays the three offices of her Head and Lord:

1. Christ is Prophet, that is teacher: "For Moses truly said unto the fathers, 'A prophet shall the Lord your God raise up unto you of your brethren, like unto me; him shall you hear in all things whatsoever he shall say to you'" (Acts 3:22).

2. He is Priest, that is self-sacrificer for our sake: "Thou art a priest forever, after the order of Melchizedek" (Heb. 5:6).

3. He is King, that is ruler: "Yet have I set my King upon my holy hill of Zion" (Ps. 2:6), "and of his kingdom there shall be no end" (Luke 1:33).

Though not all theologians are agreed as to the exact relation of Christ's offices to those which characterize His Church, we believe that the presence of these offices identifies those congregations where they appear as vibrant manifestations of the universal Body of Jesus Christ. The true Church is found:

1. Where the Word of God as revealed in the Bible is faithfully preached; there functions the office of Christ as Prophet.

2. Where the sacraments of baptism and the Lord's Supper are truly administered; there functions the office of Christ as Priest.

3. Where the congregation is aptly ruled according to the Word, and discipline is appropriately exercised; there functions the office of Christ as King.

These three are generally confessed, since the Reformation, as being the distinguishing marks of the true and visible Church. Those who occupy these offices are now known as follows:

1. Prophet: the ordained ministry, sometimes designated teaching elders.

2. Priest: the deacons, called collectively the diaconate.

3. King: the rulling eldership, sometimes called presbyters, bishops, trustees.

It may not be immediately clear just how the office of deacon displays the priestly office of Christ. We have sketched the relationship in Chapter 9, and refer the reader to that for explanation.

It can briefly be noted here, however, that the link between the priestly office of Christ and the office of deacon is the centrality of *sacrifice* in Christianity.

The Old Testament Levites brought the sacrifices required of Israel into the presence of God by laying them upon the temple altar. The Levites were thus the priestly ministers of sacrifice.

Jesus Christ offered Himself in fulfillment of the Old Testament ceremonial rites as the complete sacrifice for sins on the altar of Calvary.

Thereafter the table of the Lord's Supper became, in effect, the altar of the Christian Church, forever a memorial of Christ's self-sacrifice for His Body.

The believer no longer is required to bring sacrifices to the temple. He is, instead, required to sacrifice himself, and to sacrifice his own selfish interests, in response to the Lord's gift of salvation, visualized in the Supper and in the cleansing of baptism.

The fruits of the believer's self-sacrifice, his gifts to the Church, are no longer laid by a Levite, or priest, on an altar. They are conveyed by the deacons to where God awaits receipt of the fruits of gratitude—in the persons of the poor and needy. Thus the deacon serves in place of the Levite, and the priestly office is now fulfilled by the diaconate.

This suggests that today, as in Calvin's Geneva, it would be well if the deacons distributed the bread and wine of the Lord's Supper to the congregation—a clear symbol of their role as priests, servants of sacrifice. Deacons could, also, prepare and care for the baptismal font.

A. *RELATION OF THE OFFICES*

The three offices are not competitive. They inhere in, and serve, one Body. Oversight, however, belongs to the eldership, and extends to all functions of the Body. St. Paul's instruction to the Elders of Ephesus applies to all, as he bids them farewell for a last time: "Take heed to yourselves and to all the flock, in which the Holy Spirit has made you guardians..." (Acts 20:28).

The terms "bishop" and "presbyter," also used for the ruling elder's office in the Church, both imply oversight and responsibility.

It will follow, then, that in the very performance of their calling, the ruling eldership (however titled in your congregation) is required to supervise the faithfulness of the teaching ministry and of the deacons. It is appropriate, therefore, that the deacons report regularly to the eldership, and submit to their judgment diaconal projects involving stewardship of the Church's goods and talents.

Some diaconates may decide to keep channels of communication with the ruling elders continuously open by inviting an elder or two to sit with them in planning meetings of all kinds. Or the eldership may suggest such an arrangement—not as eldership tyranny, but as mutual concern for the best interests of the Body for which both have been called to office.

B. *INSTITUTIONS AND OFFICE*

Our discussion so far touches upon the basic elements of the deacons' understanding of office in Church. But for those who desire an analytical account of the nature of office itself, we offer the following:

1. The nature of "office" is best understand in terms of the nature of institutions. What, then, is an institution?

2. Behavior is "institutionalized" when it becomes a fixed routine or pattern. The pattern of daily work most of us do is prescribed by the job we have, whether that be in the home, school, office, shop, on the farm or wherever. An institution is created, or naturally forms, to unify the behavior of all those within it in order to attain certain ends. Thus a factory draws together the work of all employees to the end that certain products are made. An office draws together the contributions of each employee to attain certain specific ends. The home unifies husband, wife, and children into the life of a family. In short, institutions may be viewed from two perspectives:

   a. As arising out of cooperative, unified effort, or

   b. As imposing patterns, unique to each institution, upon the behavior of all included within the scope of the institution.

In either case, the meaning of "institution" is: patterned behavior toward a given end.

3. Within institutions, offices are those executive functions which facilitate the work of the whole. A true office is a function which is

essential to the institution's being what it wishes to be. Office, then, implies special function, and special responsibility.

4. It is sometimes said, especially in regard to the Church, that the idea of office is commonly conveyed in the New Testament by the Greek term *diakonia*, which may be translated as "service". This can be misleading, particularly as concerns the office of the ruling elder, unless "service" simply be understood as filling the office in accord with its appropriate functions—that of the elder being to rule.

5. It is also argued, especially in the tradition of Martin Luther, that all believers hold office in the Church. Reference is made to St. Peter's description: "But you are a chosen race, a royal priesthood..." (I Pet. 2:9). Peter is here quoting what God said to Moses as he was leading Israel across the wasteland after Egypt: "And you shall be to me a kingdom of priests and a holy nation" (Ex. 19:6). If this be understood as the priestly obligation laid upon every believer to sacrifice himself, as priest, in the service of others, all is well. But if this be misunderstood as implying that authority in the Church originates in the believers, parallel to political authority in the democratic state, then confusion results. The authority of office in the Church is delegated from the Head down, by means of His Word, not from the believer up. And this is why the only offices appropriate to the Church are those specified in the Scriptures, where the Lord lays down the qualifications required of those who fill them.

6. A misconception of office is one of the striking characteristics of the sects which have always existed alongside the Church. The sectarian mind makes light of Church office today. But true members of the Body, knowing that office in the Church manifests the offices of Christ, take the filling, and doing, and responsibility of office very seriously.

C. THE OFFICES AND THE SELF

Jesus Christ was truly God and really man. It is not surprising, then, that His offices reflect the nature of man, who was made, after all, in God's image.

Man functions as a unity, and through three faculties: mind, emotion, will.

It is evident that the Lordship of Christ reflects each of these human faculties through the divine offices:

1. Christ as Prophet is Lord over the human mind. Man is to

fashion his thoughts and judgments in the light of God's Word.

2. Christ as Priest is to govern man's emotional life, and we are to bring sacrifices of praise and goods in thankfulness and joy to Him.

3. Christ as King is to govern the human will. We are to will to do His will (law) in obedience to His Kingship.

It is obvious that the Lord chooses to exercise His control of all our faculties through the offices of His Body, the Church:

1. Over the mind by the Word preached and taught.

2. Over the emotions by diaconal conveyance of the fruits of praise to those who are in need.

3. Over the will by the guiding and, when necessary, disciplinary authority of the eldership.

So perceived and understood, the Church becomes visible as an institution, characterized by three offices, performing functions central to every society which has a future. The Body of Christ is the living presence of the Lord in history, a presence become operative through His offices, and made manifest in the life of every believer.

Chapter 8.

THE DEACON IN THE BODY

"Now you are the body of Christ and individually members of it" (I
Cor. 12:27).

The Bible speaks of the Church as the Body of Christ. This is no
offhand literary accident.

By calling the Church a "Body" the Word wants to teach us something.

Biblical metaphors are carefully chosen. When the Church is called a
Body, we may, of course, read the term casually, but the teaching
implied is not casual at all. And it, more than any other Biblical
instruction, clarifies the meaning of "deacon" in the Church. In this
way:

1. After His bodily ascension to heaven (Acts 1:9-11), Jesus chooses
to be present among mankind in another bodily form: the Church. He
might have chosen to act among us *only* through His Spirit. He might
have chosen to dwell among us *only* in His Word. But neither of these
living forces would give the Lord a bodily, incarnate presence among
us. And so He chooses to extend, as it were, His incarnation in the
flesh beyond His ascension—and until His second physical coming
(Acts 1:11)—in the form of another Body, His Church. This highly
honors the true Church—that is, the Church characterized by the three
offices of Christ. This also challenges the Church to assume a heavy
responsibility, namely to strive to be the Lord's Body. The Church is
called to be the visible Body of Jesus Christ in the form of every local
congregation—including your own!

2. It is easy for a congregation to claim in words that it is the Body
of Christ. Such words come readily to mind and flow easily off the
tongue. We can say them any time and anywhere and as often as we
please. But where will the proof be found that a congregation, meeting
regularly in its sanctuary on the corner, say, of Eighth and Main, is in

fact—and desires very much to be—the living Body of her Lord and Savior Jesus Christ? The proof appears whenever and wherever this congregation indeed behaves as the Christ would, were He living in His Body in your community. And now the metaphor of the "Body" becomes instructive. One manifestation, of course, is that a Body can speak—and the Church performs this bodily function through the lips of her ministry (to which we hope to devote another Handbook).

3. But a Body acts through other organs than just the lips. A Body has eyes, ears, feet, hands.... And as Body, the Church functions as these organs by means of its diaconate. An active diaconate demonstrates that the congregation is indeed, and knows what it means to be the Body of Jesus Christ. This Body has its own lips—the ordained ministry; and this Body has its own organs of service—the diaconate. And this Body is given internal supervision—the ruling eldership. The deed of the diaconate validates the word of the ministry: "Not every one who says to Me, 'Lord, Lord' shall enter the kingdom of heaven, but he who does the will of my Father who is in heaven" (Matt. 7:21). This applies no less to the Church as Body in its various congregations than it does to individual Christians. And the Body, as Body, "does the will" of her Lord's Father through a dedicated and active diaconate.

4. The miracles of Jesus focus much on organs of the human body. He made the blind to see, the deaf to hear, the lame to walk, the dumb to speak, and the withered hand whole.

Why? Let us re-emphasize here what we have said above:

Was our Lord healing these defects of the human body just for kindness' sake? Far more than that! He was teaching His Church that He can—and will—make useful and obedient organs out of anyone's who has faith in Him. The miracles demonstrate His power to make His Church a living and active Body in proportion to the Church's faith in Him.

The miracle-working power of Jesus Christ is revealed in the Church through her use of healed bodily organs—hands, feet, eyes, ears.

5. The office through which the healed congregation uses her organs is the diaconate.

Through the deacons the congregation sees human need within, and outside, the Body—not only sees what is conspicuous but looks diligently for needs that blind eyes never perceive.

Through the deacons the congregation hears the cries of distress and want within and outside the Body—cries that unhealed ears are deaf to.

Through the deacons the congregation hastens on legs no longer crippled, to serve with open hands no longer gnarled with greed.

The deacons are a testimony that the congregation has received the miraculous, healing power of Christ which makes it into a serving Body obedient to Him. The deacons are living and visible proof that here indeed is Christ's Body. For active eyes, ears, legs, and hands characterize only a living organism.

Still more, deacons prove that their congregation is the living Body *of Christ!* Because eyes and ears that take note of human want are indeed His eyes and ears. And feet and hands which spring eagerly to serve human want are indeed His feet and hands.

The Biblical metaphor of "Body" teaches us what the Church must be like. The miracles of Jesus teach us that He will qualify His Body to do His will. And the fact that He is the Head of His Body, the Church, teaches us whose Word it is that the Body must always hear, heed, and obey.

Chapter 9.

THE DEACON IN HISTORY

Sacrifice is at the heart of Christianity.

The Bible associates sacrifice with two symbols: the altar of the Old Testament and the Lord's Table of the New Testament. These two symbols are, in essence, one, because the altar was also the Lord's table.

It is through the symbol of the table that the New Testament deacon is related to the Old Testament Levite. Both the Levite and the deacon are ministers to sacrifice. We will try to make this relationship clear in this chapter.

The deacon who learns to appreciate the long and significant background to his office will experience a profound respect for the importance of his calling. Your office was not created yesterday. Nor was it formed by man, nor even by the Church. Rather, your office was in the divine program for the Church from its very beginning in Israel. Never think of the diaconal office as a minor calling. Do not consider it a training-ground for "more important" duty, nor meant only for younger members of the Church.

The history of the diaconal office begins with:

A. SACRIFICE

What is sacrifice?

A little child disobeys his mother. He goes out and picks a wild flower to bring her. Why? Partly because he hopes that thus he will appease her annoyance and lighten his probable punishment. But more fundamentally he wants to get "right" with his mother again by making an "offering" that will erase the wrong that separates them and troubles his conscience. Sacrifice is like that. It is an "offering" given to higher authority to undo the effects of disobedience, to make things "right" again.

Sacrifice reaches far back into the history of Christianity and of other forms of religion. We deal here only with sacrifice in Christianity, where it is fundamental, and forms the background to the diaconal office as it first emerges in the Levites. Let us trace the history.

We know that God created man good and in His own Image (Gen. 1:26-27), and that man breaks the divine law and thus alienates himself and his descendents from his Creator (Gen. 3:1-20).

Estranged from God, as a disobedient child is estranged from his mother, man early turns to sacrifice. Cain and Abel, first sons of Adam and Eve, bring their offerings to God (Gen. 4:3-4). Noah sacrifices to God after escape from the flood (Gen. 18:20). Abraham (whose name was at first Abram) builds an altar to commemorate God's promise to him of the land of Canaan for his descendents (Gen. 15:7).

When the Lord liberates Israel from slavery in Egypt, He lays down rules which make sacrifice the heart of worship. And He requires that the Levites, descendents of Jacob's third son Levi, shall be servants of the altar and in the temple later built around it. The tribe of Levi inherits no land in Canaan. So unique is their service to God and His people that they live off the gifts which are presented by other tribes to the Lord: "Therefore Levi has no portion or inheritance with his brothers; the Lord is his inheritance, as the Lord your God said to him" (Deut. 10:9).

What service do the Levites perform?

Theirs is a dual service: 1) Aaron, brother to Moses, and all his descendents are priests. They serve at the altar, making sacrifice of the peoples' gifts to the Lord. 2) All other descendents of Levi are called Levites, and their service is to prepare the peoples' gifts for sacrifice, and to care for all tasks involving the temple. We commonly read, therefore, of "the priests and Levites" as occupying offices in the temple.

For a detailed outline of Israel's sacrificial system, the deacon can consult a Bible dictionary. What concerns us here is that the temple sacrifices were of two basic kinds: 1) offerings made for sins, and 2) offerings made in thanksgiving, both for forgiveness of sins and for God's many other blessings.

B. *MEANING OF SACRIFICE*

What was the meaning of the sacrificial system imposed by God upon Israel?

And, how does this relate to the office of deacon?

The priests offered the peoples' sacrifices upon the temple altar. In so doing they foreshadow Christ's sacrifice of Himself upon the altar of Calvary. As the New Testament epistle to the Hebrews makes clear, the temple sacrifices come to their culmination, and conclusion, in the death of Jesus upon the cross. The work of the priests and Levites comes to fulfillment. The altar of the Old Testament Church then becomes the table of the Lord's Supper in the New Testament Church.

The sacrificial system has found its meaning, and the symbol of the altar has given way to the symbol of the table—though in essence both imply the same thing: sacrifice.

C. *ENTER THE DEACON*

It is a striking thing that the deacon first appears in the New Testament Church as waiting on tables! The account is familiar: "Now in these days when the disciples were increasing in number, the Hellenists murmured against the Hebrews because their widows were neglected in the daily distribution. And the twelve summoned the body of the disciples and said, 'It is not right that we should give up preaching the word of the Lord to serve tables. Therefore, brethren, pick out from among you seven men of good repute, full of the Spirit and of wisdom, whom we may appoint to this duty. But we will devote ourselves to prayer and to the ministry of the word'" (Acts 6:1-4).

Is it just a coincidence that the office of deacon arises in connection with table service—though it will soon expand to other forms of charity?

Not at all! Nothing in the history of the Church is mere coincidence.

Three tables all point to the same thing: the table called "altar" in the Old Testament; the table of the Lord's Supper; and the tables served first by deacons—all three relate to sacrifice, which remains at the heart of Christianity.

This becomes evident through a further brief look back into the Old Testament Church.

D. *FROM LEVITE TO DEACON*

Old Testament sacrifices consisted of animals, birds, firstfruits of the harvest. These were things. Things which, indeed, the giver might have used for himself. Sacrifice implies, then, self-sacrifice, too. The giver surrenders to the Lord, and to the temple, what he could have made use of. This is the first step in sacrifice: give to God what you could use for yourself.

But this is only the first step. What God sees is the heart of the giver. Does the sin-offering reflect a heart truly repentant, truly determined to amend its ways? This is what genuine sacrifice for sin required. Sacrifice is the outward symbol of an inward state; and if the heart is not true, the sacrifice is not acceptable to God. He makes this clear, again and again, through His prophets: "Has the Lord as great delight in burnt offerings and sacrifices, as in obeying the voice of the Lord? Behold, to obey is better than sacrifice, and to hearken than the fat of rams" (I Sam. 15:22). This is the Word of the Lord to Saul, first king of Israel, spoken by Samuel the Lord's prophet.

To those whose heart was not in accord with their offerings, the Lord declares: "Bring no more offerings; incense is an abomination to me....When you spread forth your hands, I will hide my eyes from you; even though you make many prayers, I will not listen; your hands are full of blood" (Is. 1:13,15).

And how, then does sacrifice become acceptable?

The Lords answers: "Wash yourselves; make yourselves clean; remove the evil of your doing from before my eyes; cease to do evil, learn to do good; seek justice, correct oppression; defend the fatherless, plead for the widow" (Is. 1:15-17). Again: "Is not this the fast that I choose: to loose the bonds of wickedness, to undo the thongs of the yoke, to let the oppressed go free, and to break every yoke? Is it not to share your bread with the hungry, and bring the homeless poor into your house; when you see the naked, to cover him; and not to hide yourself from your own flesh?" (Is. 58:6-7).

The temple sacrifices must represent willing *self*-sacrifice for others, or the temple sacrifices are unacceptable. The believer must love God above all (Deut. 6:5) and show it by loving his neighbor as himself (Lev. 19:18). This is the meaning of the sacrificial system.

But where will the believer find the strength to deny self-interest and practice self-sacrifice? How can the believer obey the command, "Wash yourselves; make yourselves clean"? Is not this just what

66

sacrifice was supposed to do? How, then, come to sacrifice with already clean hands?

We must recall, here, that Old Testament sacrifice was of two kinds: 1) for sin, and 2) in thanksgiving. The first provided clean hands for the second. The sacrifice of thanksgiving could not reach God unless it rose out of a heart cleansed of sin and thus liberated to obedience. Still more, the sacrifice of thanksgiving was acceptable to God only if it reflected the will to a life of obedience as required by God—this is the burden of the prophets, as we have observed. Not the life of perfection, for then the sacrifice for sin would no longer be necessary. But the life striving for perfection, through obedience to divine law.

But the temple sacrifices for sin only symbolized the true sacrifice for sin—Christ's self-sacrifice on the altar of Calvary. When that happened, the table of the Lord took the place of the altar, and the Old Testament Levitical office had run its course. The ministry to the altar ended. And re-appeared in a new ministry to another table: the ministry of the deacon.

The New Testament congregation gathers, now, around the new "altar" of the Lord's table as He commanded (Matt. 26:26-28; I Cor. 11:23-26). There the believer is once again confirmed in his liberation from sin and selfishness. He is once more stimulated to self-sacrifice through the gift of goods, time, talent to the Lord.

And, turning from the Lord's table, how shall the thankful Church deliver her gifts to the Lord?

Obviously, through those appointed to serve upon the table: the diaconate! Just as the Old Testament altar becomes the New Testament table, so the Old Testament ministry to the altar, the Levite, becomes the New Testament ministry to the table, the deacon!

As the Old Testament believer laid his gifts upon the altar, so the New Testament believer lays his gifts upon the table—for distribution to the needy via the diaconate. Thus the office lives on in the Church, from its beginnings in the origins of Israel to the day when the Church's Lord returns in glory!

And what could be more appropriate?

The service required by God of Israel was symbolized in the temple sacrifice, representing self-sacrifice for the neighbor. Ministering to this sacrifice were the Levites.

The service required by God of the New Israel, the New Testament Church, is in the temples where God now chooses to be found and worshipped—the persons of the neighbor. Ministering to this sacrifice are the deacons.

Thus the writer to the Hebrews first explains the transition from the Old Testament service to the New Testament Gospel, and then relates this to the believer's response: "Do not neglect to do good and to share what you have, for such sacrifices are pleasing to God" (Heb. 13:16).

It now becomes clear why all believers are described in the Scriptures (both Old and New Testaments) as being themselves "priests".

God says to Israel, through Moses: "...you shall be to me a kingdom of priests and a holy nation" (Ex. 19:6). St. Peter writes: "Come to him, that living stone, rejected by men but in God's sight chosen and precious; and like living stones be yourselves built into a spiritual house, to be a holy priesthood, to offer spiritual sacrifices acceptable to God through Jesus Christ" (I Pet. 1:4-5). And St. John writes in Revelation: "To him, who loves us and has freed us from our sins by his blood and made us a kingdom, priests to his God and Father, to him be glory and dominion for ever and ever. Amen" (Rev, 1:5-6).

A priest presides at sacrifice.

The believer as priest presides at the daily sacrifice of his own selfishness, and gives the fruits of such self-sacrifice to God: "I appeal to you therefore, brethren, by the mercies of God, to present your bodies as a living sacrifice, holy and acceptable to God, which is your spiritual worship" (Rom. 12:1). Such sacrifice can range from the smallest act of self-denial, done in obedience to divine command, through the sharing of goods, talents, time, energies with others, to the very sacrifice of life itself: "Greater love has no man than this, that a man lay down his life for his friends" (John 15:13).

And what is the office appointed from the beginning to minister to such self-sacrifice?

The office first occupied by Levite and now by deacon!

Yours is the office assigned the Church by God Himself to bring the fruits of obedient self-sacrifice by all believer-priests to the tables where God now waits to be served: the tables of the poor, the needy, the weak, the oppressed.

This *Handbook* is written to serve you in such service.

E. *TO THE REFORMATION*

The deacon is established as successor to the Levite in the New Testament Church.

Unhappily, trends soon appear which place a different construction upon the New Testament offices. By a regression we need not try to trace in detail, the Church's preaching ministry sought to be once again an Aaronic priesthood. The sacrifice of the Mass came more and more to supplant the preaching of the Word. The ministry became more and more a priestly caste. The altar assumes centrality in the Church, while the pulpit languishes. The believer's self-sacrifice through the deacons is less emphasized than the priests' repeated "sacrifice" of the Lord's flesh and blood on the Church's altars.

His office thus usurped, the deacon becomes (until the Reformation) a jack of all trades, only some of which continue the function assigned him after Pentecost.

Some of the tasks of the deacon, especially after about the fourth century when the changes described above took firm hold upon the Church, were as follows:

1. The deacon assists the bishops and the priests in the altar services, especially in caring for the utensils employed in the Mass.

2. Offerings are presented to the deacons who in turn present them to the priests, who consecrate them to God at the altar. The deacon may say aloud the names of givers as their contributions are received.

3. Deacons are sometimes assigned the reading of the New Testament "lesson" at the communion service.

4. In the absence of presbyters (ministers) at worship services, the deacon was permitted to read a sermon selected from writings of the Church Fathers.

5. Deacons often distributed the elements of the communion service when these were offered to the people. They might take them to members absent by reason of age or illness.

6. Deacons were, by special dispensation of their bishop, permitted to baptize.

7. Lacking printed bulletins, the Church often entrusted announcement of the order of the service to her deacons. They might, for example, announce when prayers were to be said, and for what or whom; when to kneel, etc.

8. By special permission of their bishop, deacons might be allowed to compose and deliver their own homilies (sermons).

9. The deacons were occasionally assigned to accept the return of erring members to the congregation by the laying-on of hands.

10. Deacons were sometimes delegated to represent their bishop at conferences, but were not allowed to cast votes nor to be seated.

69

11. Because no one was permitted to talk, or sleep, or laugh during services, deacons were often designated to maintain order by enforcing these regulations.

12. Deacons could act on behalf of their bishops in the distribution of alms and gifts.

13. As eyes and ears of the bishop, deacons were expected to take note of, and report on, the behavior of Church members.

14. When the bishop sat upon his throne, deacons often stood at his right and left hand to do his bidding.

15. Entry upon the diaconal office was prohibited before the age of 25; and in keeping with the New Testament tradition, some congregations limited the number of deacons to seven.

16. The office of archdeacon was also introduced, with these functions:

   a. To be leader among the deacons, either by their own election or designation by the bishop.

   b. To act for the bishop as his representative within the congregation and for it.

   c. To advise and assist the bishop in charities and gifts to the needy.

   d. To preach when the bishop is absent.

   e. To assist in the ordination of the inferior clergy: subdeacon, reader, singer, deaconess.

   f. To censure, as necessary, other deacons and inferior clergy.

These tasks characterize the diaconate up to the Reformation, and several may still be discerned in the Roman Catholic Church.

The deacon of today will learn little, it is evident, about the nature and tasks of his office by reference to its history in the Church from the fourth century A.D. to the Reformation—except to see the debilitating effect upon the diaconal office as the preaching ministry becomes a priestly caste.

F. *SINCE THE REFORMATION*

Reform meant, for the Reformers, restoration.

Their intention was to restore the Church to her New Testament model, especially to the offices specified by the Scriptures.

For a time, Martin Luther differed with Calvin as to the role of the Bible in defining the structure of the Church. During that period, Luther agreed with the sectarians that the Church has the right to define and fill any ecclesiastical offices she desires. Calvin maintained, on the contrary, that only the offices expressly instituted by divine revelation should characterize the Church. To this view Luther came, also, to give his support.

The Reformed Church of Calvin's Geneva restored the office of deacon to its New Testament role, and thus set a pattern followed by Reformed/Presbyterian/Congregational communions ever since, and one appearing with some modification in other denominations. The conception of the diaconal office appearing in this *Handbook* reflects the Genevan-Reformed-Presbyterian tradition. Little need here be said, therefore, by way of history.

Suffice to point out that the Genevan Church divided its diaconate by function, and made explicit and widespread use of the deaconess (see Chapter 14).

Geneva's deacons had two functions:

1. To receive, and seek out, contributions in money, goods, and skills, and to distribute them among the needy. The deacons involved in these tasks were called the "procurers". Because Calvin laid great stress upon self-sacrificial evidence of love in-deed through the diaconate, it is possible that "procurer" meant those who persistently laid upon the membership their duties, through the Church, to the poor and needy. No collection-plate was passed during the Genevan service. Gifts could be left in the money-box stationed in the narthex of the churches, or could be given on direct visit and appeal by the procurers. It is likely that careful record was kept as to each member's generosity, something which the procurers no doubt undertook to stimulate. One can even envision a particularly conscientious procurer suggesting to a delinquent parishioner that they together go over the member's tax form—a suggestion which the Genevan Consistory was likely, in extreme cases of suspected hoarding, to endorse.

2. The second function assigned the Genevan congregations' deacons is indicated by the term "hospitallier". This has reference to the fact that the central charitable institution of Geneva was called the "hospital". There the sick were lodged and cared for, and in addition the same building served as an old people's home, as a refuge for homeless refugees fleeing persecution, and as temporary quarters for any who were without warmth and shelter. The administration of the hospital was under the Genevan deacons. So was the personal care of the sick and aged and the needy. All the deacons (and deaconesses) involved in this extensive operation were called "hospitalliers". The

hospital administrators were fulltime, professional deacons. It is likely that so were at least some of those, both men and women (deaconesses), serving in the work of mercy.

Once again, in the Reformation, the pulpit wielded the sacrificing sword of the Spirit. Once again, the believer was challenged to the self-sacrifice of love. And once again, the fruits of that sacrifice were collected and distributed by the Church's diaconate. Geneva thus becomes the model, designed after the New Testament Church, for diaconal service in the Protestant Church, a model likely to spread more and more through the contemporary Catholic Church as the pulpit there increasingly wields the same self-sacrificing sword of the Spirit.

PART III

THE DEACON: FOREGROUND

Chapter 10

THE DEACON TODAY

The office of deacon, where it is retained, implies different functions in different denominations and churches.

As, for example, in:

1. Roman Catholic and Episcopal churches:

The deacon is considered a member of the clergy, generally assigned as assistant to the priest. He may exercise certain liturgical functions by specific authorization, especially when no priest is present. In practice, the office of deacon may be transitional between the seminary and the priesthood, though it may be filled by laity who have no aspiration to ordination.

The proposed Episcopal *Prayerbook* defines the office of deacon as follows: "Called to a special ministry of servanthood directly under the bishop. They are to serve all, especially the poor, the weak, sick and lonely, to study the Scriptures, to make Christ known in word and deed, to interpret to the Church the needs, concerns, and hopes of the world, to be guided and led by the bishop, and to seek not their own glory, but the glory of Christ. Also to interpret the world to the Church."

2. Eastern Orthodoxy:

The deacon is not considered a member of the clergy. His function is limited to chanting the liturgy.

3. The Lutheran Churches:

Different branches of the Lutheran Church have made various efforts, since the Reformation, to define the office of the deacon. The rise of the modern welfare state seems to have rendered the diaconate generally inoperative in Lutheranism, leaving the eldership responsible for the material as well as the spiritual concerns of the congregation.

4. Reformed/Presbyterian Bodies:

The office of deacon is generally maintained, but with a steady erosion of function as special agents of self-sacrifice. Emphasis has often primarily shifted to financial management for the congregation, the deacon becoming the "business manager" or "trustee" of the Church.

5. Other Protestant Churches:

There is a wide range of difference among Protestant communions extending from a Board of Deacons as the ruling body in the congregation on one hand, to redefining the office as "trustee" or property-holder for the Body on the other. Assuming that the welfare state now provides for the material needs of everyone, some churches have phased out the office of deacon as no longer required.

It is the contention of this book that the office of deacon reflects one of the marks of the true Church, and one of the offices of Jesus Christ. The use, or restoration or reaffirmation, of this office is, therefore, of crucial importance to the health of the Church.

Chapter 11.

BIBLICAL PROFILE:
THE OFFICE OF DEACON

A. *IN THE BOOK OF ACTS*

"...pick out from among you seven men of good repute, full of the Holy Spirit and of wisdom" (Acts 6:11).

Qualifications requisite to holding the office of deacon are first stipulated in the Book of Acts.

There had been complaint in the Jerusalem Church that certain widows "were neglected in the daily distribution" (Acts 6:1). This undoubtedly points to a flaw in the practice of that Church's having "all things in common" (Acts 2:44; 4:32). And, as we have already observed, the office of deacon first appears to amend the deficiencies of that early "New Testament communism".

The Apostles are occupied full-time with "preaching the word of God" (Acts 6:2). They instruct the Church to "pick out" seven men who are known for three traits of character. These become, then, the first outlines of the office of deacon, parts of a profile that must today characterize nominees for this high calling:

1. Of good repute:

There must be no blemish on the reputation of him who is considered for this office. Still more, he must be known for honesty, integrity, unselfishness, diligence—the ingredients of "good repute".

It must be emphasized that "repute" is in the mind of others, not in the self-image of the candidate. In accepting nomination to the office of deacon, you do not thus lay claim yourself to the required virtues. We are all well aware of our personal defects. Often the better repute one has, the less he thinks himself meriting it. The requirement is not for perfection. It is to characterize the image of the man entertained by those who know him. Let them be the judge of your qualifications to serve. They are required to choose those of "good repute".

2. Full of the Holy Spirit:

This qualification, too, has no reference to the candidate's conception of himself. Some who think themselves on intimate terms with the Spirit are seen by others as suffering great delusion. The presence of the Spirit becomes known through the doing of the works of the Spirit. And these works are described by the Apostle: "The fruit of the Spirit is love, joy, peace, patience, kindness, goodness, faithfulness, gentleness, self-control" (Gal. 5:22).

Peter puts it this way, in his testimony before the Sanhedrin: "...the Holy Spirit whom God has given to those who obey Him" (Acts 5:32). Let the nominee for the office of deacon be certain within himself that it is his sincere desire to obey God's will. God is responding by the gift of His Spirit, seen in you by others who nominate and elect you to office.

3. Wisdom:

Wisdom is more than knowledge. Wisdom cannot be taught, nor laid hold of directly. Wisdom is the fruit of obedient experience, and descends from God upon those who seek after His will to do it. Once again, let it be the judgment of others as to whether or not you possess the qualification of wisdom. It is more easily observed by others than by oneself. Indeed, the wisest often take themselves as victims of foolishness. St. James describes wisdom this way: "Who is wise and understanding among you? By his good life let him show his works in the meekness of wisdom. The wisdom from above is first pure, then peaceable, gentle, open to reason, full of mercy and good fruits, without uncertainty or insincerity" (Jas. 3:13, 17).

B. *FURTHER CHARACTERISTICS*

St. Paul lays down further Biblical requirements for deacons in his first letter to Timothy: "Deacons likewise must be serious, not double-tongued, not addicted to much wine, not greedy for gain; they must hold the mystery of the faith with a clear conscience. And let them also be first tested; then if they prove themselves blameless let them serve as deacons. The women likewise must be serious, no slanderers, but temperate, faithful in all things. Let deacons be the husband of one wife, and let them manage their households well" (I Tim. 3:8-12).

1. Serious:

How else shall the deacon approach his calling than with utmost seriousness? The dimensions of his task demand the best he can give, in all earnestness. A serious approach to his work enables the deacon to instill confidence in those with whom he has to do.

2. Not double-tongued:

"Speaking the truth in love" (Eph. 4:15) is the obligation of all Christians, an obligation which Paul stresses especially for the deacon. Deceit in word or manner will quickly alienate the deacon from those whom he seeks to serve and those whom he seeks to guide and instruct. Some of the deacon's contacts will be delicate in nature, whether they be with those who have real needs but find them hard to admit, or with those from whom the Church expects greater generosity than they display. In both cases, strict adherence to the truth is mandatory, and essential to success.

3. Not greedy for gain:

How can someone who has a reputation for greed or for miserliness be fit to solicit generosity from others? How could a diaconate concerned to build a substantial Church bank account be gladly doing the Lord's work through serving the needy?

4. Holding the mystery of the faith with a clear conscience:

The term "mystery" is not used in Scripture to indicate a puzzle, something we will never comprehend or understand. Rather the Bible uses "mystery" to indicate truths that shed light into our lives, not because we can explain them but because we believe and live by them. Paul says: "And even if our gospel is veiled, it is veiled only to those who are perishing. In their case the god of this world has blinded the minds of unbelievers, to keep them from seeing the light of the gospel of the glory of Christ, who is the likeness of God" (II Cor. 4:3-4). What is here required of the deacon is that he decline to becloud his faith by "foolish disputations" (Rom. 14:1) which serve only to trouble the conscience. Let him joyously be about his Master's diaconal business, avoiding the speculations of those who are "forever learning but never come to a knowledge of the truth" (II Tim. 3:7).

5. Let him first be tested, etc.:

Two standards are implied here:

a. A recent convert should not immediately be nominated for diaconal office. Let the congregation first have opportunity to measure his stature.

b. Diaconates should seriously consider some kind of internship program, by means of which newly elected deacons serve an apprenticeship before installation in office. Such "on the job" training could last six months, not counted as part of the deacon's term of office. The purpose is not for weeding out, but for qualifying those, who have been chosen, for the best possible service.

6. The women likewise must be serious, etc.:

The Apostle may have reference to deaconesses. This office we discuss in Chapter 14. More likely, however, the reference here is to what is required of the deacon's wife. Except for confidential matters, it is highly desirable that the deacon share his work with his wife. She may, indeed, be of great assistance to him in many ways. But such partnership requires of her a seriousness also, and a lock upon her tongue outside the home. She, like him, must "be faithful in all things." Happy is the congregation whose deacons have such wives!

7. Husband of one wife:

No doubt this is a reference to the practice of polygamy which prevailed where some of the new congregations had been established by Paul's missionary efforts. The requirement is still important in cultures where new churches are now being established where polygamy prevails. It need not, of course, be applied *against* nominees who are single or widowers.

8. Let them manage their household well:

No one is more acutely aware of his own shortcomings in this regard than the diaconal nominee. Here once again he must let others decide what impression his household management leaves upon them.

C. *SUMMARY*

The more conscientious the potential deacon is about these qualifications, the more he breathes a sigh with Paul: "Who is sufficient for these things?" (II Cor. 2:16). And by himself, no one is. But the deacon does not stand in his own competence, nor hope to serve by his own strength. And he joins the Apostle in answering his own question: "I can do all things in him who strengthens me" (Phil. 4:13).

Let each resolve to accept office, if nominated and elected to it, in the determination to rise, by grace, to its high challenges and opportunities. We are all on the way. Remember that even St. Paul was striving for obedience: "Not that I have already obtained this or am already perfect; but I press on to make it my own, because Christ Jesus has made me his own...one thing I do, forgetting what lies behind and straining forward to what lies ahead, I press on toward the goal for the prize of the upward call of God in Christ Jesus." And to those called to be deacons, the Apostle then adds (addressing, of course, all Christians): "Let those of us who are mature be thus minded" (Col. 3:12-15).

The first challenge to the mature is to accept the office.

The next is to fill it well—in the strength of the Lord!

Chapter 12.

LEVELS OF AWARENESS: FAITH AND WORKS

You as deacon will be, right now, at some level in understanding the relationship between faith and good works as that applies to your office and its responsibilities. So will your congregation. We see these levels as follows:

A. *LEVEL ONE: ARE YOU SAVED?*

At this stage all emphasis falls upon salvation by faith. No necessary relation is perceived between salvation and service.

The Bible knows this level: "For by grace you have been saved through faith; and this is not your own doing, it is the gift of God—not because of works, lest any man should boast" (Eph. 2:8-9). Assurance of salvation exists, at this stage, by itself. If the believer thinks at all in terms of charity to the needy, it is as something added to salvation. The believer's focus is far more on sharing the faith, and supporting the congregation for this purpose, than on sustaining a diaconate for service to the poor. Congregational offerings are taken for evangelism. Acts of charity are thought largely to be the responsibility of the individual believer as the Spirit moves him. Theologically, stress falls upon grace as opposed to law, on the New Testament in contrast to the Old. Talk of good works is likely to be interpreted as "the social gospel," or as a futile effort to gain heaven by one's own exertions.

At this stage in congregational consciousness, the diaconate will be optional or may be concerned solely with administrative functions.

B. *LEVEL TWO: VOLUNTARY GRATITUDE*

The believer is indeed saved by grace. This fundamental truth the Bible repeats over and over: "Since all have sinned and fall short of the glory of God, they are justified by grace as a gift, through the redemption which is in Christ Jesus" (Rom. 3:24). "As far as the east is from the west, so far does He remove our transgressions from us" (Ps. 103:12).

Thinking on such unmerited salvation, believers find themselves stirred to gratitude. Moreover, they are aware that gratitude must be more than lip-service. Does not the Prophet Isaiah condemn those "who draw near with their mouth and honor me with their lips, while their hearts are far from me" (Is. 29:13)? A judgment reinforced by the Lord Himself (Matt. 15:8-9). Much of the congregation's effort to give material expression to their gratitude may still go into support of word-evangelism, both that of the congregation itself and that of radio and television crusadists.

But gratitude may also take the form of charity. And as an arm of the congregation the deacons will try to meet human need, confined largely to that within the congregation.

Here the deacon has moved from the optional to the desirable.

C. *LEVEL THREE: MANDATORY GRATITUDE*

Reading on in Paul's letter to the Ephesians, just past the point quoted under Level One above, the believer is told: "For we are His workmanship, created in Christ Jesus for good works, which God prepared beforehand, that we should walk in them" (Eph. 2:10).

We are not saved *by* good works, true indeed, but we are saved *for* doing them, no doubt about that! Reflecting upon the import of this and similar Biblical teaching, the deacons and the congregation move into two new awarenesses:

1. Salvation is *both* individual and communal. Faith unites believers both to Jesus Christ and to His Body, the Church. Each is a *member*, that is a living part, of the whole congregation. St. Paul graphically describes what such membership in the Lord's Body, which is the Church, means in the twelfth chapter of First Corinthians. Deacons should frequently meditate alone, and discuss together, this powerful message—and should encourage its being preached to the congregation. Paul says, for example, that God distributes various gifts to members of the Church so that, by mutual service and dependence, the Body is drawn the closer together: "...that the members may have the same care for one another. If one member suffers, all suffer together; if one member is honored, all rejoice together" (I Cor.

12:25-26). Again: "Now there are varieties of gifts, but the same Spirit; and there are varieties of service, but the same Lord; and there are varieties of working, but it is the same God who inspires them all in every one" (I Cor. 12:4-6). Deacons are chosen, and supported by the congregation, to act for the whole lest anyone be overlooked.

2. Both congregation and deacons become aware that in their mutual concern for each other, the members of the Body present a powerful witness to the world: "Maintain good conduct among the Gentiles, so that in case they speak against you as wrongdoers, they may see your good deeds and glorify God..." (I Pet. 2:12). The congregation finds itself, as it were, set upon a hill, in thus being concerned for each other, and rejoice in the reminder: "Let your light so shine before men, that they may see your good works and give glory to your Father who is in heaven" (Matt. 5:16).

At this stage the diaconate is recognized as necessary, and deacons should creatively undertake to serve the needs of the Body with the resources of the Body.

D. *LEVEL FOUR: FAITH IS GOOD WORKS*

The Lord asks: "Who are my mother and my brothers?" And He answers: "Whoever does the will of God is my brother, and sister, and mother" (Mark 3:33, 35).

At this stage, in diaconal and congregational consciousness, it is perceived that faith and behavior merge. We are no longer able to separate salvation by faith from the doing of good works through faith in obedience to the will (that is, law) of God. The desire to do good, in gratitude for salvation, is now seen not simply as evidence of rebirth in Christ Jesus, it *is* rebirth in Christ Jesus. Doing good is the other face of being saved—for it is to do good that we are saved! Or, better, we enter upon salvation through obedience which is displayed in good works. This is evident throughout the Scriptures:

1. To believe in Jesus as Savior is to obey Christ as Lord: "And by this we may be sure that we know him, if we keep his commandments" (I John 2:3). Again: "If you love me, you will keep my comandments" (John 14:15). And once more: "Not every one who says to me, 'Lord, Lord,' shall enter the kingdom of heaven, but he who does the will of my Father who is in heaven" (Matt. 7:21). Those who believe obey, and those who obey believe.

2. Being wise unto salvation means building upon the Rock, which

is Christ. But such building consists in doing the good works which Christ the Rock commands: "Every one then who hears these words of mine and does them will be like a wise man who built his house upon the rock; and the rain fell, and the floods came, and the winds blew and beat upon that house, but it did not fall, because it had been founded on the rock" (Matt. 7:24-25). "Be doers of the word, and not hearers only, deceiving yourselves...he who looks into the perfect law, the law of liberty, and perseveres, being no hearer that forgets but a doer that acts, he shall be blessed in his doing" (Jas. 1:22, 25).

3. To know God is to do justice: "Did not your father eat and drink and do justice and righteousness? Then it was well with him. He judged the cause of the poor and needy; then it was well. Is not this to know me? says the Lord" (Jer. 22:15-16). "Is not this the fast that I choose: to loose the bonds of wickedness, to undo the thongs of the yoke, to let the oppressed go free, and to break every yoke? Is it not to share your bread with the hungry, and bring the homeless poor into your house; when you see the naked, to cover him, and not to hide yourself from your own flesh? Then shall your light break forth like the dawn..." (Is. 58:6-8). Again, the Prophet declares: "They shall not hurt or destroy in all my holy mountain..." Why not? "For the earth will be full of the knowledge of the Lord as the waters cover the sea" (Is. 11:9). The knowledge of God *is* the doing of right, that is, the doing of His will.

4. The believer is required to love: "Owe no one anything, except to love one another; for he who loves his neighbor has fulfilled the law" (Rom. 13:8). Again: "For the whole law is fulfilled in one word, 'You shall love your neighbor as yourself' " (Gal. 5:14). And the Lord adds this: "By this all men will know that you are my disciples, if you have love for one another" (John 13:35).

At this stage of awareness, the diaconate is perceived as registering by its activity the spiritual temperature of the congregation. The deacons witness to the warmth of love to the Body and to the world much as a thermometer registers warmth of weather.

Here the deacons are known to be indispensable.

E. TO ATTAIN LEVEL FOUR

Obviously, level four awareness is *the* diaconal goal both for the deacons themselves and for the people they serve. Can this level be sought—and found? If so, how will you go about that?

Begin with the knowledge that the life of love is not natural to us. By nature, we are ruled by self-interest. The Lord requires a life of self-sacrifice. The gradual substitution of the will to self-sacrifice for the will to self-interest is what progress in the Christian life consists of. The goal of the Church herself is promotion of the life of love in each member of the congregation. And the congregation's united progress toward this goal will be measured on the diaconal thermometer above.

How does the Church, then, go about seeking level four awareness?

1. By the preaching of the Word: "So faith comes from what is heard, and what is heard comes by the preaching of Christ" (Rom. 10:17). Faith matures more and more into the life of love under persistent preaching of the Scriptures: "All scripture is inspired by God and is profitable for teaching, for reproof, for correction, and for training in righteousness, that the man of God may be complete, equipped for every good work" (II Tim. 3:16-17). Preaching is always the key, and the congregation set on a hill by the witness of its good works is evidently the place where the Word of God is most effectively preached.

2. Those who ardently desire developing the gift of faith can seek diligently to do the works of faith. The Bible clearly specifies what works a true faith leads the believer to do: "...the fruit of the Spirit is love, joy, peace, patience, kindness, goodness, self-control...." (Gal. 5:22-23). "Love is patient and kind; love is not jealous or boastful; it is not arrogant or rude. Love does not insist on its own way; it is not irritable or resentful; it does not rejoice at wrong, but rejoices in the right. Love bears all things, believes all things, hopes all things, endures all things" (I Cor. 13:4-7). An effort to live such a life of love opens the heart to greater possession by faith.

Again and again, the Old Testament prophets and Christ Himself stress the fact that a hard heart presents a deaf ear to the Word. And the heart is hardened by persistent refusal to support the needy and to do good works among men. All who seek to open their hearts to the Spirit and the Word can prepare the soil in which faith finds fruit by doing the works of faith, through presenting themselves where the Word is truly preached.

F. *IN SUMMARY*

Diaconal service is not an accidental, optional, perhaps haphazard series of handouts given by Christians and the Church on their way to

87

glory. Diaconal service *is* the way to glory, and the more certainly the congregation is on its way to heaven the more certainly will its *works* testify to the love of God.

Chapter 13.

THE DEACON AND THE KINGDOM

The congregation which strives to live out its faith and gratitude through a wide range of diaconal services sees itself in terms of the Kingdom of God.

There is much scholarly dispute over what that Kingdom of which the Bible so frequently speaks really is. Some equate it with the Church. Others with the end of time when God will be all in all (I Cor. 15:28).

We think of the Kingdom as present wherever and whenever the will of God is obeyed among men. So it appears in the Lord's Prayer: "Thy kingdom come, Thy will be done...."

God's concern for the widow, the orphan, the poor, the afflicted points to His desire that the Kingdom be extended everywhere. Where the Kingdom is, there is charity and justice. Where charity governs and justice reigns, there can be no oppression of the weak.

The Church is instructed to pray for the coming of the Kingdom, here and now: "Thy kingdom come..." (Matt. 6:10). The Lord commands, "Seek first his kingdom and his righteousness..." (Matt. 6:33). This requires the Church to go beyond feeding the hungry, clothing the naked, and rescuing the oppressed. The Church must actively seek to expand the Kingdom in its community, that is bring the will of God to bear upon the lives of all within the scope of its influence.

The presence of the poor points to a lien upon the Kingdom. Poverty is symptomatic of deeper problems.

This means that the diaconate is challenged by human need to do more than just meet that need. The diaconate is challenged to bring in the Kingdom, that is obedience to the moral law of God, wherever its absence creates human misery. Deacons are called upon to prevent poverty as well as to minister to it.

A. *ROOTS OF POVERTY*

Deacons will want to now what are some of the root causes of poverty in their parish and community, in order to confront these with the Kingdom. Root causes like these:

1. Defects of spirit, like the hopelessness that enervates and destroys the will to produce and do work, or like the indifference that prefers handout to earning.

2. Defects of heritage, like poor training, bad work habits, inadequate education, absence of role models for incentive.

3. Defects in the system, like job markets destroyed by technology or by the closing or transfer of industry, like the flooding of the job market beyond its capacity to absorb labor.

4. Defects brought about by the greed of others, by the deliberate abuse of the weak, by theft under the color of legality.

The Kingdom is extended whenever these roots of poverty and need are discovered, analyzed, and dealt with by bringing all the resources of your congregation to bear upon them. Christian love relentlessly demands justice, in the name of the sovereign God. This is the believer's response to his own prayer: "Thy Kingdom come, Thy will be done, on earth...!" Leadership in this pursuit of the Kingdom falls to the deacons, as the arm of the Church extended to do good among men. The telltale evidence of injustice is poverty and oppression, and these come first to the attention of the diaconate.

B. *POVERTY CHALLENGES THE KINGDOM*

The existence of poverty and need is not necessarily an indictment of the poor and needy. God gives and God withholds material prosperity as He wills: "The Lord giveth, the Lord taketh away..." (Job 1:21). And those whom the Lord leaves in poverty present a dual challenge to the Church:

1. They test the Church's love of God in word to become the Church's love of neighbor in deed: "for he who does not love his brother whom he has seen, cannot love God whom he has not seen" (I John 4:20). "But if anyone has the world's goods and sees his brother in need, yet closes his heart against him, how does God's love abide in him?" (I John 3:17).

2. They are God's challenge to the Church to engage all of her resources, spiritual and material, verbal and political, to extend His

Kingdom by attacking poverty at its roots and furthering the spread of justice among mankind.

C. *SUMMARY*

This *Handbook* might have been sub-titled "A Manual of Citizenship". It points to how citizens of the Kingdom of Heaven obey their King in the use of His many gifts to them. In this sense, all that is said here is about the Kingdom.

The Kingdom of Heaven is opposed by another kingdom, commonly designated by Scripture as the kingdom of this world. This kingdom, ruled by the devil, is always portrayed as in mortal combat with the Kingdom of Heaven. It is this struggle for the allegiance of citizens which underlies all history. The Lord and Satan do battle in the human heart, and in all aspects of time and events, for the soul of each human being.

The citizenry of each competing kingdom reveal their loyalties by their conduct: "Now the works of the flesh are plain: immorality, impurity, licentiousness, idolatry, sorcery, enmity, strife, jealousy, anger, selfishness, dissension, party spirit, envy, drunkenness, carousing, and the like. I warn you, as I warned you before, that those who do such things shall not inherit the kingdom of God. But the fruit of the Spirit is love, joy, peace, patience, kindness, goodness, faithfulness, gentleness, self-control, against such there is no law" (Gal. 5:19-23).

A kingdom *is* wherever the law of its king are obeyed.

The Kingdom of Heaven lives wherever God's will is sought, is willed, and to the best of our ability is obeyed. Liberation for such obedience roots in faith, conveyed in the Word, nourished by the Church as mother of believers.

Yes, this *Handbook* is written as a manual of citizenship—in the right Kingdom! And as a manual of offensive warfare against the kingdom of the devil!

Chapter 14.

THE DEACONESS

The Lord was served in His earthly ministry by women who went with Him from place to place. So Luke reports: "Soon afterward he went on through cities and villages, preaching and bringing the good news of the kingdom of God. And the twelve were with him, and also some women who had been healed of evil spirits and infirmities...who provided for them out of their means" (Luke 8:1-3). Mark reports that at the crucifixion, "There were also women looking on from afar...who, when he was in Galilee, followed him, and ministered to him" (Mark 15:40-41). And Matthew reports the same (27:55).

It is natural that such service done to the Lord in the body should be done to the Body of which the Lord is now Head, namely the Church. And women who so serve were called from the beginning "deaconesses". Paul writes to the Church at Rome: "I commend to you our sister Phoebe, a deaconess of the church at Cenchreae, that you may receive her in the Lord as befits the saints, and help her in whatever she may require from you, for she has been a helper of many and of myself as well' (Rom. 16:1-2).

It may be that the Apostle has the deaconess in mind when he instructs Timothy, as part of the qualifications for the deacon, "The women likewise must be serious, no slanderers, but temperate, faithful in all things" (I Tim. 3:11)—though, as we have observed elsewhere, this may apply to the wives of deacons. In either case, the qualifications should indeed characterize those who serve the Church as deaconesses.

Widows who receive assistance from the Church are especially apt candidates for deaconess, and Paul prescribes their qualifications: "Let a widow be enrolled if she is not less than sixty years of age, having been the wife of one husband; and she must be well attested for her good deeds, as one who has brought up children, shown hospitality, washed the feet of the saints, relieved the afflicted, and devoted herself to doing good in every way" (I Tim. 5:9-10). What the Apostle here avoids is the Church's taking mothers out of their homes to serve as deaconesses. Rather, it is those who can turn from the care of a family now grown to the care of the family of God in a broader context who are commended for enrollment to receive, and to give, assistance.

Like the deacon, the deaconess played a prominent role in the Church of Calvin's Geneva. Deaconesses served as nurses in the city's hospital for the indigent. They cared for the handicapped and aged in their homes. They extended the hand of the Church to the needy wherever they appeared, and were the eyes and ears of the Church in discerning distress. Their work was supervised by the diaconate, which was, in turn, under the administration of the famous Consistory of Geneva.

In cooperation with, and under the general guidance of, the congregational diaconate (which is itself under the oversight of the eldership), deaconesses bring their own touch to services like these:

1. Personal ministry to the aged, the ill, the handicapped. Such ministry could include:
   a. Sickbed care.
   b. Making meals, or delivering them.
   c. Housekeeping, and mending of clothes.
   d. Provision through others for household necessities like repairs.
   e. Companionship through hours of loneliness, including reading aloud.
   f. A card ministry—remembering birthdays, anniversaries, etc.

2. Guidance to the young, especially instruction to young mothers.

3. Teaching home care, including economical and nutritious food preparation.

4. Teaching the basics of child care, and the importance of cleanliness to health.

5. Standing at the side of mothers overwhelmed by child problems, or desertion, or alcoholic husbands, or troubles with the law.

6. Teaching children Bible truths, reading to them, counseling them.

7. Developing in connection with the Church a food and clothing depot to which the indigent can come for emergency assistance. For this kind of project the deacons should gladly furnish financial

assistance.

8. Provide care and counsel for runaways, delinquents, pregnant teen-agers, unwed mothers, children at odds with authority.

9. Staff an open phone for victims of sudden trauma.

Blessed indeed is the congregation which sees the opportunities for service which the deaconess is, as woman, uniquely qualified to perceive, grasp, and master; and which, therefore, makes provision for such appointment.

Deacon and deaconess, both under the general supervision of the eldership, can work out their own inter-relationships. There can be neither time nor effort spent in jurisdictional struggle.

The probability, moreover, of competition—even in this age of liberation movements—is resolved by the Lord's own example and teaching. After washing His disciples' feet, on the night in which He was later betrayed, the Lord says to those who were to found His New Testament Church: "For I have given you an example, that you also should do as I have done to you. Truly, truly, I say to you, a servant is not greater than his master; nor is he who is sent greater than he who sent him. If you know these things, blessed are you if you do them" (John 13:15-17).

Happy is the congregation is which 'competition' as among office-bearers is always as to who can serve the rest the more. Not, however, by abdicating the administrative responsibilities correlative with each calling, but by exercising them in love.

Congregations which neglect the deaconess miss opportunities for corporate service. Deacons or deaconesses who confuse self-assertion with self-sacrifice miss the joy of their work for their Lord.

THE DEACONESS IN THE CHURCH

Though Phoebe is the only deaconess mentioned in the Scriptures, the practice of appointing women to this calling was in common use in the early Church. Certain requirements were set down for appointment as deaconess:

1. The candidate must be a widow.

2. She must have borne children and raised a family.

3. She must have been only once married.

4. She must have attained at least the age of forty years, and there was some preference for older women.

5. By way of exception, virgins of exceptional qualification were

called "widows" in order to receive appointment.

The Church applied certain restrictions upon her deaconesses, like these:

1. They were appointed to their work, not installed or ordained with the laying-on of hands.

2. They performed no priestly functions.

Tasks commonly assigned the deaconess were as follows:

1. To teach women catechumens in preparation for membership in the Church.

2. To attend the sick, especially the women.

3. To deliver messages from the bishop to women parishoners.

4. To visit martyrs awaiting execution.

5. To supervise the behavior of women in the worship services— especially true where women entered by their own doorway and sat together.

The Council of Orange, held in 441 A.D. decided to drop the deaconess, and for five or six centuries there are none in the Church. Women re-appear in diaconal service under the title of *Diaconissa*, a term often used to designate the wife of a deacon, who assisted her husband in the service of mercy.

As noted above, it is in the time of the Reformation and especially in Calvin's Geneva that the deaconess returns to serve the Church. Practice has varied since the Reformation and continues to this day to range from no deaconesses in some congregations to the installation of women as deacons in others.

PART IV

PERSPECTIVES ON STEWARDSHIP

Chapter 15.

AS SEEN FROM ABOVE AND WITHIN

A. INVESTMENT AND RETURN

Deacons seeking a clear conception of their office can profitably look at it in these terms:

1. *God and Free Enterprise*

The Lord God is a free enterpriser. This is one reason why Karl Marx, who was not a free enterpriser, rejected God.

God is a free enterpriser because He expects a return on His investments. Jesus' parables of the talents (Matt. 25:14-30) and of the pounds (Luke 19:11-27) clearly teach us that God expects interest on the talents He invests in each of us. This is implied in the Lord's command: "You, therefore, must be perfect..." (Matt. 5:48).

In short, all of God's gifts to mankind are as a divine investment upon which the Investor expects full return. And we know from the whole tenor of the Scriptures what the nature of that return should be: so putting our talents at God's disposal that others derive benefit from the gifts given to us. This is summarized in the Golden Rule: "And as you wish that men would do to you, so do to them" (Luke 6:31).

This ideal order of return on divine investment is shattered by sin. Paul vividly describes it: "...they exchanged the truth about God for a lie and worshipped and served the creature rather than the Creator, who is blessed forever! Amen" (Rom. 1:25). Paul goes on to detail the consequences of this substitution of the lie for the truth: "They were filled with all manner of wickedness, evil, covetousness, malice. Full of envy, murder, strife, deceit, malignity, they are gossips, slanderers, haters of God, insolent, haughty, boastful, inventors of evil, disobedient to parents, foolish, faithless, heartless, ruthless. Though they know God's decree that those who do such things deserve to die, they not only do them but approve those who practice them" (Rom. 1:29-32).

The divine Investor is willfully defrauded of His return. At the heart of this theft is false worship. Men bow before their own lusts instead of before their Creator, because they are in bondage to the Devil, author of the lie!

2. *Out of Egypt*

Israel's bondage in Egypt symbolizes mankind's bondage to sin and Satan. The Lord's liberation of Israel from Egyptian bondage symbolizes His liberation of all true believers from bondage to self-interest and Satan, through the self-sacrificial death of Jesus Christ. On Jesus the Lord laid "the iniquity of us all" (Is. 53:6), so that by faith the believer is "free from the law of sin and death" (Rom. 8:2).

What, then, is this "by faith" which frees us from Egyptian bondage? It is the gift of God which sets us once more in the position of returning God some interest on His investment in us. Our gifts and talents are liberated from bondage to self-lust, and freed for service to others in the name of God. To all those liberated by faith are the parables of the talents and of the pounds addressed.

3. *Then What?*

Believers are not left in the dark as to how the Lord wants interest upon His investment of talents and gifts. The Word of God sheds light upon the ways in which interest accrues. God Himself connects our liberation with obedience to His commandments: "I am the Lord your God, who brought you out of the land of Egypt, out of the house of bondage. You shall have no other gods before me..." (Ex. 20:2-3). Liberation is under the Law, not from the Law: "Think not," the Christ says, "that I have come to abolish the law and the prophets; I have come not to abolish them but to fulfill them. For truly, I say to you, till heaven and earth pass away, not an iota, not a dot, will pass from the law until all is accomplished" (Matt. 5:17).

The commandments are summarized in the divine requirement to love God above all and our neighbors as ourselves (Luke 10:27). These are the twin guides to producing interest upon God's investment in ourselves.

The motif of investment-return appears in the Great Commission of the New Testament. The Apostles are mandated by the Christ to build His Church. First, they are to preach the good news (gospel) of liberation. Those who believe the good news are joined to the Church through baptism. And the Church is then obliged to teach them all that the Lord commands, which is how to produce a return upon God's investment in them (Matt. 28:19-20). And what the Lord commands is

62072

nothing else than what was summarized by the commandments given Israel after liberation from Egypt, and expounded by the Prophets throughout Israel's history—and further applied by the Apostolic epistles to the New Testament Church.

4. God's Agents

Like any prudent investor, God does not leave His return to chance. He pursues it. And His agents in this pursuit are the deacons of His Church.

The diaconal office is by no means, then, incidental to the role of the Church and Kingdom. The diaconate is everywhere indispensable to return on God's investment in the Church. Deacons are the link between the Owner and the vineyard, appointed to bring the firstfruits from grateful laborers to their sovereign Lord.

B. CONSCIENCE

The diaconate has a strong ally in the conscience.

Consider carefully, therefore, what the conscience does.

We do not say, "what the conscience *is*." Fruitless hours of speculation can be spent on what conscience *is*. It can be questioned whether or not all persons have a conscience, and if so whether it is acquired by birth or developed by environment. Avoid such detours by focusing upon how conscience behaves, what it does, and why that can be enlisted in diaconal service.

1. What Conscience Does

The term "conscience" impies "knowing together," or "knowing with," at one and the same time: from "con" meaning *with* and "science" meaning knowledge.

What, then, is known together by conscience? Two things: 1) the divine Law, spelled out in the Ten Commandments and inscribed by God upon the human heart as part of the divine Image in each human being; and, 2) the action one has done, or contemplates doing; the thoughts and purposes one entertains; in short, all behavior. Conscience brings Law and conduct together, and judges behavior by the Law. Conscience is the inner courtroom where God's Word and our conduct meet for judgment. Conscience is God's witness in each human heart: "...what the law requires is written on their hearts, while their conscience also bears witness..." (Rom. 2:15). Paul is here speaking of those to whom the Law did not come by special revelation, the Gentiles.

Conscience monitors behavior, makes demands upon it in the name of the Law. And in response, the believer can strive to keep his conscience clear of accusation against him by seeking to obey God's Law—and here conscience becomes ally to the Church and her diaconate. St. Paul says to the Roman governor Felix: "So I always take pains to have a clear conscience toward God and toward men" (Acts 24:16). That is to say, the Christian always takes pains to love, which is obedience to the Law.

2. *Bridge to the Particular*

Conscience plays a unique role in the obedient life.

It is often said that the Bible falls short of particulars in laying down regulations for Christian obedience. We are never expressly told, for example, how much we may keep for ourselves of all the goods which God gives us. We are not informed as to whether money should be given to one charity or to another, or whether it is right to enjoy good food and drink while many starve. The Bible declines to be an ethical recipe book. The Word only reveals general mandates and universal commandments.

Why?

Because God provides conscience to be the bridge from the general and universal Law to the particular act. Conscience is, so to speak, the elbow where the vertical command coming down from God governs the horizontal deed done among men.

The Bible is geared to conscience. The Word is addressed to conscience, and should be preached to conscience. Out of the struggle to do the revealed will of God in daily living, conscience emerges ever more sensitive and helpful. Conscience is the agent of Christian maturity.

3. *Always Reliable?*

It is easy to dispute the trustworthiness of conscience. "Let your conscience be your guide" is indeed not always a guarantee that what follows is in full accord with divine Law. The conscience requires a constant tutor—the Word of God. Believers bring conscience to the worship service to school it the better in awakening response to the Law—the version written on the conscience vibrating in harmony with the preaching of what is written in the Scriptures.

Estranged from the Church, and indifferent to the Bible, conscience may indeed become more and more wayward and less and less reliable: "And since they did not see fit to acknowledge God, God gave them up to a base mind and to improper conduct" (Rom. 1:28).

But aroused again and again by the Word preached, tutored by the Word studied, and disciplined by an alert eldership, the believer's conscience serves as the living voice of the Word, "accusing or else excusing" what he thinks, says, and does (Rom. 2:15, KJV).

4. *And the Deacon*

Conscience is always on the deacon's side. Because conscience is always requiring love, which for the deacons means generosity toward the poor and needy.

Still more, deacons should see themselves as conscience to the congregation. Yours it is to prod the stingy, to bless the generous, to bring the delinquent in charity to the attention of the ruling body in the Church.

Yours it is, also, to stimulate preaching directed upon conscience, aimed to awaken it by repeated clarion notes from the Word.

Conscience is there. We need not, and could not, create it. But how exciting a challenge to enlist its voice in your efforts to serve the Church through obedience to the divine Law.

Chapter 16.

TWIN MYSTERIES

A. THE MYSTERY OF POVERTY

"The Lord makes poor and makes rich" (I Sam. 2:6).

Could not God immediately feed all the world's hungry?

Indeed, He could!

This is evident from the miracles done by Jesus with the loaves and fishes. He reminds His disciples: "Do you not remember the five loaves of the five thousand (Matt. 14:17-21), and how many baskets you gathered? Or the seven loaves of the four thousand (Matt. 15:34-38), and how many baskets you gathered?" (Matt. 16:9-10). Twice the Lord multiplied a lad's lunch into a meal fed to thousands of men and women, with plenty left over.

God fed Israel with manna, rained from the sky in the wilderness, and even varied the diet with the meat of quail (Ex. 16). He instructed ravens to feed the prophet Elijah with bread and meat, morning and evening; and provided that the supply of meal and oil should not fail in the home of the widow of Zarephath "for many days" (I Kings 17:6, 8-16).

There is more than enough evidence in Scripture to assure us that God could, at will, satisfy human need around the globe.

But He does not.

Why not?

Because the needy serve God's purpose, and have their own recompense for so doing.

1. *God's Purpose*

How shall those who truly love the Lord manifest their love for Him in deeds? How shall believers give their Savior material expression of their love when, in fact, all is already His and He, being perfect, needs nothing?

God provides the needy to solve this problem. He wills to be sought, found, and served in the poor. This is clear from what has already been said about investment in heaven. It is clear, too, from the parable of the Last Judgment, where the Lord equates gifts made to the poor as made to Him: "Truly, I say to you, as you did it to one of the least of these my brethren, you did it to me" (Matt. 25:40).

The poor and needy are God's surrogates. We serve Him through them. That is why there are poor in God's world. And to compensate for the burden of poverty, as we shall see, God gives the needy special blessing.

2. *Secular Explanations*

The secular mind attempts many explanations for poverty. Behind them all, the Bible gives us but one fundamental account: "The Lord makes poor..." (I Sam. 2:6).

The difference between the secular explanations and the Bible's account is of crucial importance to the deacon. For the deacon the poor are not so much a problem as an answer. God provides the needy so that the deacon can reply to the question: why give? and why give in money and material goods?

Secular explanations account for poverty from some inferred cause, like: the poor are lazy; the poor are shiftless; the poor cannot handle money, do not know how to save, cannot restrain their desires, lack employable skills, can't hold a job, won't take orders, are victimized by their own sub-culture, etc. All of which may be, indeed, God's means to poverty. And, as secondary causes, they do provide the deacons with the challenge to set right what can be amended. There will always be poor enough in the world so that the Lord can bless every diaconal effort to prevent poverty. But the underlying meaning of poverty is the Lord's will to provide opportunity to the true believer to display love in deed. This becomes evident in the fact that countless millions of poor humans slave at jobs from dawn to dusk and remain poverty-stricken just the same. God makes poor....

Jesus tells a parable (Matt. 20:1-16) which enforces what is revealed through Samuel. A householder, Jesus says, goes out in the marketplace to hire laborers for his vineyard. Some he finds and hires early in the morning, some later in the day, and still others well toward evening. At day's end, the householder instructs his steward to pay each worker the very same wage. Some who had labored through the heat of day complain that those who had worked but a little get the same reward. To which the householder (God) responds: "Am I not

106

allowed to do what I choose with what belongs to me?'' (Matt. 20:15).

God, the Creator and owner of all things, does His will with the world's goods. He makes poor and rich, by giving and withholding what is His own.

We note, in passing, that poverty is the stuff of which revolution is made. Marxism rests its appeal on the misery of the proletariat. The Bible, too, has a response to that misery: obedience among the rich and powerful to the commandments of God.

Moses takes account of this option in addressing the Church as it appeared in the form of Israel: "But there will be no poor among you...if only you will obey the voice of the Lord your God, being careful to do all this commandment which I command you this day'' (Deut. 15:4-5). This, then, becomes the New Testament Church's ideal: there need be no poverty around the world, if only God's commandment to love were universally obeyed. Such should be the goal of missions and evangelism!

God does, indeed, make poor. So the Scriptures teach. But He does so, as it were, against His will. God's command to love Him above all is fulfilled in that love for neighbor which makes the elimination of poverty its prime goal. Such elimination of poverty is among the mandates laid upon the diaconate.

Jesus is, alas, so certain that the commandment of God will not be universally obeyed, that He can say: "The poor you always have with you'' (John 12:8). Marxism will not, either, scourge poverty from the face of the globe. As Moses himself had acknowledged: "For the poor will never cease out of the land...'' (Deut. 15:11)—not, that is, on account of our disobedience.

3. Divine Compensation

God goes out of His way, however, throughout the Bible, to reveal an intense concern for the poor whom He provides as opportunity to the rich, in ways like these:

a. God hears their cries of distress: "For the Lord hears the poor...'' (Ps. 69:33). "Hears'' means, in Scripture, "acts upon''. God responds to the pleas of the oppressed and needy. Many a head lies restless upon its pillow because God has heard the groans of those oppressed by its owner. Many a business failure took first root in deceit against the unwary. God hears when the victims of injustice cry to Him.

b. God supplies spiritual strength to the poor so that they may transcend their lives of grinding hardship: "For thou hast been a stronghold to the poor, a strength to the needy in his distress" (Is. 25:4). The endurance of the oppressed in the face of apparently insurmountable odds is God-given. The peace that may pervade a poor dwelling descends from above. The sweet sleep of the dead-tired may contrast with the restlessness of the rich. God makes poor, and compensates in His own way for their tragedy.

c. Though poverty commonly affords little hope of temporal escape for those caught in its toils, God promises that, "the needy shall not always be forgotten, and the hope of the poor shall not perish forever" (Ps. 9:18). The Lord lifts the eyes of the needy beyond the narrow horizons of their time-bound lives, and gives them hope which lays hold upon another, fairer world.

d. The promise given the poor is precise and explicit: "'Because the poor are despoiled, because the needy groan, I will now arise,' says the Lord; 'I will place him in the safety for which he longs'" (Ps. 12:5). The veil between time and eternity wears thin in poverty, and God lets the needy look easily beyond the narrow confines of their earthly lives. Consider the triumphant songs of the oppressed!

e. To accomplish these things among those whom He has made poor, God endows them liberally with faith: "Has not God chosen those who are poor in the world to be rich in faith and heirs of the kingdom which He promised to those who love Him?" (Jas. 2:5). This is why the risen Christ can instruct St. John to write to the Church of Smyrna, "I know your tribulation and your poverty (but you are rich)..." (Rev. 2:9). Poor in goods, but rich in faith and sure promises!

f. It is not surprising, then, that Mary magnifies the joy of Jesus' birth by singing that the Lord has "exalted those of low degree; He has filled the hungry with good things, and the rich he has sent empty away" (Luke 1:52-53). Jesus is food of hope and promise of liberation to the poor. But those rich who will not share their goods, in Jesus' name, find nothing in the Christ for themselves. Their hands full of unshared possessions, they are sent spiritually empty away by a Lord they will not serve with their hoarded goods. And the Christ Himself confirms His mother's prediction, saying at His home in Nazareth: "The Spirit of the Lord is upon me, because he has anointed me to preach good news to the poor" (Luke 4:18)—words taken from the Prophet, said many years before (Is. 61:1). God compensates those whom He makes poor in goods with the riches of the Good News of Jesus Christ.

g. Having made the poor vulnerable to the greedy, the Lord keeps jealous watch over their treatment: "The Lord enters into judgment with the elders and princes of his people: 'It is you who have devoured the Vineyard, the spoil of the poor is in your houses. What do you mean by crushing my people, by grinding the faces of the poor?'" (Is. 3:14-15). The wicked prove themselves wicked by taking advantage of those whom the Lord has made temporally defenceless: "In arrogance the wicked hotly pursue the poor...he lurks in secret like a lion in his covert; he lurks that he may seize the poor, he seizes the poor when he draws him into his net" (Ps. 10:2, 9). But God takes special note of evil done to those whom He has made poor. For that sin He destroys Sodom, raining down fire from on high (Gen. 19:24-25).

h. It was Sodom's fatal crime that she neglected the poor, and exploited those whom God had rendered weak: "Behold, this was the guilt of your sister Sodom: she and her daughters had pride, surfeit of food, and prosperous ease, but did not aid the poor and needy" (Ezek. 16:49).

4. *In Summary*

Why, then, has God made many poor, and expends such concern over them?

Deacons should reflect, as they review what has been said so far, on the parable of the rich man and Lazarus (Luke 16:19-31).

What was the poor beggar doing at Dives' gate? All he asked for food was the scraps discarded from the rich man's sumptuous table. He seems to do Dives no service. He waits in vain for love expressed in charity. Then Lazarus dies, and lo, he appears in heaven!

Why?

Because, no doubt, he had richly served God's purposes by patiently bearing the heavy yoke of poverty. Lazarus accepted without complaint the burdens laid by God upon his shoulders. And what service, then, did Lazarus do for God?

He put Dives to the test.

God made Lazarus materially poor so that Dives might be spiritually blessed. Opportunity to show love for God in doing good to Lazarus was on Dives' very doorstep. He could not come or go from his residence without observing the knock of God upon his hard heart.

Dives failed the test. He, too, like Lazarus, died—and went straight to hell!

The Lord could no more graphically portray the role of the poor in God's world. At issue in this drama, which is played everywhere around the world, was not so much Lazarus' need as Dives' soul. At issue everywhere that poverty appears is God's test of man's soul. For the poor it is a question of patient endurance of God's yoke. For the rich it is a question of love working through material goods.

And the judgment is sure: "Depart from me, ye cursed, into everlasting fire prepared for the devil and his angels. For I was hungry and ye gave me no food, I was thirsty, and ye gave me no drink..." (Matt. 25:42).

The mystery of poverty is that God uses the needy to stand in His stead among all the nations of the world. Because their yoke is burdensome, God lightens their plight with excess of faith, hope, and love. And through them God tests:

1. Those whose service to Him is in talk only, mere lip-service.

2. Those who cannot resist the temptation to take advantage of the weak.

3. Those who, in their eagerness to display their love, seek Him out in the needy where He may be found, and give of their goods, time, talents, and skills to them.

B. THE MYSTERY OF WEALTH

"The silver is mine, and the gold is mine, says the Lord of hosts" (Hag. 2:8).

No sound perspective on the Church's duty toward the wealthy is possible apart from this revealed truth: all wealth, however acquired, is God's, let out on strictly temporary loan to whoever is its temporal possessor. So crucial is this fundamental Christian economic maxim that we repeat it, and urge that the congregation be persistently reminded of the Lord's repeated declaration: "for the world and all that is in it is mine" (Ps. 50:12). Israel's King David, who himself accumulated vast public and personal sums in preparation for building the Lord's temple in Jerusalem, declares: "Both riches and honor come from thee, and thou rulest over all" (I Chron. 29:12).

Even the very effort through which anyone acquires temporal title to God's material gifts is itself His donation: "You shall remember the Lord your God, for it is he who gives you the power to get wealth" (Deut. 8:18).

All this, we repeat, is background and context for the Church's approach to the mystery of wealth.

110

1. *In Exchange*

In exchange for His gifts, as we have pointed out, the Lord exacts return. God is, as we have said, a free enterpriser, demanding interest on His loans to mankind in proportion to the gift: "Everyone to whom much is given, of him will much be required" (Luke 12:48).

But how shall the recipient of wealth know what is "required" of him in exchange for its temporal use?

Only those who ask this question seriously receive an answer: "It is written in the prophet, 'And they shall all be taught of God' " (John 6:45; Jesus is quoting Isaiah 54:13).

And how does God now teach?

By His Word, the Holy Scripture, most authoritatively as that Word is preached *in* the Church by those ordained *by* the Church to the task: "And how are they to hear without a preacher? And how can men preach unless they are sent?" (Rom. 10:14-15).

To use a Biblical illustration, the world is the Lord's vineyard, and "Who plants a vineyard without eating any of its fruit?" (I Cor. 9:7). In a more restricted sense, we may transpose the language of the prophet to say, using "Church" instead of "Israel": "And the vineyard of the Lord of hosts is the Church, and the members of it are his pleasant planting" (Is. 5:7).

It is within the Church that the question is most seriously asked: how shall we know what the divine Owner of the vineyard whose fruits we enjoy "requires" of us? It is within the Church that the answer is seriously supplied: "Thy word is a lamp to my feet and a light to my path" (Ps. 119:105). It is within the Church that the call goes out: "O house of Jacob, come, let us walk in the light of the Lord" (Is. 2:5). And it is within the Church that the scientific light shed by economics upon the uses of wealth is set in the light of the inspired Word: "...in thy light shall we see (our) light" (Ps. 36:9).

2. *What Does The Church Say?*

The Church says—or should say—concerning what God requires of those whom He has made wealthy only—and all—what the Bible says. Human research and investigation, however thorough, will not suffice. Classical or Marxist economics is not enough, and leads astray if not set in His light. The tenant cannot dictate to the Landlord the conditions of his labor or nature of his rent. The tenant—man—can only strive to learn God's rules and to do them lest he face eternal eviction. For if the Landlord's will is ignored, His reaction to such rebellion is sure: "What will the owner of the vineyard do? He will come and destroy the tenants and give the vineyard to others" (Mark 12:9). And, indeed, the inexorable passage of time brings new tenants into the vineyard and old tenants to inevitable judgment, where ignorance will be no excuse for disobedience.

What, then, does the Church have to say about wealth and its responsibilities?

This question can be answered only on two levels: 1) the teaching of the Scriptures on economic and other matters can be and has been organized into general perspectives, but 2) there is no "Christian economics" which can coerce what the pulpit will speak to the rich—or to the poor. The pulpit is free. Its freedom is guaranteed by obedience to the Word, and to the Word alone. No economics can antecedently prescribe what the Word will say to the rich—or to anyone else—as a text is exegetically applied to the life of the congregation. The sermon is—or ought to be—an adventure. The Word always runs far ahead of where the Church is, and the obedient pulpit brings tidings from tomorrow to today. No "Christian" economics dictates content to preaching; it is formulated in the preaching.

We will, therefore, suggest Biblical perspectives on the obligations of wealth to its Donor, but a living Word can only be spoken into the ear of the rich from the lips of a faithful pastor. Indeed, the Word preached at large to the congregation is particularized in the ear of each who *hears* its syllables. What is said by the pulpit, from the Word, to the wealthy is heard by each in exact proportion to his capacity to hear: "He who has ears to hear, let him hear" (Matt. 11:15). So the Lord expressed the thought we are wishing here to stress, namely that the Word spoken comes alive only in those able truly to "hear" what the Lord is saying on the lips of His ordained servant.

And who, then, comes with ears able to hear?

Only whoever comes desiring, passionately desiring, to have the Word of the Lord addressed to himself: "...seek the Lord your God, and you will find him, if you search after him with all your heart and with all your soul" (Deut. 4:29).

The Word truly preached will be heard by all truly desirous to know the will of the Landlord. He will hear who knows himself a tenant for limited duration, eager to know, because eager to do, the Landlord's good pleasure before He returns to demand an accounting of the use made of His good gifts (Matt. 21:33, 40). Such tenants seek out where the Word is faithfully preached, and will hear what the Lord requires of them.

But he who is rebellious at heart, determined to dispose of "his" wealth as he alone sees fit, will not really hear the Lord's Word even if he forever attend upon its proclamation: "The word of the Lord came to me, 'Son of man, you dwell in the midst of a rebellious house, who have eyes to see, but see not, who have ears to hear, but hear not, for they are a rebellious house'" (Ezek. 12:1-3). Rebels in the vineyard will demand, or devise, their own science of economics, claiming that the Word is economically silent or illiterate. And to them it is!

3. *Why To Each?*

Does the preached Word in fact speak to all while being heard (if heard at all) by each?

Indeed, how else can it be? For each of God's image-bearers is unique. If no two snowflakes are ever alike, will two persons ever be? Each of us is a first and only edition. So God acknowledges, and addresses us individually in the Word said to all but particularized by each.

Do you feel that in our mechanized society all slots are alike, and rob everyone of individuality? Anyone can push the broom, bake the pie, tend the machine, occupy the office, farm the land, or teach the class? Maybe so. But that is not the issue when our God-ordained uniqueness is in view. Anyone, or almost anyone, can do your job, but only you can accumulate what doing the job does to the doer! The work may be the same, but each "you" who does the work is unique. And the self that emerges from a lifetime of experience is unlike any other self made by God. It's not what we *do* that passes into eternity, but who we become by doing. And who we finally are is the living deposit of each day's doing, either in the light of the Word of God or the twilight of the word of man. God meets us uniquely because otherwise He would not meet us at all. He seeks out each of us—by name: "He who has an ear, let him hear what the Spirit says to the churches. To him who conquers I will give some of the hidden manna, and I will give him a white stone, with a new name written on the stone which no one knows except him who receives it" (Rev. 2:17). Despite appearances to the contrary, life is opportunity to individuality, and the Word which is addressed to all celebrates the uniqueness of each by speaking to each where he lives.

The Bible does not permit, therefore, simplistic solutions to the mystery of riches, like these:

1. That the rich should give all their wealth away. The Bible nowhere prescribes this.

113

2. That the Bible depreciates wealth. On the contrary, the Bible equates wealth with divine blessing.

3. That the Bible views having great possessions as evidence of lack of charity. God rather embraces those to whom He has given wealth from the age of the Patriarchs to the present.

The Word speaks uniquely to each of us to ward off such simplistic exegeses.

4. *Abuse of Texts*

We take note of certain Biblical texts often mistakenly employed to resolve the mystery of wealth, like these:

a. We have already observed that a rich young man, often called the rich young ruler, approaches Jesus with a question: "Teacher, what good deed must I do, to have eternal life?" The Lord points him to the Law. The young man claims to have kept the Law from his youth. Then Jesus adds: "If you would be perfect, go, sell what you possess and give it to the poor, and you will have treasure in heaven; and come, follow me" (Matt. 19:16, 21).

Can only the poor follow him? And is this a mandate laid on all who are rich: "Go, sell what you possess and give it to the poor"?

It would be recklessly simplistic so to interpret the story.

Such total divestiture was not required of Zacchaeus, chief tax collector of Jerico. Zacchaeus was blessed by the same Lord who admonished the rich young man to sell all, when Zacchaeus declared: "Behold, the half of my goods I give to the poor..." (Luke 19:8).

Sell all, then? Or half? Or...?

We are saying that no generalizations can be derived from simplistic exegesis of selected texts. Clearly, the Lord dealt then as His Word does today, uniquely with each who come seeking direction for the use of his wealth.

Joseph of Arimathea was "a rich man" (Matt. 27:57), who fulfilled prophecy (Is. 53:9) because his riches gave him access to Pilate to secure the body of Jesus for burial in Joseph's new-hewn tomb. Jesus Himself and His disciples were supported by those "who provided for them out of their means" (Luke 8:3), and Paul is befriended by the wealthy on his journeys (Acts 16:40, for example). Abraham and all the Patriarchs were very rich and companions of God, as was King David who was both rich and the prototype of Jesus.

In short, no simplistic inference can be carried over from the advice given the rich young man to the obligations of all the rich who seek to please God. Rather, it becomes obvious that the Word of the

Lord addresses, all across history, each of the wealthy in a unique way.

b. Immediately after the rich young man rejects Jesus' advice, the Lord has the following discussion with His disciples: "And Jesus said to his disciples, 'Truly, I say to you, it will be hard for a rich man to enter the kingdom of heaven. Again I tell you, it is easier for a camel to go through the eye of a needle than for a rich man to enter the kingdom of God.' When the disciples heard this, they were greatly astonished, saying, 'Who then can be saved?' But Jesus looked at them and said to them, 'With men this is impossible, but with God all things are possible'" (Matt. 19:23-26).

It is easy to infer from this conversation that only those who shrug off all their riches can squeeze through the strait gate onto the narrow road that leads to eternal life (Matt. 7:14). An easy, but simplistically mistaken inference.

Why were the disciples "astonished"? Had they hitherto supposed that the rich were guaranteed first entrance upon the Kingdom? And, therefore, with their exclusion no one at all would make it? So they seem to say: "Who then (if not the rich) can be saved?" And perhaps this was their mistaken assumption: first the rich, blessed by God with abundance, and then the poor, less favored from above. But "Jesus looked at them," St. Matthew tells us. Why? Is it a look of surprise? Of disappointment? How little they understand of His coming, and teaching! Can riches ever pry open the gates to the Kingdom by being given away? Does wealth unlock the strait gate? Of course not!

Entrance upon the Kingdom is quite irrespective of wealth. It is by faith revealed in obedience, also a gift of God: "With men this is impossible, but with God all things are possible"—that is, only God can make the dead soul live, and change the alien into a true citizen of the Kingdom.

That the temptations of wealth do indeed threaten entrance upon the Kingdom is true. We shall take note of that below. But neither the abundance nor the absence of riches, as such, governs eternal destiny. The soul passes through the eye of the needle by grace, not by selling all it has.

c. "Do not lay up for yourselves treasures on earth..." (Matt. 6:19).

Is this an admonition against the acquisition of wealth?

It is, if the acquisition is "for yourselves"!

It is, then, if the purpose is for saying: "Soul, you have ample

115

goods laid up for many years; take your ease, eat, drink, and be merry" (Luke 12:19). Such acquisition characterizes the "fool" (Luke 12:20).

But wealth legitimately acquired may also become capital which, in a free society, has the power to organize human energies into productive enterprise. Goods and services useful to God's world are called into existence by energies assembled and structured for productive efficiency by capital and those characterized by integrity and qualified by talent to accumulate and manage it. Such accumulation of treasure need not be, though it can be, solely "for yourselves". It is not forbidden by Scripture.

Still more, as already pointed out, wealth is power. Would that much more of such power were put to the service of the Kingdom by those who have it, and who hear the Word of God addressed to them! The hope of the weak for justice is largely dependent upon the power of wealth, and upon its influence enlisted for them by the rich who hear the Word of the Lord. The support of Kingdom causes depends heavily upon the wealthy. Social change in directions pointed by divine Law is most readily, and bloodlessly, accomplished through the power of sanctified wealth.

d. "Son, remember that you in your lifetime received your good things, and Lazarus in like manner evil things; but now he is comforted here, and you are in anguish" (Luke 16:25).

The speaker is Abraham, who is in heaven comforting Lazarus the poor beggar who lay unattended at rich Dives' gate and now enjoys the bliss of eternity. He is addressing Dives who once "was clothed in purple and fine linen and who fared sumptuously every day" (Luke 16:19), and now, after death, is in hell.

Does this mean an antithesis: rich here, poor there; poor here, rich there?

Hardly, for the very Abraham who speaks had been himself very rich, had enjoyed his "good things" on earth, and now appears in heaven.

Time is indeed the vestibule to eternity. Dives gets where he is by reason of his behavior—or rather, misbehavior—in time. But was hell, then, the "compensation" for his riches?

No, for God Himself is the donor of riches. Hell is Dives' destiny because he accounted God's gifts as solely for his own sensual benefit. He arrives in hell not for what he had but for what he lacked: "But if any one of you has the world's goods and sees his brother in need, yet closes his heart against him, how does God's love abide in him?" (I

John 3:17). Blind of eye, lacking love, Dives does not see Lazarus' need. Deaf of ear, lacking love, Dives does not hear Lazarus' weakening pleas. Hard of heart, lacking love, Dives eats and drinks and makes merry like the fool who says in his heart, "There is no God" (Ps. 14:1)—and spends eternity, therefore, in keeping with his profession.

But it is lack of love, and not God's good gifts to him in his lifetime, that determines Dives' destiny. The Bible does not teach that wealth, in itself, is cursed by compensation with evil after death.

5. *The Mystery*

But this is the mystery of wealth: that God's good gift can so readily become man's idol. And in the service of the gift instead of the Giver man goes the broad way to destruction (Matt. 7:13).

Wealth may come in many ways. Seemingly, it may be, by accident or luck, one comes into a fortune. Or by inheritance. Or through hard work, or shrewd investment, or careful saving. Who would know, without the light of the Word, that behind the scenes the ultimate Giver of all riches is God!

Wealth may come in many forms. We concentrate in this chapter on material goods. But there are gifts of talent, of beauty, of warmth of heart, of skills, of qualities of spirit—many that money cannot buy, and some far more rare than money, like artistic abilities. But always the gift can become the god, God's good perverted by man unto his damnation, "because they exchanged the truth about God for a lie and worshiped and served the creature rather than the Creator, who is blessed forever! Amen" (Rom. 1:25).

The Word, therefore, surrounds wealth with warnings, to which we shall attend. But we stress the point here that these warnings do not include the requirement that he who is blessed with abundance is thereby required to give it all away. There are, we repeat, no such simplistic alternatives for avoiding the burden of responsible use of God's good gifts. The key to responsible employment of wealth comes from the same Hand that provides the goods—it is in His inspired Word, given to the Church for proclamation to congregation and world. There the mystery of wealth is set in the context of obedience to the Giver.

6. *Mistaken Options*

Not only are some Biblical texts misinterpreted as regards the use of riches, as suggested above, but we believe that what are today called "theologies of liberation" also abuse Scripture for mistaken purposes. We take brief note of this error.

Theology of liberation has followed upon theology of revolution, both largely expounded in Central and South America, though with European roots, and both generally developed by Roman Catholic theologians. The motivation is sincere, and the point of departure very real:

a. Theology of liberation grows out of the observation and experience of human misery and of man's grim inhumanity to man. The awesome misery of the utterly destitute—the mystery of poverty—so common in the Third World provokes pity, rage, and despair. Pity for the helpless, miserable destitute, unable to provide for themselves and, still worse, for their starving and stunted children. Rage against those wealthy enough to help, but coldly, brutally unwilling to do so, and against those utterly indifferent to it all. And despair that so often the Church seems so little concerned, so cowardly, and so ineffective. Quite naturally, those who cannot sleep with the moans of misery echoing in their hearts seek license in the Scriptures for revolution and sometimes seek cooperation with Marxists to achieve it. Using the models of Israel's liberation from Egypt—the Exodus—and of Christ's triumph over the power of darkness at Calvary and through the empty tomb—Christ the Liberator—the theology of liberation seeks to take history into its own revolutionary hands. Starting from the Bible, these theologians sooner or later subdue the Word to their own ultimate designs. Theology of liberation is not obedient response to the abuse of wealth.

b. Consider, for example, this: if we can be appalled, as we should be, by human degradation, how much more must heaven be outraged by man's perversion of God's gifts into instruments of exploitation, how much more must God be anguished by human selfishness and unconcern. We may be sure, therefore, that the Bible has always reckoned seriously with precisely the gross iniquities that drive sensitive souls into plotting revolution. Indeed, the Bible always has: "Vengeance is mine, and recompense..." (Deut. 32:35). "For we know him who said, 'Vengeance is mine, I will repay.' And again, 'The Lord will judge his people.' It is a fearful thing to fall into the hands of the living God" (Heb. 10:30-31). Time and again, the Word of the Lord assures us that "The Lord is not slow about his promise as some count slowness..." (I Pet. 3:9). The day of judgment, far more terrible than any mundane revolution, awaits the merciless: "Then he will say to those at his left hand, 'Depart from me, you cursed, into the eternal fire prepared for the devil and his angels; for I was hungry and you gave me no food, I was thirsty and you gave me no drink, I was a stranger and you did not welcome me, naked and you did not clothe me, sick and in prison and you did not visit me.' Then they also will answer, 'Lord, when did we see thee hungry or thirsty or a stranger or naked or sick or in prison and did not minister to thee?' Then he will answer them, 'Truly, I say to you, as you did it not to one of the least of these, you did it not to me.' And they will go away into eternal punishment..." (Matt. 25:41-46). The Lord is aware, far more keenly aware than are we, of man's inhumanity to man. His judgment already begins in the unease which the inhumane endure, in the absence of joy which beclouds their seemingly happiest moments, and His judgment concludes in eternal damnation.

What is of crucial importance to the theologian is not revolution but proclamation. Are the rich courageously warned, again and again, that something worse than revolt threatens them if they hoard God's goods against human need, and use God's gifts to exploit God's children: "I tell you, my friends, do not fear those who kill the body, and after that have no more that they can do. But I will warn you whom to fear: fear him who, after he has killed, has power to cast into hell; yes, I tell you, fear him!" (Luke 12:4-5). That is, fear God! Let the Church so warn mankind against the "day of wrath when God's righteous judgment will be revealed. For he will render to every man according to his works: to those who by patience in well-doing seek for glory and honor and immortality, he will give eternal life; but for those who are factious and do not obey the truth, but obey wickedness, there will be wrath and fury" (Rom. 2:5-8). Let theologians demand such preaching!

c. *Political* revolution, which seeks freedom for proclamation and for obedience according to conscience, *is justified* by Scripture, and has given the Western world the liberties we now enjoy. But *economic* revolution, along Marxist lines, has enthroned tyranny wherever it has been successful, and has destroyed the freedom of preaching without which a society becomes its own prison. Marxist revolution has sometimes provided bread at the expense of liberty, but the world observes that the Solzhenitsyns who speak for multitudes declare "that man does not live by bread alone, but by everything that proceeds out of the mouth of the Lord" (Deut. 8:3), quoted by Christ against the Devil, (Matt. 4:4). Theology of liberation, so long as it substitutes economic for political Exodus, only points to the substitution of one tyranny for another.

d. Finally, theology of liberation via Marxist revolt assumes that

119

evil has an explanation and, therefore, a rational cure. This is not a Biblical, but rather a secular premise. Evil surfaces in human exploitation and callous greed. Evil tramples on the destitute in the persons of the greedy. But evil is without explanation. Evil has parentage—the Evil One—but no ground. Evil responds to no "why" or "wherefore". Hard heart, blind eye, deaf ear—the origin of these is hidden in "the mystery of iniquity" (II Thess. 2:7). The Bible assigns no cause for human depravity which may be isolated by social or psychological or economic analysis, and then cured by revolt. Marxism attributes evil to economic relations, and then assumes that abolition of such relations cures evil at its source. The dimensions of this mistake are evident in the new crop of evil which Communist tyranny so abundantly produces.

The Bible knows but one source of man's inhumanity to man. It is the depraved human heart. And the Bible knows but one cure for depraved hearts—the indwelling of Christ, via His Word, which makes new what was depraved: "Therefore, if anyone is in Christ, he is a new creation; the old has passed away, behold, the new has come" (II Cor. 5:17).

We are not endorsing the substitution of "faith" for obedience, nor the preaching of heaven as substitute for social justice. We are saying that the Bible sets the Word of God, faithfully and fully and courageously preached, in the fore of man's pursuit of social righteousness. The world may give up on the Word of God and turn to the words of Marx. But the Church can never forget that the only lastingly liberating power available to man in history is the Bible truly preached: "For as the rain and the snow come down from heaven, and return not thither but water the earth, making it bring forth and sprout, giving seed to the sower and bread to the eater, so shall my word be that goes forth from my mouth; it shall not return to me empty, but it shall accomplish that which I purpose, and prosper the thing for which I sent it" (Is. 55:10-11). This is the Word of the Lord. Simon Peter confesses to Jesus: "Lord, to whom (else) shall we go? You have the words of eternal life..." (John 6:68). But to those who despair of the Word's power to effect social change, there is the Lord's warning: "He who rejects me and does not receive my sayings has a judge: the word that I have spoken will be his judge on the last day" (John 12:48).

Either the Church and her theologians trust the power of the Word to transform social evil, or that Word will on the last day judge the Church herself for apostasy.

We therefore believe that the Word fearlessly preached, from every pulpit free to speak it, is far more productive of social righteousness than the threat or even the success of Marxist revolt.

Moreover, we believe that the Exodus is not the symbol of successful *economic* rebellion. It was the passage from bondage to the opportunity freely to serve Jehovah. The Exodus is a model for political, but not for economic, revolution. The goal of the Exodus is the right to worship: "And you shall say to Pharaoh," God says to Moses, "Thus says the Lord, Israel is my first-born son, and I say to you, 'Let my son go that he may serve me'" (Ex. 4:22-23). And the Exodus in time produces the proclamation: "...proclaim liberty throughout the land and to all the inhabitants thereof" (Lev. 25:10). To such revolution, the kind that gave democracy to one country after another in the West after the Reformation, the Bible lends support. And for such revolution the Exodus serves as a model, as does the Christ who liberates us also from Egyptian bondage, that we may freely serve Him.

For the path out of Egypt leads directly to Sinai where God reveals why He liberates His people, then and now: "I am the Lord your God, who brought you out of the land of Egypt, out of the house of bondage: You shall have no other gods before me..." (Ex. 20:2-3).

We observe, then, that theology of liberation is not the Bible's approach to resolving the obligation of riches to the God who gives them. While, at the same time, we believe that the Bible does endorse political revolution where it is necessary to secure freedom of the pulpit and liberty of obedience according to conscience.

What, then, is the Bible's approach to man and his wealth?

7. *Biblical Perspectives - General*

What the Lord requires of each of His children as return upon His gifts to them will be specifically heard, we have observed, by each in the Spirit-guided conjunction of Word proclaimed, of willing ear, and in the light of circumstances peculiar to each listener.

But the Bible does provide certain perspectives which deacons can employ for teaching themselves and helping their congregation see the obligations of wealth. First, general perspectives like these:

a. The Christian must seek to put himself and all his time, talents, and goods at God's disposal. Not at God's disposal as we wish or think that to be, but at God's disposal as He graciously reveals His will in His Word. This is the true believer's response to the First of the Great Commandments: "You shall love the Lord your God with all

121

your heart, and with all your soul, and with all your strength, and with all your mind..." (Luke 10:27; Deut. 6:5). To love God is to obey Him. The believer obeys; the obedient believe. Of this, rich Abraham is prime example. Thus to love God according to the First Commandment is deliberately to put oneself and all one has under His directives as revealed in His Word. The wealthy who turn to the Church—its preaching ministry, its ruling eldership, its serving diaconate—for guidance from the Scriptures as to appropriate use of their goods, set themselves in the right posture for doing good stewardship.

A parallel, in the Church, of such docility—teachableness—appears in the relation between the preaching and the Word. The obedient pulpit serves the inspired text even as the preacher employs his own words to expound and apply it. "He who hears you," the Lord says of such preaching, "hears me" (Luke 10:16). How do human words become God's? By *obedience* to the text. The preacher whose sole desire is to obey the Word of the Lord as he shapes his thoughts, and phrases his sentences, attains this awesome authority: what he says, in obedience to the text, God in Christ says! Similarly, in close parallel, the believer who submits what he *does* with his wealth to governance by the Word may know that what *he* does God is doing with, and through, him. This is obedience to the First Great Commandment.

b. A second general Biblical perspective is opened by the Second of the Great Commandments: "thou shalt love thy neighbor as thyself" (Luke 10:27; Lev. 19:18). Obedience to God results in service to neighbor. Love of God is authenticated by love for man. It is striking that St. Paul sets this priority in his great hymn to love in the first letter to Corinth: first love, that is to say, the will to obey the Word, and then all else; but, lacking love, all else too becomes nothing: "If I give away all I have, and if I deliver my body to be burned, but have not love, I gain nothing" (I Cor. 13:3).

The Word of God works, as it were, by indirection. It achieves one end by seeming to aim at another. Seeking the open hand and generous heart, the Word points us to love. Given love, all else follows; lacking love, no good can come. Therefore, the Apostle concludes: "Make love your aim..." (I Cor. 14:1). Therefore all that is commanded us in the Law is summed up in: Love...! The Church which preaches love, as duty to obey rather than as warmth of emotion, is a Church where the fruits of love will be achieved as by-product.

The Two Great Commandments, therefore, are the general Biblical guidelines for the proper use of all God's gifts.

8. *Biblical Perspectives - Specific*

In the context of the Commandments, the Bible lays down more specific perspectives on the proper use of wealth:

a. There are repeated warnings against letting possessions become masters rather than remaining servants:

1) "No one can serve two masters; for either he will hate the one and love the other, or he will be devoted to the one and despise the other. You cannot serve God and mammon" (Matt. 6:24).

Man is capable of two loves, two servitudes, but not at the same time. He can love, that is obey, God in the service of neighbor, or he can love gold in the service of self. The Word of the Lord comes to oblige us to choose, not only once but day after day: "Behold, I set before you this day a blessing and a curse: the blessing, if you obey the commandments of the Lord your God, which I command you this day, and the curse, if you do not obey the commandments of the Lord your God, but turn aside from the way which I command you this day, to go after other gods which you have not known" (Deut. 11:26-28).

The same hand may grasp with greed *and* give a smattering away, but the heart can only serve one master: God or self. Moses puts the alternatives again: "I call heaven and earth to witness against you this day, that I have set before you life and death, blessing and curse; therefore choose life, that you and your descendants may live, loving the Lord your God, obeying his voice, and cleaving to him; for that means life to you and length of days..." (Deut. 30:19-20). Think not that this choice was only presented, ages ago, to people long since gone from the face of the earth. It is precisely the choice set before us now, and always: "therefore choose life"! Surrender yourself and all you have to the will of the Lord as revealed in His Word! For not to serve Him *is* to serve the Adversary. The heart can have but one guiding star. There is no dual citizenship as between the Kingdom of Heaven and...another.

2) Riches not put to God's disposal threaten the very roots of the spiritual life. In His parable of the sower, Christ teaches that the Word once received may yet be choked out by "the cares of this world and the deceitfulness of riches" (Matt. 13:22). Wealth does not itself stand as neutral over against the soul. What is not freely committed to control by the Word quickly becomes enemy to the Word, and threatens to throttle the voice of the Lord and darken the light of His revelation. Enemies of obedience are the fingers of greed and the showy tinsel of affluence.

123

3) St. Paul goes so far as to charge that "the love of money is the root of all evils" (I Tim. 6:10). Here, as elsewhere, the Scripture is not condemning wealth as such. It is the *love* of money that is condemned. For love always makes of its object an end in itself.

4) The Wisdom of Proverbs reinforces the same truth: "Do not toil to acquire wealth; be wise enough to desist" (Prov. 23:4). Once again, warned against here is the pursuit of wealth as an end in itself, or as solely the means of gratifying one's own selfish desires.

5) Summary: Biblical passages like these, which might be multiplied, establish perspectives upon wealth in terms of two absolute alternatives: either, 1) we place our goods of all kinds at God's disposal under His Word, or 2) these good gifts become an intolerable burden weighting the soul toward hell and hardening the heart against all appeals from the needy.

b. The Bible also opens suggestive perspectives upon specific economic relations; we instance but an illustrative few—it will be fruitful for deacons to search out and discuss others also:

1) *Pay wages promptly and in full:* "Behold, the wages of the laborers who mowed your fields, which you kept back by fraud, cry out; and the cries of the harvesters have reached the ears of the Lord of hosts" (Jas. 5:4). This admonition of the Lord's Word is as timely today as when the Apostle penned it. All employers owe it obedience in terms of their own business affairs.

2) *Be generous:* "When you reap the harvest of your land, you shall not reap your field to its very border, neither shall you gather the gleanings after your harvest. And you shall not strip your vineyard bare, neither shall you gather the fallen grapes of your vineyard; you shall leave them for the poor and sojourner: I am the Lord your God" (Lev. 19:9). Economic circumstances change, but God does not. Though he has every *legal* right to do so, the owner or employer is *not* to extract every penny he can—remember the needs of those employed by you, or within reach of your generosity.

3) *Be scrupulously honest:* "You shall do not wrong in judgment, in measures of length or weight or quantity. You shall have just balances, just weights, a just ephah (measure of grain), and a just hin (liquid measure): I am the Lord your God, who brought you out of the land of Egypt" (Lev. 19:35-37). The same Lord our God has brought us, too, in Christ, out of Egyptian bondage to Satan, to ourselves, and to our possessions. In Egypt anything goes, but not among those for whom the Lord is God. Among them, there must be absolute

integrity in every transaction, including refusal to buy cheap and sell dear, if no value be added in between.

4) *Pay labor what it is worth:* "I will be a swift witness...against those who oppress the hireling in his wages, the widow and the orphan..." (Hag. 3:5). Do not take advantage of the defenceless in your employ. Do not league with necessity to drive hard bargains, pay starvation wages, or demand overtime without remuneration.

5) *Avoid usury:* "You shall not lend upon interest to your brother, interest on money, interest on victuals, interest on anything that is lent for interest" (Deut. 23:19). The Church since Calvin has distinguished between the right to take interest on commercial loans, which are not in view here, and taking interest on loans made to a neighbor in his necessity. Risk capital owes the payment of interest. The needy brother, if he cannot pay, may not be threatened for either interest or even the loan itself. Such is the Biblical teaching.

6) Summary: thoroughly and courageously preached, the Bible opens compelling perspectives upon the economic relations which produce wealth, and into which wealth enters. It is easy to see that these texts, and many which might be added to them, simply focus on particular relationships the light shed by the obligation to love. Or, to put it another way, Biblical economics specifies what the Lord requires by saying: "So whatever you wish that men would do to you, do so to them; for this is the law and the prophets" (Matt. 7:12).

9. *The Biblical Summary*

What the Bible teaches concerning the obligations imposed by God in the gift of riches is summed up by St. Paul in words that explain themselves: "As for the rich in this world, charge them not to be haughty, nor to set their hopes on uncertain riches but on God who richly furnishes us with everything to enjoy. They are to do good, to be rich in good deeds, liberal and generous, thus laying up for themselves a good foundation for the future, so that they may take hold of the life which is life indeed" (I Tim. 6:17-19).

This summary of the Bible's perspectives on wealth should be preached, and pondered, and obeyed in the Church of Jesus Christ. Deacons should be doing all they can to make this so.

10. *Twin Mysteries: Concluding Observations*

The aim of Christianity is fellowship with God.

The conditions for entering upon such fellowship are prescribed by the Holy Scriptures: "Jesus answered him (Judas, not Iscariot), 'If a man loves me, he will keep my word, and my Father will love him, and we will come to him and abide with him' " (John 14:23).

God gives us life and time for the sole purpose of beginning a fellowship with Him which will be consummated in eternity: "...and I heard a great voice from the throne saying, 'Behold, the dwelling of God is with men. He will dwell with them, and they shall be his people, and God himself will be with them...' " (Rev. 21:3).

God adds to life and time all other gifts of talent and goods, and provides in His Word instructions for making these into means for facilitating fellowship with Him. Mysteriously, and without explanation, He blesses many with poverty and some with riches. In both instances, God's design for promoting our fellowship with Him through the right use of His gifts may be frustrated by our disobedient use of them.

The Church has equal obligation to preach and teach the Word to poor and rich alike: "Hear this, all peoples! Give ear, all inhabitants of the world, both low and high, rich and poor together!" (Ps. 49:1-2). And this, as regards riches and poverty, is the substance of the Church's teaching: "The Lord giveth, the Lord taketh away; blessed be the name of the Lord" (Job 1:21); "And your ears shall hear a word behind you saying, 'This is the way, walk in it!' " (Is. 30:21).

In this light we make the following observations:

1. It is as difficult for the rich to acknowledge that all their possessions are God's gifts as it is for the poor to recognize that their want is God's provision. Preaching both, and diaconal teaching of them, will not be popular.

2. Materialism is as likely to characterize the poor as the rich— the one longing to acquire riches, and the other determined to hoard them.

3. Materialism may also characterize social reformers, even "Christian" social reformers, whose goals in practice often decline to crassly economic levels.

4. A noisy, pretentious concern for the poor may cloak a deep envy of the rich.

5. Intellectual reformers do not hesitate to use the poor as a lever upon the public conscience, not so much to alleviate poverty in itself as to attain their own manipulative ends.

6. Unlike some child psychologists, the Bible never hesitates to motivate behavior by promise of reward. Christ offers the rich young man what should have been a tempting alternative: "Sell all that you have and distribute to the poor, and you will have treasure in heaven..." (Luke 18:22). Surrender the temporal, and acquire the eternal—who offers a better bargain, and promises greater reward? It is some indication of the blindness induced by riches that this probably shrewd business man turned the Lord down. But the Word promises reward, both temporal and eternal, for obedience. So should the Church! The Bible also, of course, guarantees grim "reward" for disobedience, especially on the Day of Judgment, and no one lays more emphasis upon that than our Lord Himself!

7. Our own materialism tempts us to interpret every Biblical reference to riches and to poverty in terms of material goods. It is evident, however, that the Word uses both "rich" and "poor" with far broader connotation, like:

a. The Biblical "poor" are those who know that their most basic needs for time and eternity *cannot* be met short of the Gospel, as the Bible presents the Gospel—namely, the power of God to make disciples out of rebels. These, whatever their material wealth, are the true poor to whom "the Gospel is preached" (Luke 7:22) and who gladly surrender all they have to God's service (like the man who commits all he has to buying a field where the Word is hidden—Matt. 13:44). Such "poor" are those who, because they know their own emptiness (however much they have in the ways of goods), are "filled with good things" by the birth of the Lord (as Mary sings in her "magnificat," Luke 1:53). Such "poor" are those to whom "the kingdom of heaven" belongs because they know that God alone can give citizenship in that kingdom (Luke 6:20). These "poor" may be destitute or may be blessed in material possession, but their poverty is the only gateway to the eternal "riches" (Luke 16:11). Only God really knows who among us are such "poor," though their fellowship with Him will be suggested by their eagerness to put themselves and all they have at the disposal of His Word. The goal of the Church, in this context, is to alert us all to our *real* poverty!

b. Conversely, the Bible often derides the "rich" for their blindness, meaning those who are unaware of needs more profound than earthly goods can supply. These "rich" may possess great measures of wealth and talent, but they may also be materially destitute and greedily seeking riches—in either case their trust is in riches or power or acclaim and their ambition is to acquire them. These are the "rich" sent "empty away" from the birth of Jesus, like those who filled the inn that first Christmas Eve and ignored the stable (Luke

1:53). These are the rich who are castigated by the Prophets, warned by the Lord, and condemned by the Apostles, for putting God's gifts to their own service and trusting in the creature rather than in the Creator.

c. Unless the deacon bears these Biblical uses of the terms "poor" and "rich" well in mind, he is apt to confuse the instruction which the Word gives on wealth and poverty. The Bible does, indeed, speak directly to riches and poverty as such. Much of this *Handbook* is an effort to highlight just these Biblical perspectives. But each reference in the Scriptures must be carefully tested as to what riches and which poverty are being discussed.

8. We conclude these observations with two illustrations of how a text may be confused by imposing materialistic interpretation upon its terms:

a. One of the most stringent Biblical admonitions concerning possessions occurs in St. Matthew's account of Sermon on the Mount: "Therefore do not be anxious, saying, 'What shall we eat?' or 'What shall we drink?' or 'What shall we wear?' For your heavenly Father knows that you need them all. But seek first his kingdom and his righteousness, and all these things shall be yours as well" (Matt. 6:31-33).

Much is written about the Kingdom of Heaven. What does it mean to seek it first? And how, then, will food, drink, and clothing come tumbling after?

Quite simply, as already discussed in chapter 13, a kingdom exists where citizens swear allegiance to a king and undertake to obey his laws. All those who profess fidelity to God as their King and strive as loyal citizens to do His will constitute the Kingdom of Heaven in its temporal manifestation. Citizenship in God's Kingdom is not in conflict with political allegiance to any state which does not restrict liberty of worship and conscience. Indeed, the Christian is required by God to be a good citizen of such a nation. This is what the Lord implies by telling Pilate, "my kingdom is not of this world" (John 18:36). Citizens of his Kingdom are interspersed among all nations. There is not, and cannot be, a geographical Kingdom of Heaven located among the world countries. God's Kingdom has no geography—and expands across all geography!

To seek, then, the righteousness of God's Kingdom means simply to do God's will with all our might and all our gifts and talents. And will this, then, bring down a flood of riches? Yes, if it be remembered, now, that "riches" come in far more forms than just the material. But the Lord is speaking, in the text, directly to material goods: food, drink, clothing. How are these "ours" by first seeking the Kingdom's righteousness? Because all goods are, as it were, not really ours but simply on lease to us from the Giver *until we put them to His service!* Goods kept wholly for ourselves never do, really, pass from temporal lease to permanent possession. None of these is invested in heaven for permanent possession. We get lasting ownership only of those gifts we put to work here for the Kingdom, according to the King's Word: "all these things shall be yours as well."

b. "Sell your possessions, and give alms; provide yourselves with purses that do not grow old, with a treasure in the heavens that does not fail, where no thief approaches and no moth destroys" (Luke 12:33).

Some moralists call this a counsel of perfection. We think of it as fitting into the Biblical perspectives we have been outlining.

It is obvious, on reflection, that by no means all of God's gifts to us can literally be sold. Only material possessions can. Moreover, many of God's most obedient servants, like the Patriarchs, did not divest themselves of all their material goods. What, then, is meant here by "sell your possessions"?

To sell is to transfer title, done in consideration of a certain return. When, in consideration of a certain need, we place goods at the disposal of another, or place our time and talents in the service of another in love, we do fulfill the condition of the Lord's command to "sell" possessions. The purpose of goods is to serve. When we put the power lent us by great possessions into the service of justice benefitting those who need justice, this is as surely "selling" our goods as is turning them into money. Yes, let those who are influential so "sell" their possessions for the benefit of the needy. They will discover that the promise of reward is sure: "a treasure in the heavens that does not fail".

9. A final word: the Bible takes for granted that we know from experience how much "rich" and "poor" measure. The Word gives no definition of either. We know that the poor in a wealthy nation may be rich by contrast to the destitute in a deprived nation. We could stumble long and frustrate action indefinitely by demanding a definition of "rich" and "poor" before putting ourselves and our gifts at God's command. Let that not be so where deacons are active and alert.

The needy become visible, not by definition but to the eye

seeking out opportunities for obedience. Whoever seeks fellowship with God by finding Him where service can be rendered to man will find the needy without ever defining them. Let the deacon believe this, and pursue with diligence the ingathering of gifts and the organized distribution of these wherever need appears.

He or she is poor, right now, who needs something which another could give. He or she is rich, right now, who has something another needs. Often such needs can be measured, and met, in terms of material goods, passing through the loving, diaconal hands of the Church. As often, or perhaps oftener, human needs cry out for other forms of wealth, in compassion, concern, human interest, time, companionship, a smile, a word, a note, a call, a hand, a ride, a prayer.... By "selling" these the Kingdom is formed.

PART V

CIRCLES OF SERVICE

PART V.
CIRCLES OF SERVICE

How successful is your diaconate?

Successful, that is, in the Lord's service, as measured by meeting your immediate tasks, by the range of your extended outreach, and by your integration of the whole congregation in corporate diakonia?

To help a diaconate gauge its standing among the various levels of service open to this arm of the Church, we invite you to imagine a series of concentric circles, each indicating a broader range of diaconal activity. These are discussed in the seven chapters that follow.

We urge you to consider carefully the level of diaconal achievement you have reached, and to place yourselves in the circle that represents. Then let the next higher or broader circle become a challenge you strive to meet, and so on with perfection always your ideal: "You, therefore, must be perfect, as your heavenly Father is perfect" (Matt. 5:48).

Chapter 17.

FIRST CIRCLE

SERVING THE CONGREGATION

"...the laborer deserves his wages" (Luke 10:7).
"In the same way, the Lord commanded that those who proclaim the gospel should get their living by the gospel" (I Cor. 9:14).
"All things should be done decently and in order" (I Cor. 14:40).

SCOPE

Challenges and opportunities facing deacons in the context of what we are calling the First Circle of Service are discussed in three main sections, as follows:

I. The diaconate provides for the material concerns of the congregation:

    A. General survey

    B. Methods of Giving

    C. The Deacon as Trustee

II. The diaconate provides for instruction and information to help the congregation fulfill her diaconal calling:

    A. The Deacon as Teacher

    B. The Deacons' Newsletter

III. The diaconate provides encouragement and guidance to assist the congregation in the practice of stewardship:

    A. The Diaconal Visit

    B. Criteria for Giving Outside the Congregation

    C. The Deacon as "Elder"

135

PART I. PROVISION FOR THE MATERIAL CONCERNS OF
THE CONGREGATION

A. *GENERAL SURVEY*

Practice varies among congregations, and denominations, as to the role of the diaconate in the dollars-and-cents affairs of the Church. "Counting pennies" is not, for some, diaconal service, and the business affairs of the congregation are delegated to others. Oversight of all monies received by, and expended by, the congregation is considered by others as diaconal responsibility.

There is, we believe, no principle at stake. We take, therefore, the broadest view of diaconal service, including all business aspects of congregational life, while segregating detailed discussion of these aspects in the Appendix on "The Deacon as Trustee". We begin the First Circle of Service, then, with:

1. *Paying the Bills*

In sending out the seventy, the Lord instructs them to accept whatever is set before them in the homes of those who take them in: "eating and drinking what they provide, for the laborer deserves his wages" (Luke 10:7). Jesus thus enunciates a universal principle, common throughout the Scriptures: the laborer must be paid for his work. This is no less obligatory within the Church than anywhere else.

It is true that in his sad farewell to the Elders of Ephesus, St. Paul reminds them that during the three years he spent among them, "these hands ministered to my necessities, and to those who were with me" (Acts 20:34). And we know from Acts 18 that Paul's trade was tentmaking (18:3). There have been, therefore, "tentmaking ministries" across the history of the Church, staffed by those who provided for their own material necessities. But these are, properly, the exception. For St. Paul discusses at some length, in the ninth chapter of First Corinthians, the right of the ministry to be supported by the congregation: "Who serves as a soldier at his own expense? Who plants a vineyard without eating any of its fruit? Who tends a flock without getting some of the milk?" (I Cor. 9:7).

Why, then, does Paul himself decline such material return upon his own labors? Because the Gospel is new in the world. And it has competitors who indeed make a good living as traveling salesmen of sensational religious humbug. And Paul wants no such charge leveled at the Gospel of Jesus Christ. And so he writes: "Nevertheless, we have not made use of this right, but we endure anything rather than put an obstacle in the way of the gospel of Christ" (I Cor. 9:12). Indeed, he counts it his one opportunity for boasting, properly, and his reward for risky service, that he pays his own way: "What then is my reward? Just this: that in my preaching I may make the gospel free of charge, not making full use of my rights in the gospel" (I Cor. 9:18).

We make no criticism, therefore, of "tentmaking ministries," but stress the Biblical "right" of those who serve the congregation to adequate remuneration. This will include all those employed by the local Church, each of whom contributes in his and her own way to the smooth operation of the Body.

Involved also is provision for the congregation's physical plant and its auxiliary services. Sanctuary and classrooms well constructed and cared for, adequate in size and equipment, play a fundamental role in the work of the Church in the world. Deacons should take appropriate pride in seeing to it that all facilities are adequate and well cared for. There are those, and always have been some, who declaim against Church structures. The Body of Christ, however, has as much claim upon dignified and beautiful housing as does any other institution— nay, far greater claim. Let building and grounds bespeak the reverence due His presence among those who seek to serve Him.

If the congregation has use for car, bus, parish house, radio and TV outreach, and the like, these too must be provided under the broad umbrella of diaconal responsibility, to say nothing of competent janitorial service, office and classroom help and supplies, care of lawn and grounds, denominational quotas, and all else that serves the material substratum of congregational activity. What the Church thinks of herself will also be reflected in how the Body is housed and served "at home".

We take special note of some strange reluctance to pay Church employees, and often especially the ministry, comparably to other professional services. Though often schooled as long and rigorously as other professionals, pastors seldom are compared with these when salaries are being set, and demands "beyond the call of duty" are being taken for granted. We have discussed in our *Elders Handbook* the importance of adequate remuneration for the ministry, and merely summarize here by repeating that any laborer in the Lord's vineyard *is* worthy of his hire—and the deacons should ever be on the alert to see to it that this is true in their congregation. They should be ready, when necessary, to justify salaries, and to explain the "right" of congregational employees at all levels to adequate fringe benefits and vacations. Especially important is the question of how well the ministry is provided for if at retirement the pastor is obliged to enter the housing market and purchase his own dwelling, while the congregation retains title to property which has enjoyed steadily rising real estate values.

Deacons would do well to study whether potential candidates of high competence choose other professions than the ministry for financial reasons as they move out of your own congregation into the world. Do so in the light of First Corinthians, Chapter Nine!

2. *Keeping the Records*

In the Appendix on "The Deacon as Trustee" we discuss in detail the essentials of handling congregational monies. In advance of that discussion we observe that diaconates wisely interest themselves in matters like these:

a. The development and exercise of proper procedures, like:

1) Creation and up-dating of a procedural manual including clear instructions for handling of funds, a chart of various financial accounts, and relevant job descriptions.

2) Outline system of proper record-keeping and financial reporting.

3) Separation of various funds into: general, benevolence, property, endowment, etc.

4) Provision for quarterly statements to: eldership or trustees, the general membership, the auditing committee.

5) The annual audit.

b. We urge, also, the development of prudent practices like:

1) Counting committees of two, with regular rotation.

2) Weekly counting.

3) Cash deposits by a committee of two, wisely at a 24-hour bank.

4) Discourage keeping cash in the building.

5) At least two must have combination to the safe, if there be one, and it is preferably opened by these together unless used for general office supplies.

6) Receipts through numbered envelopes should be posted weekly.

7) Send quarterly statements to all members, whether or not contributions have been received.

8) Acknowledge all contributions from outside the congregation,

at once.

We commend to those who act as congregational treasurer: Loudell O. Ellis, *The Church Treasurer's Handbook,* published by Judson Press, Valley Forge, PA 19481, as the most useful guide we know to this important service.

B. *METHODS OF GIVING*

Extracting money from reluctant pockets is an ancient art. The development of TV has provided this art with the widest range it has ever enjoyed. The diaconate finds itself in competition with highly skilled competitors in pursuit of the congregational dollar.

Without resorting to the ballyhoo or hard sell of some "faith ministries," deacons have employed various means for meeting the church's budget and providing for the needy.

Some of these methods are:

1. *The budget system:*

Each member is "assessed" an equal share of the total budget. This share is defined by dividing the total budget by the number of church members. Contribution is made weekly or monthly, and record is kept by the deacons for members' income tax purposes. For purpose of record, budget envelopes are distributed to each member annually, each set with its own number. It is important, of course, that deacons keep these figures in strict confidence, indeed that only a few members of the diaconate see the records. Members who are delinquent, however, should be discussed by the deacons so that an approach to them can be planned and executed. Members who flatly decline to support the congregation, but who have, so far as the deacons can ascertain, the means to do so must be reported to the eldership or ruling body of the church for discipline.

Do not hasten to discipline. Do not quickly report the names of those quilty of delinquent giving to the eldership or council. Why not? Because this also reflects upon the diaconate. Yours, too, is a spiritual calling. The extent of its challenge is measured by the size of this *Handbook.* The deacon is also a teacher. The delinquent donor is simply a poor pupil, a challenge to your skills and tenacity. Work with him or her, pray for and with and about these in your deacons' meeting and alone. Try to impress upon them the principles of Biblical steward-ship. Go, perhaps, from a little bit of progress to the hope of more. Only after such devoted effort, done with an eye to the delinquent's own spiritual growth, should you refer the completely "hardened" member(s) to the ruling body for the discipline such must receive.

2. *Proportionate giving:*

Mechanically this method operates like the budget system. It differs in that each member is expected to contribute in proportion to income. Instead of asking a fixed contribution from each member, the church suggests that each give, say, from four to six percent of net income. The percentage figure can be reviewed each year, in the light of past experience and anticipated budget. This method meets the "can't afford it" excuse which may be heard under the budget plan, but does involve the deacons in trying to estimate whether various members are carrying their proportionate share of the load. It is important that deacons work at this, and give advice to the delinquent, if the method is not to break down.

3. *Sliding scale giving:*

The intention here is to fit contributions still more closely to the member's ability to pay. The lower the income, the lower the percentage of it asked by the Church. Deacons establish income brackets, and indicate for each bracket what percent should be budgeted for the congregation. Expected contributions increase progressively with higher incomes. In this way the greater burden is borne by the wealthier families, and those in lower income brackets can give more to other causes while doing their fair share in support of the Church. Here again the deacons must sort out those who seem to be doing less than they ought.

4. *Voluntary contribution:*

This method makes no use of budget envelopes and deacons keep no individual records. After the congregation adopts the annual budget, the membership is impressed with the necessity of providing it. From time to time, at least quarterly, the deacons advise the church as to its financial status. Apart from general admonition, the deacons have little to do in the way of giving guidance and encouragement in particular cases. For income tax purposes they are only able to divide the year's total income by the membership.

5. *Faith-promise or faith-pledge giving:*

Often used for special drives, this method can also be employed to meet the congregational budget. It is based on unsigned pledge cards, usually provided at a special meeting of the congregation at which budget needs are fully explained. After the card is handed in, fulfillment of the pledge is between the member and his conscience, under the eye of God. Substantial contributions are often raised by this method for special causes, like missions. For meeting the annual budget it is simply a special form of voluntary giving as described above.

6. *Every member canvas:*

One of the common methods of meeting the budget. It rests upon a serious effort to acquaint all the membership with the financial needs of the Church. This can be done through the mails, by special meeting, in the deacons' newsletter, or by communication from the pastor or council. Then pledge cards are distributed by mail or at the Church, or may be taken personally by elders (or trustees) and deacons to members' homes. Incoming pledges are tabulated, and until the budget is fully subscribed the effort is repeated. Budget envelopes are generally then employed to keep record of members' giving, with the usual responsibility upon the deacons of admonition to good steward-ship.

Deacons should be on the alert for other methods used successfully by churches, and be willing to discuss and, if desired, experiment with these. Basic to the success of any method is educating the congregation in the Biblical doctrines of stewardship, to which much of this *Handbook* is devoted. Giving should be a joyful testimony to the Lord's infinite goodness. The deacon should think of himself as a means to this witness by each believer.

7. *Deferred Giving*

Deacons are no doubt aware that giving by bequest, or through "living trust," etc., has become a popular form of stewardship, often promoted by organizations seeking this source of income.

Deacons should make themselves generally familiar with the various types of such giving, and do well to know who among them, or in the congregation or community, is expert in these matters, for two reasons:

a. So you can give advice to those contemplating such bequest in response to campaigns for funds of this sort, and

b. So the deacons can consider setting up a program of this kind for your own congregation, developing funds intended to support particular projects.

We remark in this connection that one aspect of everyone's stewardship is making a will. Countless bitter contentions among heirs could be avoided if a will were in effect, governing the division of an estate. It is a diaconal responsibility to encourage heads of house-

141

holds in the making, and up-dating of wills. Free advice should be offered, with guaranteed confidentiality, by deacons themselves. And lawyer-members of the congregation should be encouraged to make such service available to those who feel they cannot afford legal counsel in preparing the orderly disposal of their goods, however limited, after death. All this could, of course, include encouraging remembrance of the Church and allied causes in the formulation of bequests.

SUMMARY

All of the methods discussed above are techniques. They are simply means adapted to getting the fruits of faith and obedience efficiently gathered and handled, and duly accounted for.

It is not likely that the Bible exhibits a preference for one method over another. But the Bible does require support of congregational ministry in its broadest sense. That the pulpit ministry be properly provided for is, as we have noted elsewhere, stressed by Paul in I Corinthians, chapter 9. That the diaconate, as serving hands of the congregation, be amply supported is the thesis of this *Handbook*, abundantly taught by Scripture. That an accounting be kept of the fruit borne for the Lord in these ways by each member of the Body comports with the stress laid in the Bible upon God's concern with good order. These principles do not restrict freedom in giving; they provide for it. Law always guarantees liberty.

It may well be that progressive development of the computer and credit card will one day enable the diaconate to gather its funds by such means. The passing of the collection plate was never an element in the liturgy of early Reformation churches. Gifts were left in boxes set for the purpose in the narthex of the church, and were also collected personally from the members by the deacons. That each congregation might have its own small computer, and each member use his credit card for contribution is not impossible—even sometime soon.

Whatever the future, deacons must always be prepared to use the most efficient means to get the Lord's work done.

C. *THE DEACON AS TRUSTEE*

Depending on denominational policy or congregational preference, some or all of the deacons may be appointed trustees of the Church.

142

Others may have a separate board of trustees to relieve the elders and deacons of the work and responsibilities involved in care for the material concerns of the congregation.

Still other churches assign trustee functions to standing committees on building and grounds, and the like.

To serve those diaconates who are given trustee responsibilities, we include in Appendix I to this *Handbook* a detailed discussion of the deacon as trustee.

PART II. PROVISION FOR INSTRUCTION AND INFORMATION

A. *THE DEACON AS TEACHER*

The Key to the congregation's practice of good stewardship is, of course, the pulpit. And the special stewardship required of the pulpit ministry is faithful and courageous preaching of the inspired Word of God. It is the Word which bears the fruit of obedience. So the Lord teaches, for example, in the parable of the sower, whose seed falls upon various kinds of soil and does so with various kinds of result (Matt. 13:1-9; Mark 4:1-9; Luke 8:4-8). "The sower," our Lord says, "sows the word" (Mark 4:14).

When the Word preached falls into receptive lives, it brings forth "grain, growing up and increasing and yielding thirtyfold and sixtyfold and a hundredfold" (Mark 4:8). Some of such yield will flow through the hands of the deacons into service of the needy.

The deacons' basic concern, then, in the education of the congregation to good stewardship is that the Bible be faithfully expounded and applied, in the worship services, in study groups and societies, and, it may be, in mid-week services. While the deacons are particularly interested in preaching directed expressly upon the Biblical principles of good stewardship, they may be sure that the Bible works by indirection also. That is, all doctrines established by the Word, all attitudes governed by the Word, and all faithfulness stimulated by the Word will contribute to generous hearts and open hands.

The deacon as teacher, then, concerns himself first of all with urging faithful preaching, and supporting it.

In addition, the diaconate should accept responsibility for becoming more and more the "experts" in the particular doctrines of stewardship, like those expounded in this *Handbook*, and for further developing these in terms of the local congregation. Members should feel free to turn to deacons for advice, and for discussion of particular problems: do I "owe" this to the Lord? should I support that cause? What is a fair gift? May I keep...? Should I will...?

And, finally, the deacon as teacher should undertake to familiarize the congregation with basic principles of.stewardship, with particular problems and opportunities facing the congregation from a diaconal point of view, and with emergency matters—through a deacons' newsletter, discussed in the next section.

B. *THE DEACONS' NEWSLETTER*

Communicate!

Tell the story!

Let the word get around!

In short, one key to diaconal success is letting the congregation know the what and the why of deacons' work. An effective means to this end can be a deacons' newsletter. If you already produce one, plan it to associate the congregation more and more in your work. If you do not have one, consider things like these:

1. *Format:*

a. This means the shape and form of the newsletter. Begin modestly. Use, perhaps, a single mimeographed sheet which can be run off in the Church office, or done cheaply outside.

b. Consider moving to a four-page letter when you hit your stride. This can be produced by folding over a double-letter-size sheet, produced by mimeograph or some inexpensive copying process by a local firm.

c. Keep the letter modest, neat, attractive.

d. Find someone in the congregation who can draw or design an attractive heading for the letter, using a title someone thinks of, like *Service In-deed, Diakonia, Helping Hand,* etc.

e. Keep the articles short, easy to read. The style can be simple. Just get the message across.

2. *Content:*

a. The purpose of the letter should be twofold: 1) to develop a congregational understanding of diaconal stewardship and its principles, and 2) to keep before the congregation actual needs and accomplishments involving their diaconate.

b. Consider schooling the congregation, one step at a time, in

144

some of the ideas suggested in this *Handbook* (we have no objection to your quoting whole paragraphs if you like).

c. Describe some of the problems and challenges facing you as deacons, keeping private matters, of course, out of print.

d. Provide on-going information on the financial status of the congregation, trends in expenses, in giving, in inflation, etc.

e. Evaluate faith ministries operative in your area, being careful to let the facts speak for themselves and support any conclusions you draw.

f. Give background information prior to fund drives, before the every-member canvas, annual budget meeting.

g. Explain opportunities for broader outreach.

h. Point to needs that could be met if volunteer time and talent were offered. Report on progress in such areas.

i. Stimulate contribution of food and clothing to the congregation's family assistance depot, or to that operated by a number of congregations together.

j. Encourage special and appropriate contributions at holidays; get out help for the aged and ill for spring cleanup and winterizing.

k. In sum, make the newsletter a running account of diaconal service being done, needing doing, and "out there" waiting to be found and met.

l. Consider a question-box where questions can be posed and answered.

m. Make the newsletter a source of information concerning public assistance programs not everyone is likely to have heard of.

3. *Frequency:*

a. If you are just starting out, begin modestly, but try to meet some regular schedule, like quarterly. Experience may suggest more, or even fewer, issues. Perhaps you can do a deacons' column in a newsletter already published in your congregation as a starter.

b. In conjunction with the annual pledge drive or budget meeting is a good time to launch.

c. Do not give up too readily if at first no enthusiasm is expressed.

4. *Cooperative or regional newsletter:*

a. Diaconates engaged in cooperative projects might well issue reports from time to time as to progress, needs, etc.

b. Regional diaconal organizations could well issue their own occasional letter.

c. Neither of the above should be substituted for the congregational letter, but the same articles on the principles of diakonia could be used in both.

SUMMARY

What you wish to do via a newsletter is to keep before the congregation an awareness of their deacons' presence and activity on behalf of the Body. Just to let them know that you're around, and why, and how—and what they could be doing to participate more and more in the witness of your work. You *can* do that! And both the Church and the needy will bless you for it, as will the Head of the Church who knows all that goes on in, and for, His Body!

PART III. PROVISION FOR ENCOURAGEMENT AND GUIDANCE

A. *THE DIACONAL VISIT*

The pastoral visit by minister or elder, or both, has had a constructive role in congregational life ever since the Reformation. Many congregations still wisely provide for it (see our *Elders Handbook* for concrete suggestions).

Visits to congregational homes by the deacons, however, have generally been limited to "pledge week," to special pleas for particular needs or programs, or to efforts to ascertain surmised needs.

But have you ever thought of regularly scheduled visits by the deacons to the entire membership? If so, we suspect you have found such visits very valuable; if not, we urge that you consider such a program.

1. *Purpose*

It is the thesis of this *Handbook* that diaconal service, within and without the congregation, is required by the Lord of His Body, and is a key form of witness to the community. Because this is Biblical, the deacon holds a key office in the Church. How appropriate it is, then, that deacons and other members come to know each other well, and freely discuss together the diaconal outreach of the Body. There is no better way to achieve such understanding than by the personal, scheduled visit.

Moreover, we believe, as already suggested, that the deacon should

146

be busily instructing the congregation in the principles of stewardship. One way to do that is by carefully planned face-to-face conversations between the deacons and the other membership.

We are not thinking, then, of the social visit perhaps embroidered with some few comments on the congregational budget. We are thinking of a carefully conceived "educational" program, designed to involve the Body more knowledgeably and enthusiastically in serving through the deacons as hands, eyes, ears, and willing feet for its risen Head.

2. *Methods*

a. The deacon and elder assigned to a district, or section, or "household" of the congregation could together make scheduled annual visits to all families under their immediate care. This would have certain advantages, like these:

1) The elder represents the spiritual and doctrinal concerns of the Church.

2) The deacon represents the material expression of these concerns.

3) Their combination in the one visit emphasizes the Biblical stress upon proving faith by works.

4) The presence of the elder confirms the Church's official endorsement of the diaconal programs discussed.

5) Both elder and deacon hear, and can report back, the members' reaction to the work of the congregation in both its doctrinal-spiritual and diaconal forms.

b. Annual visits could be alternated between deacons and elders, probably going out in teams of two. This would also have its advantages, like these:

1) Focusing the visit upon spiritual-doctrinal matters on the one occasion, and upon particular diaconal projects on the other.

2) Underlines, for the deacons, their full competence to instruct the Body in principles of stewardship.

3) Might enable the deacons to pursue more frankly any problems they may have with a particular family's generosity without the hint of disciplinary authority suggested by the presence of an elder.

Each congregation will decide which form will suit its aspirations. What we wish to stress here is the importance of a planned and scheduled program of visiting which involves the diaconate.

3. *Benefits*

We have already suggested, in a general way, the benefits which can be anticipated from diaconal visiting. Specifically, we think of these:

a. Such a program conveys to the Body a sense of the importance which should be attached to diaconal service.

b. It means that the deacons themselves take their calling seriously. This will be, under divine blessing, contagious.

c. Affords the deacons opportunity to explain in detail the challenges and opportunities for service facing the congregation.

d. Permits a frank discussion of what diakonia costs, and of the blessings it provides.

e. Enables the deacons to learn of hitherto untapped resources of time and talent and interest which they can focus upon need within and without the congregation. How often those who decline to volunteer are nonetheless simply waiting to be asked!

f. Provides opportunity for the deacons to discover hitherto unknown needs.

g. Serves to generate a spirit of united cooperation in obedient service.

h. Gives members opportunity to suggest neglected avenues to diakonia, and perhaps to volunteer in meeting these.

4. *Preparation*

Visits will be blessed in proportion to the preparation made for them. We suggest:

a. Close cooperation with the ministry with an eye to preaching that time and again stresses diakonia, and "kicks off" the annual visiting season with particular emphasis on what is going to be done.

b. Careful planning by the diaconate of the themes to be emphasized for the season, such as:

    1) Discussion of aspects of stewardship (see Part I).

    2) Discussion of perspectives on diakonia (see Chapter 12).

    3) Teaching drawn from parables which apply to diakonia (see Chapter 24).

c. Planning what information will be shared, what issues stressed, this season.

d. Deciding in what areas the deacons would like to solicit information or convey it.

e. Preparation of specific questions which might be posed to stimulate conversation to open the visit, like:

    1) Suggestions for serving the elderly better?

2) Suggestions for meeting the needs of youth, especially orphans or victims of broken homes?

3) Successful service programs known to this family by experience, from relatives, reading, etc?

4) Diakonia and rising inflation?

5) Diakonia and the welfare state?

What we are suggesting, in short, is that the visit be *planned* so that questions which can elicit more than just "Yes" or "No" responses serve to get the discussion off the ground. People enjoy giving their input, if once the initial barriers are broken.

f. Be sure you know the names of all members of the family you are going to visit, and a little about each of them: school or work, interests, services to the congregation, activities in the community, etc. Not for the purpose of socializing, but as context for the visit and whatever may arise during it.

g. Know what stewardship principle(s) you intend to stress on this visit, and find the time to get them in. Over a period of years deacons can thus give a "course" of instruction on Biblical stewardship.

h. Pre-arrange the visit by phone, bulletin, newsletter, etc.

i. Pray individually and together for blessing on the visiting program.

5. *During the Visit*

a. Be on time!

b. Do not overstay!

c. Keep the conversation on your pre-arranged program, without robbing it of all flexibility and spontaneity.

d. Try to get everybody in, including the children and youth.

e. Know which member of the team will open, who will pray, who will read Scripture (and what; bring your own Bible).

f. Decline to argue, but listen carefully to complaints and promise to bring these under discussion among the deacons (or elders). If desirable, agree to return "answers".

g. Keep in mind that the purpose of your visit is constructive, and that its goal is the better serving of the Body of Christ in the world.

6. *After the Visit*

a. Report to the diaconate (and/or eldership) on the visits.

b. Make use of what has been learned, of skills to be used, problems to be met, etc.

c. Reflect personally and together on the "success" of your plans, what can be done better, what was useful, and so on.

149

d. Be especially concerned to act upon any needs discovered, like the name of a lonely person, a child needing a Big Brother or Sister, repairs to be made, driving required—and the discovery of skills to do these things.

SUMMARY

The alert diaconate will find these suggestions simply points of departure for a visiting program which will be of growing benefit to the congregation and the deacons in their combined witness to the community where God has placed His Church.

B. *CRITERIA FOR GIVING OUTSIDE THE CONGREGATION*

The Gospel has no competitors.

But the local congregation is exposed to intense competition for the diaconal dollar. Appeals pour out over radio and television networks for the support of "faith ministries" both in evangelism and in the support of the needy abroad. These appeals compete with the congregation and her deacons for the members' support.

How shall the deacon deal with this competition?

He must begin by recognizing that many members will not consider "faith ministry" appeals as competitive to the Church. Without undue argument, the deacon must seek to establish the local congregation as "first" on the member's gift list, indeed as top priority among the member's financial responsibilities.

As a stewardship task force, however, the deacons must undertake development of congregational sensitivity to wise versus unwise giving. What do the members know about those who beat the airwaves for aid? What do the deacons themselves know about them and their causes? But how can prudent stewardship be done in ignorance?

The diaconate must become stewardship counselors to the congregation, in regard to giving, in ways like these:

1. Acquire and file financial reports from all those making appeals for funds or other forms of support in your area, whether by direct mail, radio, television, or magazine advertising. Keep up-to-date!

2. Acquaint the congregation with the existence of such a file, and urge its use. Offer photocopies of financial statements to all who ask for them.

3. Make your own diaconal analysis of financial reports received. Depend upon those deacons, or invite in others, who have some experience in finance and fund-raising. Consider, for example, ratio of overhead to accomplishment, how income is accounted for, what goes into auxiliary expenses. Make such analyses available to the congregation, with objective comment.

4. Inform the congregation as to all groups refusing to submit financial statements.

5. When, in your considered judgment, the absence of a financial report or the character of one submitted suggests an unreliable person or organization, dare to say so.

6. As a rule of thumb: no taxation without representation is an old and valuable political principle; here its parallel is: no liberality without accountability.

SUMMARY

It is tempting, and easy, to leave full responsibility with each member as to support of "faith ministry" pleas for funds. And so, indeed, will many members desire to have it left. But such individualism is at odds with the concept of "the Body" which is the Church. Deacons owe the membership all the information they can obtain and circulate (say, through their newsletter) concerning responsible giving—for which both member and deacon are and will be held responsible before the Lord. It's a touchy business, but who ever promised the conscientious deacon a rose garden?

C. THE DEACON AS "ELDER"

In small congregations, the deacon often doubles as elder (or trustee) and vice versa. Sometimes one elder and one deacon will function as a team for a given district. In some denominations and churches little distinction is made between the two offices.

For a complete study of the office of elder we refer the reader to our *Elders Handbook,* but offer here the following summary:

1. *The Nature of the Elder's Office*

a. Authority:

The elder serves under divine appointment and receives his authority from the Lord, not from the congregation—even though he be democratically elected.

b. Accountability:

The elder is accountable to the Lord, according to His will as expressed in the Scriptures, and the congregation owes "submission" to the eldership: "Obey your leaders and submit to them" (Heb. 13:17), not as fellow believers only, but "as men who will have to give

151

account" (Heb. 13:17).

c. Priority:

Deacons expected to serve also as elders, and members of the congregation nominated for these offices, should count it high priority opportunity, and should decline to stand only for the weightiest of reasons.

d. Safeguards:

To guard against excesses or misuse of office, the Bible maintains the following principles:

1) Plurality: the Word always speaks of the eldership in the plural, the rule of more than one in the congregation. Decisions by the eldership must be reached democratically.

2) Parity: neither the teaching elder (pastor) nor the chairman of the meeting excels the rest of the eldership in status or authority: "For you have one Teacher, and you are all brethren" (Matt. 23:8).

3) Unity: cooperation and unity within the eldership becomes a model for the congregation. Unity of the congregation with its denomination—classis, synod, presbytery, conference, etc.—builds the Church of Christ in the world.

2. *Responsibilities of the Elder*

Responsibility is correlative with authority. A profile of the elder's responsibilities emerges from two Biblical sources:

a. The names given the office: the Bible uses interchangeably the Greek terms "presbyter" and "episcopos" for the office of elder, both implying the authority and responsibility of oversight and super-vision.

b. The tasks assigned the office of elder:

1) To keep watch over themselves in terms of doctrine and life: "Watch over yourselves" (Acts 20:28), and "be examples to the Church" (I Pet. 5:3).

2) To keep watch over the congregation, "Watch over the church" (Acts 20:28) and, "Take oversight over the flock" (I Pet. 5:2), involving:

a) Control of the worship service, the purity and power of the preaching, music and choir, special elements in the liturgy, attendance.

b) Visiting the membership, with special concern for those in any kind of spiritual distress or need. May be done by elder-deacon teams.

c) Promotion of obedience, encouragement to godly life, and

exercise of discipline.

3) To "feed the Church of God" (Acts 20:28) through:

a) Provision of adequate pulpit ministry, and full support of same, with conscientious supervision of the minister's doctrine, life, and preaching.

b) Appropriate and timely administration of the sacraments.

c) Special concern for the training of the young through catechism or church school, and involvement with them in facing the temptations of the age.

d) Making sure that the special needs of the sick, the shut-in, the aged, the bereaved, the mentally handicapped, and those suffering emergency problems are not being ignored.

3. *The Elder's Trust*

The elder is entrusted with a very precious treasure, one which belongs to the Lord by reason of purchase: "...which he has purchased with his own blood" (Acts 20:28). This is the Church over which the elder is appointed overseer.

4. *The Elder's Challenge*

The Lord and His elders have an enemy who seeks the souls of the flock: "Your adversary the devil prowls around like a roaring lion, seeking some one to devour" (I Pet. 5:8). And the devil finds his kind of missionaries: "Savage wolves will come in among you, not sparing the flock; and from among you men will arise speaking perverse things" (Acts 20:29-30).

The elder is therefore challenged: "Be alert!" (Acts 20:31).

Equip yourselves with "the whole armor of God" so graphically described by St. Paul in his letter to the Ephesians (Eph. 6:11-17).

Chapter 18.

SECOND CIRCLE

SERVING THE CONGREGATIONAL NEEDY

"So then, as we have opportunity, let us do good to all men, especially to those who are of the household of faith" (Gal. 6:10).

"And if your brother becomes poor, and cannot maintain himself with you, you shall maintain him..." (Lev. 25:35).

SCOPE

In the language of the fig tree, the congregation through the First Circle of diaconal service bears leaves for itself. Leaves are indeed indispensable to the life of the tree. But their purpose is to enable the tree to bear fruit. And fruit-bearing begins where the deacons reach out in service to the congregational needy.

We discuss such service in two sections with a number of specific suggestions and a sample case study:

I. Meeting Obvious Needs

We are thinking here of the needs that by themselves come to the deacons' attention. Such needs most commonly occur in the form of financial hardship, but we consider also other types of want.

II. Challenging the Congregation

Even a small congregation is mostly an untapped reservoir of time, talent, skills, and compassion waiting to be organized for use in serving needs within the Body, and we envision a challenging and expanding program of mutual aid and benefit as deacons steadily relate untapped aptitudes to unmet needs.

III. Determining Need

When word is received that a person or family in the congregation suffers real hardship, but gives no evidence of it that the deacons can observe, how shall it be determined if, indeed, such need does exist? We suggest ways in which this can be accomplished.

PART I. MEETING OBVIOUS NEEDS

A. *MATERIAL NEEDS*

Need is most often clothed in lack of money or goods, but is rarely limited to such obvious dimensions. We take note of poverty in goods because it is hardest to hide and, often, easiest to overcome, at least temporarily. Moreover, as observed before, man's handling of his material possessions in relation to those in material need is a sure index of the state of the soul.

The Bible is obsessed with the plight of the poor. Deacons will profit by doing their Bible reading, whole books at a sitting if possible, with pen in hand to underline God's mandates concerning care for the poor. The diaconate can learn to recognize variety, though it may rarely encounter them all, in the forms of material poverty:

1. *The destitute:* these are not only without goods but without hope. So beaten are they by hunger, indifference, suffering that no star illumines their horizons.

2. *The indigent:* these are long time in poverty. They have adjusted to life at subsistence levels, to an absence of celebration. Their children receive no gifts; their shelter lacks all refinement; repairs cannot be made. The future is grey, only more of the same.

3. *The poor:* they are somewhat emancipated from either of the above categories, but live ever at the brink of indigence or destitution. Lacking in reserves, they fear calamity before it occurs. They may, in defiance of common sense, spend extravagantly on one token of the good life, a car or television set or the weekend binge. They may be unskilled in the management of income, inept at the care of property, ignorant of the basic aptitudes essential to home making.

4. It is evident that the challenge presented to the diaconate by poverty, in any of its forms, is at least three-fold:

a. Immediate needs must be met, but:

1) What share of such need is, or should be, provided by public relief? The deacons should be certain that all sources of public support are enlisted, if possible supplied through the diaconate's hands.

2) What other sources of aid are available but so far untapped? Does Medicare or Medicaid apply? Has it been sought? If necessary, are free or inexpensive clinical or dental services to be had?

3) How can diaconal funds, and support in kind, be best applied?

b. The duration of required assistance must be estimated. Is this a temporary or long-term emergency? If probably long-term, then:

c. The situation must be studied and analyzed. Is poverty the symptom, or result, of other, underlying problems? Can these, if so, be isolated and attacked? For example:

1) Is there illness, physical or mental, which has reduced the bread-winner's capacity for work? Or is the family a broken circle, lacking one or even both parents? Is there a responsible head of the house?

2) Is old age and unemployability the problem?

3) Is absence of training or education responsible for unemployment?

4) Is alcoholism involved? If so, for how long?

5) Does the family know how to manage what income it has, or had? Know how to set priorities? Able to discipline wayward desires? Willing to try?

6) Has "welfare statism" set in, as a passive willingness to live on assistance?

Difficult as these kinds of problems will be to resolve, they cannot even be attacked until discovered. But if diaconal assistance is to be both a rescue and rehabilitating operation, such questions must be raised and answered to the best of the deacons' abilities.

Diaconates can learn a great deal about meeting poverty and its contributing factors by careful analysis of their encounters with it, and by bringing in for discussion reports and articles dealing with the poor. Comparison of one diaconate's experience with that of others can also be instructive.

Needs which are at bottom material in character do not always wear the bleak face of poverty. They may sometimes surface in well-clothed despair. More than one suicide can be traced to "success" over-extended, with finally no place to turn. But such a haven of last resort should ever be at hand in the diaconate. And it should be known in the congregation that this is so, and that full confidence will always be honored. Need is need, be it in rags or bib and tucker. Involved is always a human being who is also a brother or sister in the Lord. How senselessly tragic for your congregation if anyone caught deep in a financial bind dared not appeal to his friends because of pride nor to the deacons for fear of rejection. Or if the victim did not even imagine that deacons cared!

Material needs may root in temporary unemployment, with payments falling due. The need is there. Lectures on extended credit can come later. The diaconate should be there to tide over the crisis, and to assist in job-finding.

Families burdened with the care of "special" children, or crippled adults, may live in quiet desperation while repairs to home go unmade, car deteriorates, health care is ignored, and diet falls victim to progressive inflation. Let such learn that deacons care, because the Lord cares, and will gladly help with what He gives them to administer. Nursing home expenses rise steadily. Are they outrunning someone's ability to pay and yet live somewhat normally? Are families caught between the cost of a parent in a rest home and children growing up?

Need may rise with crushing force out of calamity and threaten to overwhelm the otherwise self-sufficient. Be it accident, marital tensions, unexpected reverse in business, loss of limb or eye or mobility—be sure that the hand of the diaconate is extended to see the crisis through.

B. *OTHER DIMENSIONS OF NEED*

The need may be emotional:

1. The elderly in the rest home may be lonely, neglected (or thinking so) by children, pastor, and the Church, and outliving friends. Regular visits on scheduled basis, and persistent admonition to careless children are diaconal roles.

2. The lonely and seemingly friendless of any age—a card or call or brief visit enable the diaconate thus to display the love of the Body for the isolated member. The gift of a book or record, being sure that the television set is in repair, an invitation to an outing—the imaginative diaconate will think of all these and more.

3. The specially burdened, by a wayward child or unfaithful mate or from rigid and un-understanding parents; the orphaned; the widowed; the rejected—all would find a gleam of sunshine in a word, a call, a card, a gift....

The need may be spiritual:

1. The deacons supplement the pastoral and elders' ministries with expressions of their own share of concern in ways suggested above.

2. Deacons, too, bear the Word of the Lord, and can make sure that spiritual needs come to the attention of ruling and teaching elders, too.

The need may be almost incidental, and easily ignored:

1. Emergency transportation.

2. Regular rides to shop or clinic or friends.

3. Warm meals on schedule to the elderly or when mother is away or ill.

The need may be complicated:

1. The Bible leaves no doubt of God's care for the widow and the fatherless: "You shall not afflict any widow or orphan" (Ex. 22:22). The Lord "executes justice for the fatherless and the widow" (Ex. 10:18). "Cursed be he who perverts the justice due to the sojourner, the fatherless and the widow" (Deut. 27:19). Jesus uses a widow in his parable of the unjust judge as illustrative of God's willingness to hear those who cry to Him for justice (Luke 18:1-8)—and if God, then so also must His Church be listening. Deacons cannot overlook instances coming to their attention of the abuse of the weak by the strong in the congregation, whatever form the offense may take: overcharging, underpaying, exorbitant interest, inhuman treatment. If it is a matter of support for aged widows, St. Paul has explicit instruction: "If a widow has children or grandchildren, let them first learn their religious duty to their own family and make some return to their parents" (I Tim. 5:4). If it is a matter of injustice, let deacons and elders together join in disciplinary action. The Church may not look the other way, when God in heaven is hearing cries from the weak being trampled by the strong.

2. The Bible frowns upon the taking of interest upon loans made to relieve a brother's need. Calvin led the way, in the sixteenth century, in discriminating between loans made for business ventures (on which interest is legitimate) and loans made to brethren in desperate need (on which the Bible clearly forbids taking interest, or even demanding return of principal): "If you lend money to any of my people who is poor, you shall not be to him as a creditor, and you shall not exact interest from him" (Ex. 22:25). "You shall not lend upon interest to your brother, interest on money, interest on victuals, interest on anything that is lent for interest" (Deut. 23:19).

The deacons may not close their eyes to appeals made to them against brethren who violate these commands. It may be that the diaconate must have on hand a modest sum for the relief of such borrowers, even as they strive to illumine the heart and mind and will of the creditor.

3. An alert diaconate will be on the lookout for ways in which they can take the initiative in helping meet the material and other needs of those in the congregation who are not in poverty but have a hard struggle to make ends meet. You will find, for example, that some

Catholic parishes have established model, flourishing credit unions which are able to loan at moderate rates to members who may also share in modest profits. Cooperative buying is widely done to the advantage of the participants. Yours could join other diaconates in creating these.

Deacons must, however, be alert to division within the congregation which might be introduced by members who are merchants and whose business seems to be threatened by a cooperative. Proper arrangements between the merchant and the cooperative can be advantageous to both if carefully worked out in advance. It may well be, too, that those who would purchase from the cooperative would not be likely customers for the merchants anyhow—this could be surveyed in advance. Every effort must be made, in any case, to avoid dissension before a cooperative is launched. But the challenge is there! Think on it!

PART II. CHALLENGING THE CONGREGATION

The Lord lays His tithe upon our goods as token of His similar claim upon all our other talents and gifts. The diaconate is challenged to weave the full range of congregational skills into a tapestry of mutual support and service as first-fruits of the joy of salvation.

Deacons serve the congregation's needy as representative of the whole Body and its Lord. This is within the scope of the Second Circle of obedience. As the deacons succeed, however, in drawing the talents of others into service of the needy, the diaconate will move also into the Third level of service, discussed in detail in the next chapter.

A. *TITHING TALENTS*

The forms of human need—material, emotional, and spiritual—discussed in the preceding pages are but illustrative of the many ways in which members of the Body require the services of the Church. Responsibility for grappling with these needs rests first of all upon the deacons. But it is evident that deacons should make deliberate and undiscouragable effort to enlist the cooperation of other members of the congregation in serving the Lord by the alleviation of need, in ways they are specially qualified to walk by virtue of talent, gift, education, time, skill, interest. In ways like these:

1. *Learning from others:*

The deacons' efforts to understand poverty and its causes can be greatly enriched by discussion with social workers, welfare directors, police officials, economists, bankers, lawyers, and the like. Draw these into deacons' meetings. Schedule public meetings where poverty is discussed. Learn, and help others to learn, the realities of destitution, indigence, and economic hardship.

Similarly, the deacons should draw upon members of the congregation who can instruct them in whatever areas problems emerge, to help them handle diagnosis, cause, and cure. Deacons should go after any knowledge and experience possessed by anyone in the congregation which facilitates diaconal service, on the ground that all knowledge and expertise belongs to the Lord.

2. *Enlisting others:*

Deacons represent the Body in the service of others. But the representative does not entirely replace those who are represented. Gifts funneled through the diaconate are indeed as given directly to the Lord, but they should be regarded by the giver as tokens of his own willingness to serve. And it is one of the exciting opportunities laid upon the diaconate to organize and direct just such congregational participation in doing good to those in need.

Deacons should spend time studying their own Church. From such study they should develop a profile of congregational skills and talents. There will be a wider range of endowments in most congregations than the deacons may at first suppose. Place them in categories, like these:

a. *Professional:* the need may call for professional service or advice, in law, in business, in money management, in medicine, in relations with government. Deacons should know who in the congregation can provide, either free or for modest fee paid by the diaconate, these and similar services in cases of need. Who can prescribe drugs least expensively, by generic rather than trade names? Who can cut through legal tangles? Who can deal with the law? Who can counsel a child in trouble, or parent in despair? Who can liberate the victim of the loan shark?

b. *Mechanical and vocational:* the problem may be fixing a screen door, repairing a broken fixture or window, stopping a leak, tuning a car motor, making more nutritious meals, mending clothing; or it may be training or re-training for other job opportunities, finding an apprenticeship, getting a chance to prove abilities in another kind of work, taking a chance on a parolee. Who can share his technical skills or vocational know-how toward meeting such needs?

c. *Personal:* perhaps a child needs a Big Brother or Sister whose patience will be steeled by love. A single parent needs a reliable baby-sitter and aid in paying the bill. The aged ill may need a daily call. The temporarily bed-ridden may need care. The troubled spirit cries out for counsel, while the family in tension needs a soothing concern.

3. *Schooling:*

Bringing the God-given talents in the congregation to bear upon the kinds of need surfacing in the Body is not going to be easy. Beginning with the conviction that all talents and skills, however developed, come from God, the deacons must undertake two unending pedagogical tasks:

a. *Schooling themselves:* in the light of Part I of the *Handbook,* deacons must fully convince themselves that the Church has a lien of at least a tithe upon all the goods and abilities with which the Lord has endowed His Church. The deacon must find himself taking for granted that those upon whom he calls for service to the needy "owe" the Lord such service. The deacon does not beg. He asks no favors. He simply points members to duty, the doing of works "worthy of their repentance" and membership in the family of God. Still more, the deacon opens the door of opportunity for that sharing of goods and talents which alone justifies their possession. Through the deacon the Lord is saying, "as you did it to one of the least of these my brethren, you did it to me" (Matt. 25:40). And, through the deacon the Lord is warning, "as you did it not to one of the least of these, you did it not to me" (Matt 25:45). Which means that deacons who do not open doors of opportunity for service, when such opportunities exist, rob their brethren of liberating obedience. All this must become second nature to the deacon who is dedicated to fulfilling his crucial office.

It is easier, of course, to suggest taking this approach than to take it. The deacon who works himself into the frame of mind which looks upon his appeal to the membership as offering them an *opportunity* for giving may anticipate some resistance, if not hostility, to this perspective. Deacons do well, therefore, both individually and collectively to fortify themselves with frequent reference to St. Paul's vivid descriptions of the mutual dependence of the members of a body upon each other. Consider: "For the body does not consist of one member but of many. If the foot should say, 'Because I am not a hand, I do not belong to the body,' that would not make it any less a part of the body. And if the ear should say, 'Because I am not an eye, I do not belong to the body,' that would not make it less a part of the body... But as it is, God arranged the organs in the body, each one of them, as he chose. If all were a single organ, where would the body be? As it is, there are many parts, yet one body...that the members may have the same care for one another. If one member suffers, all suffer together; if one member is honored, all rejoice together. Now you are the body of Christ and individually members of it...." (I Cor. 12:14-16; 18-20; 25-26).

Paul stresses the same theme in Romans 12:3-8.

The deacon is not mistaken in believing that each member owes to the Body whatever he can contribute to the needs of other members. Otherwise he would not be a *member*. This is what the Lord clearly teaches through St. Paul, and elsewhere through Israel. And therefore the deacon is not mistaken in seeing his calling as enabling each member openly to show his understanding, through obedience, of what membership in the Body of Christ involves.

Oh yes, there may be opposition to this point of view. But it is, none-the-less, God's point of view. Act on it!

b. *Schooling the congregation:* Once again, use the newsletter and exert steady pressure upon elders and pulpit to instruct the Body in its obligations to its members. Beyond such general admonition, the deacons must engage in personal persuasion. Those with unwilling hearts must be "saved" from their stubborn blindness. As pointed out in Chapter 12, the doing of good is not optional for the Christian. And the deacon is situated precisely where the doing of good can be observed in the passage from word to deed. Nor is the deacon blameless if many words of love produce in fact but few deeds of kindness.

c. Whatever the kind of service required within the Body, the diaconate should school itself to know where to turn for just that service, within the Body, Thus three related blessings are achieved:

1) The need is met, blessing the recipient.
2) Good is done, blessing the donor.
3) Christ is served, blessing the Church, and witnessing to the world.

B. *SUGGESTIONS*

Following are some suggestive ways in which either the deacons, or other members of the congregation organized by the deacons, can be of specific service to congregational needs:

1. For the elderly and the widow: ·

a. Assistance when seasons change: storm doors, windows, yard cleanup, etc. General home and yard care.

b. Assistance in coping with energy costs: insulation, improved burners on furnace, changing furnace filters, etc.

c. Assistance in filling out forms and making necessary contacts with service agencies: medical and Medicare, insurance, special grants, etc.

d. Snow removal, shopping, trips to the doctor or out visiting.

e. Special concern for the recently widowed: emergency needs, filling out forms, caution against rash decision, protection against exploitation, etc.

2. For emergencies:

a. Legal advice.

b. Eligibility for food stamps and other grants.

c. Assistance in finding suitable shelter, emergency clothing, food.

d. Aid in finding available insurance or compensation payments, including unemployment insurance or workman's compensation.

3. Miscellaneous:

a. Special efforts on behalf of unemployed youth: seeking jobs or job training, special projects at or for the Church, neighborhood cleanup, etc.

b. Making available: wheelchair, hospital bed, assistance in twenty-four hour nursing care, etc.

c. Assistance to the deaf and the blind, including provision of special devices to serve their needs.

d. Care for handicapped children while their parents have some vacation from their exacting obligations.

Like the needs that stimulate them, the varieties of diaconal response are infinite. All depends upon the deacons' enthusiasm for doing an imaginative and creative work for their Lord as He wills to be found in the needs of those who share the same congregation.

C. *CASE STUDY*

We offer the following true story as illustrative of the application of some of the suggestions made above, thoughtfully applied to the local situation.

Mr. and Mrs. Doe (not their real name) are the parents of three children, and the family belongs to the local congregation.

Mr. Doe is a semi-skilled worker, making modest wages. Recently he was demoted, reducing his income. He has a rather authoritarian attitude in the home, and thinks it demeaning to assist his wife with household chores. He distrusts banks and credit unions, and prefers to keep his financial affairs to himself.

Mrs. Doe is the more progressive of the two, but is handicapped by never having been taught the basics of home economics before marriage. She purchases food unwisely, depends heavily upon pre-cooked items, and serves a lot of "junk" food to the children. She defers attention to a nagging, chronic medical problem to save money.

The family has financial problems, aggravated by Mr. Doe's recent demotion. To make a down payment on their home, the Does borrowed at high interest, and in two years they have managed to pay off only $200 on the principal. Bills are paid with money orders, more costly than a checking account. The medical bills for the birth of the last child remain unpaid.

The needs of this family are discovered because Mrs. Doe calls the wife of one of the deacons to discuss her medical problems. Jane visits the family and perceives the dimensions of their need. She at once undertakes to school Mrs. Doe in household management. The deacons discuss what has been discovered, and work with the somewhat reluctant Mr. Doe to accomplish these things:

1. A checking account takes the place of paying bills by money order.

2. The doctor's bill is paid and Mrs. Doe is thus enabled to seek attention for her own problem.

3. The finance company loan made for the down payment on the house is replaced with a regular bank loan, to be paid by payroll deduction through arrangement with Mr. Doe's employer. The diaconate's offer to co-sign for the loan was not required by the bank.

4. After much encouragement, and with the assistance of a deacon, Mr. Doe applies for the food stamps to which his family is eligible (the sum came to $125 per month!).

The family was established on a more sound financial footing, meals and household management were much improved, and the Does now know that the hand of the Body undergirds them. The deacons, of course, keep in touch with the situation, and the deacon's wife pays regular visits (this she might well do as an appointed deaconess—see Chapter 14).

PART III. DETERMINING NEED

Deacons may become aware of need, or be informed of it, which the needy themselves are reluctant to admit or to seek assistance for. The effort to help begins, then, with the delicate and sensitive task of securing open lines of communication. To achieve this, we make the following suggestions:

A. *Initial contact:*

Make the initial contact personally or by telephone. This will be done either by one deacon selected by the diaconate for the task or the deacon in whose "district" the needy ones reside. Set up an appointment for a confidential meeting or visit. This first conversation should be conducted by the one deacon. It is easier to deal with what may be intensely personal matters when but one representative of the Church is at first involved.

B. *During the first visit:*

Open the conversation informally, perhaps on a social or other matter of common interest at the time.

Lead the discussion to the concern of the Body for the well being of each and all her members. Use, if you wish, an approach derived from Part I of this *Handbook*. What concerns you is that the needy person or family fully understands that yours is an errand of obligation: the Church has a duty to know, and to meet, the varied needs of her membership. You have come, therefore, neither to pry nor to gossip—and you will, of course, guarantee the strictest confidentiality. You have come on the Lord's errand, and in this spirit they can both receive and trust you.

As you move toward the needs of this particular person or family, lead the conversation from the general or even commonly known to the more personal. Start, for example, with unemployment or medical bills or emergency matters of which presumably many have knowledge as regards this member. You can then move to obligations which may have suffered from demands like the above: mortgage payments, utility bills, monthly payments, and other fixed items. Then you can inquire as to more personal matters: groceries, clothing, childrens' needs, even recreation and postponed dental visits, and the like.

Your aim is to discover *where* this person or family is hurting in

166

ways that the Church in general, and her deacons in particular, can help. If you meet stubborn resistance, try to ascertain why. Is it determination to make it on their own? If so, assure them that all assistance can be considered a loan from the Lord, to be repaid with interest as He provides. Is it fear of being known as deadbeats or chiselers, looked down upon in the congregation? If so, guarantee secrecy—and keep it! (Nothing can so much harm a diaconal program as a blabber-mouth deacon; this must never occur!) In short, if you cannot break through, do not despair nor surrender. Take your leave, ponder the problem, perhaps discuss it at the next deacons' meeting—and try again! Try until you succeed, if you know the real need *is* there.

If you do acquire a hold on the financial problems involved, do not make promises your colleagues might think extravagant. Simply indicate that you will report in confidence the degree of need to the diaconate, promising a return with their response.

C. *After the visit:*

Decide whether immediate help is required or whether you can wait until the next deacons' meeting. If it is an emergency, secure whatever authority is required (there should be provision for this in the regulations which govern your diaconate) and provide the assistance.

When a decision has been made along regular channels to provide aid, see to it that action is immediately taken. If financial assistance is being given directly, be sure that now two deacons are involved. Going alone would invite the interpretation that you, rather than the Church, are assisting; and it is always wise to handle money in the presence of a witness. This can be, if that proves necessary, easily explained to the needy member.

D. *The use of money:*

If the payment of bills is involved, we suggest that the needy member normally be given the funds necessary to make the payment as approved by the diaconate. If, however, there is some evidence of financial irresponsibility, the suggestion might tactfully be made that the bills approved for payment be handled by the diaconate.

E. *Follow up:*

Be sure that the case remains on the diaconal agenda until the emergency is over. Provide, or provide for, appropriate counseling in the handling of money, or the search for employment, or the consolidation of bills if these be required. Hit or miss concern, generated by the momentary appeal, could in the long run be more harmful than none.

Cases like these try the deacons' skills and patience, but will be, on solution, a source of lasting satisfaction to both the needy and the Church.

Chapter 19.

THIRD CIRCLE

CONGREGATIONAL EXTENSION

We have just observed that the scope of diaconal service at the second level is determined by the kinds of need which become apparent in the congregation.

SCOPE

The scope, now, of the Third Circle of Service depends mostly on the range of diaconal vision. How can the hands of the Body reach out, by way of your hands, to further congregational life among those dependent upon it?

We are thinking of service extended particularly to three groups within the Body:

A. For the Children
B. For the Adults
C. For the Elderly

It is likely that some suggestions made below were already stimulated by what has been said in our previous chapter. We are willing to believe, however, that setting in a different perspective may enliven the same idea.

A. *FOR THE CHILDREN*

1. *Christian education:*

We need not attempt to make here a case for Christian education. The desire for it is rapidly spreading across the USA and elsewhere. Briefly, this desire rests upon the sound premise that there should be a fundamental harmony of goals and values between the home and the school. The Bible is to be as much honored and as normative in the one as in the other.

Countless parents willingly undergo "double taxation" to pay for both public and private, Christian schools. Some families manage to do this only through sacrifice. Other families are unable to pay the double bill. Here, obviously, is opportunity for the deacons to serve.

Once again, the background to such service must lie in a congregation united by the pulpit in an understanding of the importance of the issue. The case need not be made by critique of public schools. They serve an important, indeed indispensable, purpose. The case rests upon the premise stated above: the Christian seeks an education for his child which shares the same basic beliefs about God, man, and world which are taught in the Church. The better this be understood, the more willing will be the congregation's extension of its service in this circle.

Deacons can approach the support of Christian education in several ways:

a. Some congregations contribute through their regular budget, allotting a specified amount per child to whatever Christian school he attends.

b. Some congregations take regular collections to be devoted to Christian education on an allotment basis.

c. Some congregations associate Christian education with the Church itself, often holding classes in the Church plant, and paying teachers as employees of the congregation or congregations involved.

d. Deacons may make each family which sends a child or children to a Christian school the object of individual concern, supporting to the extent of need.

e. Parents whose children are beyond the school age, and those who are blessed with more than average wealth, are often urged to help shoulder the load imposed upon other families who have school-age youngsters. The deacons can play a facilitating role in this.

Whatever the method, the point to be stressed is the mutual obligation accepted by the whole congregation, through the diaconate, for the Christian schooling of its youth.

2. *Special education:*

God provides, for His own reasons, that some families receive special children either by birth or adoption. By "special" we mean, as is commonly implied, "in need of special care and education".

More and more is being done for special children by local boards of education. This may seem, to some parents, to suffice. But the grounds for seeking Christian schooling for other children apply as much, or even more, in the case of the special child. But such education is often

170

almost prohibitively expensive unless the costs are shared by the diaconate. The deacon can not only channel congregational funds into such need, but he can facilitate inter-congregational efforts and can sometimes receive public funds also.

The deacon should be aware of the terminology currently used to describe different types of special need, like these:

a. *Mentally impaired:* retarded, lower than normal intelligence, handicapped mentally in some way.

b. *Physically impaired:* bodily deformaties often contributing to lower than normal mental development.

c. *Orthopedically impaired:* physically deficient in some respect, but with normal mental development.

d. *Physically- or health-impaired:* needing a special environment to function normally, as for example allergic or asthmatic children.

e. *Behaviorally impaired:* lacking any indication of mental or physical handicap, yet unable to function normally at home or in school—a group which receives little special attention at the present.

Parents are often happy to find any form of educational facility which will serve children with such problems. But the alert diaconate, concerned with the extension of congregational witness, will at least discuss the possibility of providing Christian schooling in their area for these children. Methods of raising the funds may be similar to those mentioned above, with, no doubt, an appeal to private foundations and public agencies.

B. *FOR THE ADULTS*

Special children often become special adults. Normal adults sometimes suffer mental and emotional stress which temporarily or even permanently commits them to institutions of mercy. In such institutions both the special and the "defeated" adult are apt to be forgotten by all but a few. Such neglect must be met and overcome by the Body acting through, and under the guidance of, its deacons. Remember factors like these:

1. *Support and care:*

Share in expenses through one of the ways suggested above for handling Christian education. Plan regular visits, both for yourselves and by others who have a gift (especially among the retired) for spreading cheer and an ear for listening. Encourage gifts of denominational literature, appropriate reading, etc. Remember cards on

171

birthdays, holidays, etc. Get others to send these through "card chains" assigned to members of Church societies, for example.

2. *Leadership:*

Try to participate in the administration of local institutions of mercy by encouraging members of the congregation, or of the diaconate, to serve on the board, participate in fund drives, do volunteer "advertising," etc. Appear before boards with suggestions, and attend membership meetings. All with an eye to improving the service of the institution to the community, and broadening its base of support.

3. *Information:*

Keep the congregation informed of the services and needs of various institutions which do, or might, serve congregational members.

4. *Types of service agencies:*

    a. Adoption agencies serving congregation and community.

    b. Counseling agencies for individuals, families, alcoholics, unwed mothers, prisoners released from jail, children in trouble at school, etc.

    c. Rehabilitation agencies for ex-alcoholics, drug addicts; sheltered workshop programs; training centers for the handicapped.

    d. Health care agencies of various kinds.

    e. Agencies associated with the United Fund and other umbrella units—often a catalog or listing of such agencies is published by the parent fund.

There is a lot to learn about the ways in which the modern city tries to meet diaconal needs arising outside the Church. Deacons will not only expand their outlook by finding out about such services, but will be all the more able to integrate specifically Christian services with those offered at public or foundation expense.

C. *FOR THE ELDERLY*

There were special needs in Jerusalem because the Holy City attracted many elderly Jews seeking to spend their last days there. Christian congregations in other cities shared their goods with the Jerusalem needy as the Church spread outward. St. Paul writes to Rome: "At present, however, I am going to Jerusalem with aid for the saints. For Macedonia and Achaia have been pleased to make some contribution for the poor among the saints at Jerusalem; they were pleased to do it, and indeed they are in debt to them, for if the Gentiles have come to share in their spiritual blessings, they ought also to be of service to them in material blessings" (Rom. 15:25-27).

For the aged it often is a case of those who have hitherto supported the congregation now needing the support of the congregation as earnings cease and inflation nibbles at retirement income.

Deacons should be aware of every member who is in a rest or retirement home. They must know, too, who among the elderly should be thinking of making such a transfer, especially those who are held back by the expense. They should be in touch, also, with those taken to the hospital and probably unable to bear all the cost. All to the end of being of service in the name of the Lord.

The challenge here is parallel to that as regards care for the impaired: sharing in expenses, keeping the Church informed, sending cards, visiting, involvment on boards and at meetings.

Deacons should also be alert to the services which the elderly can render to the congregation, especially if some assistance in goods or transportation is provided. Retirees have a pool of talents which can be tapped for diaconal work: visits, letter and card writing, prayer chains, calling, knitting, sewing, even instruction in house-keeping and cooking. For the men there can be work on the church lawn, in the building, planting flowers and bulbs, pruning. Reading to shut-ins and invalids and those who are losing their sight is always welcome and rewarding.

Service to, and in exchange service from, the elderly unites with the Church those saints who have for long years been a mainstay for others. The creative diaconate will consider such forms of extension an exciting part of its calling.

Chapter 20.

FOURTH CIRCLE

SERVING THE NEIGHBORHOOD

"So then, as we have opportunity, let us do good to all men..." (Gal. 6:10).

"Let your light so shine before men, that they may see your good works and give glory to your Father who is in heaven" (Matt. 5:16).

The Church is required by her Lord to assume responsibility for the needy in her "parish," that is, her *neighbor*hood. In response to this obligation, the deacons move into the Fourth Circle of Service.

SCOPE

A neighborhood is where neighbors live.

The summary statement of the second table of the Law is brief and to the point: "You shall love your neighbor as yourself" (Mark 12:31; Lev. 19:18). What, then, the Church does diaconally for herself, she owes also to those of her neighborhood. How far the boundaries of a congregation's neighborhood may in fact extend will depend upon how resourceful the Body and her deacons are determined to be—that is, how obedient to the Lord's commandment the Body is.

We discuss this Fourth Circle in terms of:

A. Problems

B. Solutions

C. Concrete Suggestions

A. *PROBLEMS*

Reaching out to need in the Church's neighborhood is beset with problems, like:

1. *Should the congregation really do so at all?*

There are those who believe in all sincerity that the financial and talent resources of the congregation must be diaconally funneled within the Body. The resources with which God blesses His people belong, it is believed, to those among them who are in need.

It may even be argued that the vivid description of the Last Judgment in Matthew 25 implies that the Lord is served only in "the least of these my brethren" (v. 40), limiting the range of "my brethren" to membership in the Church.

But it is evident from the texts cited at the head of this chapter that such an interpretation of "my brethren" is in error. The "neighbor" referred to in our Lord's summary of the divine law bears no connotation of fellow membership in the Church—its reference is obviously to those whom we encounter, who are close at hand. Moreover, Christ defines who is the "neighbor" in His parable of the Good Samaritan, and makes clear there that it is need and not fellowship that obliges us to be neighbor to the needy (see chapter 24, A and C). Indeed, the Lord chooses as characters in this dramatic story members of two peoples who were then at odds with each other—the Jew (no doubt meant by "A man was going down from Jerusalem to Jerico..," for no Samaritan dwelt in Jerusalem) and the Samaritan. Still more, here the Lord lays stress upon "being" a neighbor: "Which of these three, do you think, proved neighbor to the man who fell among the robbers?" And He lays the obligation of such neighborliness upon everyone: "Go and do likewise" (Luke 10:25-37). It is the Church above all, then, as the Body of the living Christ, which is required to "do good to all men...."

The Lord goes still further in obligating the Church to service of its neighborhood: "But I say to you that hear, 'Love your enemies, do good to those who hate you, bless those who curse you, pray for those who abuse you'" (Matt. 6:27). And the Spirit inspires St. Paul to write: "If even your enemy is hungry, feed him; if he is thirsty, give him drink; for by so doing you will heap burning coals upon his head" (Rom. 12:20).

The Church is bound by her Lord's commands. Service to the neighborhood is not optional. It is obligatory.

This obligation is further enforced by the example of Israel. The Jews were a chosen people. St. Paul outlines what this meant: "They are Israelites, and to them belong the sonship, the glory, the covenants, the giving of the law, the worship, the promises; to them belong the patriarchs, and of their race, according to the flesh, is the Christ..." (Rom. 9:4-5). The Jews carefully distinguished themselves from those of other races, even when members of those races dwelt among them in Palestine. These others were called "sojourners" or "strangers". But the Lord goes out of His way to oblige the chosen people to feel obligation toward those who are not of the Body: "When a stranger sojourns with you in your land, you shall not do him wrong. The stranger who sojourns with you shall be to you as the native among you, and you shall love him as yourself; for you were strangers in the land of Egypt: I am the Lord your God" (Lev. 19:33-34). Transferred to our times, this command of God clearly obligates the Church to care for the needy in its neighbor-hood.

Moses emphasizes the same obligation in various ways, like this: "When you reap your harvest in your field, and have forgotten a sheaf in the field, you shall not go back for it; it shall be for the sojourner, the fatherless, and the widow; that the Lord your God may bless you in all the work of your hands" (Deut. 24:19). Again, the "neighbor" is placed on the same footing with the needy who are within the "family"—so it was for the Church when it was the people of Israel, and so it must be for the Church today as the living Body of Christ.

We repeat: diaconal service to the neighborhood is not optional. It is obligatory!

2. *Can the congregation serve its neighborhood, or parish?*

It could be admitted that the faithful congregation does indeed owe diaconal ministry to its parish, while the objection is brought that no congregation can in fact afford such service. This problem breaks down into two aspects:

a. The deacons may not have the financial resources requisite to reaching outside the congregation. If this is true because the people are in fact poor, and giving all they can, the Lord does not require what He does not Himself also provide for. What anyone can give, after all, is only what the Lord has blessed him with having. In the fifth chapter of Leviticus, for example, God makes special exceptions in what is required of the poor. What the deacons must then strive to keep alive in the consciousness of the congregation, however, is the obligation laid upon the Church to serve its neighborhood *in so far as it can.*

b. More likely, however, congregational patterns of giving do not provide the deacons with the funds which reaching-out requires. If this be so, the diaconate faces a dual challenge and opportunity:

1) To strive in every way, through word of mouth, newsletter, public meetings, and by urging the pulpit to speak forthrightly to this issue, to "educate" the congregation to the full extent of its diaconal obligations.

2) To draw upon congregational resources in talent and expertise (as discussed above under the Second Circle) for meeting parish needs "in kind". What one may not be inclined to give in money, he or she might be "educated" to give personally in skill, time, compassion. In such giving, both donor and recipient are blessed, and the Lord is served. Creative diaconates can stimulate such giving if they bear steadily in mind our Lord's command: "Let your light so shine before men, that they may see your good works and give glory to your Father who is in heaven" (Matt. 5:16). Fueling such light with the energies of talent and good will is the kind of love for neighbor that diaconates are uniquely called upon to stimulate and organize and focus. A congregation sluggish in shedding such light probably reveals a diaconate sluggish in its perception of the Lord's commands.

3. *But should the Church do via the diaconate what individual believers are called upon to do?*

This is, of course, the question that can be put to having a diaconate at all. But if it has been only grudgingly conceded that the congregation ought to care for its own needy, the objection may be put all the more strongly when parish outreach is proposed.

It is instructive here to observe that Jesus uses two figures of speech in describing our obligation to our neighbors (Matt. 5:14). One is the figure of a lamp: men do not "light a lamp and put it under a bushel, but on a stand, and it gives light to all in the house." This, surely, has reference to the good works done by the individual, an obligation he cannot shift to the Church or the diaconate. The other figure, however, is that of a city: "A city set on a hill cannot be hid." It is as a city, a communion of saints, an organized and living Body, that the Church is to shine before the world. She does so in her acts of corporate obedience, in which the diaconate serves as hands, feet, and advising mind. What the diaconate does, the whole "city of God" does—and thus is "set on a hill" for all in the parish, and beyond it, to see and "give glory to your Father who is in heaven."

4. *But what about being taken in by the chiseler?*

There are chiselers! And the deacon must never forget that often they are "professionals" and he is an amateur. There are those whose occupation is "working the churches"—often in the evenings and on weekends, when checking into such credentials as they offer is difficult.

How shall the Church serve the real needs of its neighborhood without being taken in by the pro's?

Get help!

Learn at first hand from those in your community who are experienced in welfare just how the chiseler works, what his or her "line" is likely to be, and what kinds of questions you can ask to expose the fraud. And then spot cheaters, and resist them. The Lord has harsh words for some kinds of human being: "Do not give dogs what is holy and do not throw your pearls before swine, lest they trample them under foot and turn to attack you" (Matt. 7:6). These hard words extend beyond diakonia, but they also set a diaconal standard: the chiseler is out!

This is so important, because chiseling makes genuine aid to the truly needy so much more difficult, that deacons should invite welfare experts to "role-play" with them: the expert taking the part of the chiseler, and the deacons seeing how quickly they spot telltale indications that they are being "had".

The more the word gets around that your diaconate intends to serve the needy in your parish, the more attempts will be made to get in line—until you have made it clear that you know how to discriminate honesty from fraud.

When in doubt, give prudently and sparingly the first time, so you will not have mismanaged much of the Lord's goods if you are misled.

What the chiseler makes doubly difficult is generous diaconal stewardship of the Church's gifts. There is, on the one hand, the welfare artist so well known to relief agencies; and there is, on the other hand, the model of the Lord Himself, who "went about doing good and healing all that were oppressed by the devil" (Acts 10:38). And St. Matthew typically reports, that "many followed him, and he healed them all..." (Matt. 12:15). Moreover, in the case of the ten lepers —as we have observed elsewhere in this volume—the Lord cured all ten of their loathesome disease, knowing full well that only one would return to give thanks (Luke 17:11-19). Even the Syrophoenician woman, whom the Lord Himself likened to "the dogs," received her desire that He cast a demon out of her possessed daughter (Mark 7:25-30). The Bible, like the creation itself, abounds with instances of the prodigality of God—all is abundance, life to the overflowing. Those who would represent God among men must be no less generous!

In short, the chiseler is a challenge rather than a threat. He who comes to cheat must be detected, exposed, and refused until he makes confession and genuinely intends to cheat no more: "Let the thief no longer steal, but rather let him labor, doing honest work with his

179

hands, so that he may be able to give to those in need" (Eph. 4:28). What a transformation might be wrought by proper caution and through experienced instruction: from chiseler to giver! The Spirit can, through you, accomplish that! To the chiseler as chiseler, let the diaconal hand be extended, but closed; to the chiseler who can be turned 'round and set on the road to renewed self-respect, let the diaconal hand reach far beyond the first mile (Matt. 5:41-42). Your hand is, after all, that of Him who came "to seek and to save the lost" (Luke 19:10).

Here is a set of questions useful in detecting the chiseler:

1. *Name: (Mr., Mrs., Miss):*   *Age:*
2. *Address:*
3. *Phone #:*
4. *Wife/Husband's Name:*   *Age:*
5. *Head of Household Social Security #:*
6. *Children's Names:*   *Sex:*   *Age:*
   a.
   b.
   c.
   .....

7. Is the person/family currently a client of or receiving help from any agency or organization? If yes, which ones and what services?

8. *Family Income:*
   Source   *Amount (Gross, Net?)*
   a.
   b.
   c.

9. What is the problem? *(be specific)*

10. What is/are the person/families needs? *(be specific)*

11. How and why did the problem arise? *(be specific)*

12. What has the person/family done to try to solve the problem? *(be specific)*

13. Has the person/family asked any other churches, agencies, organizations, persons, etc. for assistance with this problem?

   A. If yes, which ones?   What assistance, if any, was given?
      (be specific)
      1.
      2.
      3.

   B. If no assistance was received from some or all of the above, what reason(s) were given by each?

B. *SOLUTIONS*

As we have discussed the problems inherent in this Circle of Service, we have also suggested directions in which solutions may be sought. In addition, the suggestions made in the Second Circle apply here. Just as the congregation must be led to bend all its gifts, talents, skills, and goods to the meeting of its own needs, in Circle Two, so the deacons aiming at this Fourth Circle must strive to enlist the Body in the witness of service to its own neighborhood.

No one supposes that this will be easy, nor go without question or opposition. Of course not! Many will be the arguments to show that your congregation "cannot" or "may not" reach out to its neighbors with a helping hand. But if these be many, the deacons' counter-arguments must be more! For it is the Lord's will that His Body be like a city set upon a hill, radiating His love through its deeds.

C. *CONCRETE SUGGESTIONS*

Service to the parish will be carried out in terms of the needs that appear there. Often these will duplicate the kinds of need requiring the kinds of service which appear within the congregation. There are, however, other kinds of opportunity, like:

1. Provision to the neighborhood of information of general interest:

   a. As to programs which deal with alcohol and drug abuse.

   b. As to lectures and seminars and counseling services on family problems.

   c. As to coping with inflation and energy conservation.

   d. As to programs intended to deal constructively with neighborhood concerns like safe streets, activities for youth, ways to alert city hall, etc.

   e. Notice of Bible study groups, coffee house ministries, child care opportunities, etc.

   f. Information on how to prepare for retirement, how to meet emergencies, how to get inexpensive legal and medical advice, etc.

2. Planning to provide fellowship:

   a. For the elderly.

   b. For singles and single parents.

   c. For children and youth.

   d. For those with special problems, physical, mental, social.

Chapter 21.

FIFTH CIRCLE

SEEKING OUT THE NEIGHBORHOOD NEEDY

"When you give a dinner or a banquet, do not invite your kinsmen or rich neighbors, lest they invite you also in return, and you be repaid. But when you give a feast, invite the poor, the maimed, the lame, the blind, and you will be blessed, because they cannot repay you. You will be repaid at the resurrection of the just" (Luke 14:12-14).

Diaconal responsibility extends beyond waiting for cries of anguish. It includes seeking out neighbors in want whose needs are real but unadvertised. So it is, as already observed, within the congregation. So it must be, also, in the neighborhood. This is the Fifth Circle of Service.

SCOPE

Our discussion focuses upon the problems, and responses to them, which service in the Fifth Circle encounters.

A. *PROBLEMS/SOLUTIONS*

Seeking out need, especially outside the congregation, poses severe problems. One of our tasks as maturing humans, someone has said, is to know what we see rather than to see what we know. We are all quite able to look upon human need, often right on our doorsteps, without knowing that it is truly *need* that we see. The world's poor are not only hidden deep inside the world's cities, or huddled in shacks around the cities' perimeters, but are in fact simply invisible to many who could help them. The Bible frequently equates the blind eye and deaf ear with the stony heart, just as the Lord equates an absence of fruit with stony soil (Mark 4:16). And it is the Lord who must replace the stony heart with the heart of flesh, one which opens the eyes and ears to human need and guides the diaconal hand to alleviate it: "A new heart

I will give you, and a new spirit I will put within you; and I will take out of your flesh the heart of stone and give you a heart of flesh. And I will put my spirit within you, and cause you to walk in my statutes and be careful to observe my ordinances" (Ezek. 36:26-27).

Once again, the priority of the Word preached, through which the Lord makes this exchange of stony heart into heart of flesh, is the key to diaconal outreach. And we stress this once more: your "success," deacons, begins with the pulpit, and your every effort to encourage and undergird your pulpit ministry lays the foundation ever more securely for your own service!

Consider the following:

1. Do you, as deacons, *really want to know* what forms of human need exist in the streets surrounding your Church? Can you come to worship service, time after time, and not even want to know if there be hunger, pain, distress, loneliness, frustration, injustice behind the doors and windows you pass—known, of course, to the Lord, but ignored by you as His Body? Yes, that indifference is likely; but so, you know, it should not be! Pray for a heart of flesh!

2. Does your congregation *really want to know* the same things listed above? No, it is quite natural that they do not. But the basis of the Church is not the natural, but the supernatural! What a challenge it is for you as deacons to alert those who want to see, but do not know where to look, the needs which the Lord knows and wants His Body to meet! And, still more, to aid in opening the eyes and ears of those who do not care to acknowledge human need, so that they gradually can come to "see" clearly what is before their faces. Yes, as the Word from the pulpit breaks the hardened heart, so you can set lenses upon the eyes being liberated, to behold the "neighbor" in what had been the unseen alien!

3. What is discussed in points 1 and 2 above is, of course, the heart of the deacon's problems in every aspect of your work. To be able to "see" what needs attention, to "hear" what needs response, begins in a heart turning from self-interest to self-sacrifice. Such turning is schooled by the Word, and is what the Church exists primarily to accomplish through the agency of the Spirit, working with and through the Word preached and taught. That the pulpit courageously speaks the Word of the Lord, and the diaconate distributes the fruit of such sowing of the Word, is the oversight responsibility of the eldership. And so the three offices of the Church are at one, in the one Body of the Lord, to do His work in the world.

184

4. In their neighborhood outreach, as observed before, the deacons must be sure that all sources of public assistance are fully used by the eligible needy within their parish. You must know what public funds and services are available, and how they can be obtained. Then you must lead those to them who, for one reason or another, have not gone on their own. Keep abreast of changes in the welfare laws. Know what kinds of private funds, loans, grants, assistance in kind are offered in your community. If none of the deacons is himself a lawyer, be sure to enlist legal aid from within the congregation (or outside it, if necessary) to assist the needy in getting their legal rights, what the Bible repeatedly calls "justice".

5. Deaconesses, joined by women of the congregation, should be encouraged to establish a clothing and food depot for aid to the needy of the neighborhood. These resources can be tied in with local welfare agencies, who will screen recipients for aid. Deacons should encourage, and financially support, such efforts, while enlisting the cooperation of the elders and ministry in publicizing it. Far better that used clothing come here to enrich the poor and bless the donor than that they be featured in "garage sales" to enrich the owner.

6. Careful cultivation of "connections" with welfare and relief agencies can result in making the deacons active participants in the work of these bodies. In some localities both charitable foundations and governmental sources are willing to channel at least some of their monies and goods through responsible diaconates. Deacons can stress the dual advantages of this arrangement:

a. The welfare agency is assured that the assistance goes where, and for what, it is appropriated, and

b. The diaconate knows that human need is being met in its parish, and is able to attach a "return address" to such charity: "the love of God constraineth us" (II Cor. 5:14). Considerations of separation of Church and state bend, here, to the fact that God is sovereign over both, and it is He who wills that need be met. For the state "is the minister of God to you for good" (Rom. 13:4).

7. Mennonites, Quakers, and other religious groups have earned an enviable reputation for quietly appearing at the scenes of natural disasters to assist in cleanup and rehabilitation. Creative diaconates will plan similar means of letting their light shine before men, so that God may be honored through their obedience. Work and relief teams, combining various skills, can be organized, perhaps out of neighboring congregations—men and women who, perhaps by virtue of retirement,

can find time to serve for a few days or weeks in places of temporary emergency need.

8. Diaconates of neighboring churches should consider banding together to hire a fulltime diaconal consultant to be eyes, ears, and facilitator in discovering and coordinating relief of parish needs.

We will discuss the fulltime deacon-at-large, or better, diaconal consultant, under section A, The Regional Conference, of the next chapter.

B. *THE FIFTH CIRCLE: SUMMARY*

Here the deacons strive to focus the resources in money, time, and talent which God so generously provides the congregation upon needs in the neighborhood which do not advertise themselves. The task is never easy, and probably always beyond completion. But it is, no doubt, a task assigned every congregation which hears the Lord's command to be as a city set upon a hill.

C. *A CASE STUDY*

The following is true:

An elderly woman is blind, but manages to live alone in her own apartment, with some assistance from time to time.

This particular winter is a severe one. The lady's landlord has financial problems. Although the lady's rent includes payment for her gas heat, the landlord fails to pay her bill. The gas company sends out a representative to shut off the blind woman's gas. She protests that her bill was paid with her rent, but the service man has his orders.

The woman remembers the Church, and manages to get word to a deacon of her plight. He makes the necessary contacts, suit against the landlord is threatened, a judge indicates that a substantial fine will be levied if the blind woman's gas is not immediately restored by payment of her bill.

The landlord pays.

A serious need has been discovered and met in the name of the Lord.

Chapter 22.

SIXTH CIRCLE

COOPERATIVE DIAKONIA: NATIONAL/INTERNATIONAL
"For I will not venture to speak of anything except what Christ has wrought through me to win obedience from the Gentiles, by word and deed..." (Rom. 15:18).

The Church universal is one.

The diaconate universal is one.

In the Sixth Circle of Service, the congregational diaconate lifts its eyes to its universality, beginning with diaconates close at hand, extending to diaconates serving states, provinces, or regions, and focusing on international opportunities for witness in-deed for Jesus Christ.

SCOPE

Beginning with reasons for cooperative diakonia, we turn then to:

A. The Regional Conference

B. The National Diaconate

C. International Diakonia

D. And the Great Commission

E. Appendices: Model Constitutions

NATIONAL/INTERNATIONAL SERVICE

There are many reasons why deacons should reach out to cooperate with diaconates of other congregations and other manifestations of the universal Body of Christ; among such reasons these:

1. Cooperative effort can draw upon a broad range of talents, gifts, resources.

2. Cooperation can focus preplanned effort upon extensive or intensive emergency situations.

3. Cooperation can become a mutual learning experience, one diaconate teaching and learning from another.

4. Cooperative effort reflects the basic, universal unity of the Body

of Christ: "There is one body and one Spirit, just as you were called to the one hope that belongs to your call, one Lord, one faith, one baptism, one God and Father of us all, who is above all and through all and in all" (Eph. 4:4-6).

5. St. Paul himself set the pattern for cooperative diakonia by collecting funds in the provinces for the needy in Jerusalem: "At present, however, I am going to Jerusalem with aid for the saints. For Macedonia and Achaia have been pleased to make some contribution for the poor among the saints at Jerusalem..." (Rom. 15:25-26). Paul discusses this diaconal aspect of his ministry, in greater detail, in the eighth and ninth chapters of the Second Letter to Corinth. From the beginning, therefore, the Church has, as one Body, cared for her needy wherever they might be. Developing from this model are regional, national, and international diaconates.

We offer the following suggestions for regional and national/international diaconal cooperation.

A. *THE REGIONAL CONFERENCE*

The term "Conference" here does not refer to scheduled meetings. It refers to a number of diaconates joined together by regional organization. The Conference will, of course, include among its activities both regular and special regional meetings.

The Conference develops out of boundaries set by membership in a presbytery or classis, and may come to include several adjacent such bodies. Churches which exist independently of regional ecclesiastical union can structure a diaconal Conference along municipal, state, provincial, or other regional political boundaries. The primary purpose of the Conference will be to facilitate the kinds of advantages suggested above, and can include purposes unique to the region.

1. Organization or Structure:

   a. Planning for the creation of a Conference can be initiated by any diaconate, at a meeting to which representatives of other neighboring diaconates are invited.

   b. The permanent organization of the Conference should provide for delegated participation by each diaconate wishing to be involved, probably through two members.

   c. Provision may well be made for the membership of one or more pastors of participating congregations.

   A constitution must be drafted, probably by a committee

assigned to the task, and its provision for officers and executive committee carried out (see appendix to this chapter for a model constitution).

2. Purposes for creation of the Conference might be specified as:

a. To promote the effectiveness of congregational diaconates by way of common assistance, educational and inspirational meetings, sharing of methods, mutual approach to private and public support sources, etc.

b. To provide a guiding oversight of needs and how they are being met within the regional area.

c. To promote the discernment of human need within the region through:

1) Contact with established social agencies.

2) Surveys of member congregations.

3) Appointment of permanent committee on emergency situations.

d. To assign dealing with discovered needs to the nearest, or best qualified, diaconate, with assistance from the whole as required. *It should not be the intention, nor the practice, of the Conference to supplant local diaconates!*

e. To deal, however, by means of its own committees with problems which encompass the entire region or occur outside the reach of any local diaconate.

f. To circulate a regular newsletter designed to educate the membership, and to call attention to challenges and opportunities within the region. The spirit of the Conference may well depend upon the quality of the newsletter, and the editor should be carefully chosen and staunchly supported.

g. The Conference can deliberately undertake on-going projects, like some of those listed below. These will perform a service in the region, and will constitute activities around which interest is woven with unifying effect.

h. Public funds are sometimes available for distribution through the agency of the regional diaconal Conference, especially when it can be demonstrated that thus the money most efficiently reaches its goal. Conference executives should constantly be on the lookout for this possibility, as well as for money and assistance in kind offered by private agencies, companies, merchants, etc.

i. The Conference could employ a part-time or full-time deacon-at-large, or better, a diaconal-consultant, assigned the responsibility of seeking out need and supervising its alleviation. See Appendix B to this chapter for model job description—diaconal consultant.

j. The Conference could be involved in projects like the following, which are offered only as a suggestive list:

1) Assigning to local diaconates the rehabilitation of alcoholics, drug addicts, ex-delinquents, those released from jail.

2) Finding employment for the jobless, assisting in retraining for the otherwise unemployable, job placement for youth and the handicapped.

3) Establishing a home for abused children or wives.

4) Establishing a family counseling center.

5) Supporting or providing a home for unwed mothers, especially during pregnancy—and providing follow-up after the baby arrives.

6) A crisis center, and twenty-four hour telephone service for runaway teenagers and others suffering traumatic experiences.

7) Hospitality center for seamen and military personnel.

8) Emergency family services involving utility turn-offs, food, financial emergencies.

9) Training courses in family management and home economics.

Because the Church was delinquent in seeing and meeting needs like these, the state was obliged to fashion its own forms of diakonia. An active diaconal Conference can turn the trend back toward a diakonia done by the body from whom loving service is most appropriate—the Church of Jesus Christ.

2. Preparation for disaster:

a. No area is immune from disaster, in common or uncommon form. The regional Conference should be the diaconal planning center for meeting emergencies when they strike—planning done in consultation with the local Red Cross and other emergency groups.

b. Advance disaster planning should include the following:

1) Selection of buildings suitable for emergency shelter.

2) Contact with businesses for guaranteed supply of items like cots, blankets, heating units—perhaps available through national guard armories.

3) Means of emergency transportation to hospitals, etc.

4) Lists of persons experienced in physical and emotional therapy.

5) Designated leaders to assume responsibilities for diaconal

services in time of emergency, coordinated in advance with local emergency groups.

6) Sources for the provision of food, field kitchens, sanitary services.

c. While the Conference should never undertake planning or action solely on its own, there will be ample challenge to be met when tornado, flood, fire, earthquake, ecological mishap, or the like strikes.

3. In summary: diaconates which are now members of a regional Conference should be ever on the alert for ways to vitalize it the more. Diaconates lacking a regional body should consider the creation of one. The motive is always twofold: 1) to render service of love to the Lord who wills to be found in the victims of need; and, 2) thus to bear witness to the Body of Christ which is set on a hilltop by diaconal obedience.

See Appendix A to this chaper for model constitution for a diaconal conference.

B. *THE NATIONAL DIACONATE*

Reasons for establishing a national diaconate, cutting across denominational lines, are essentially those for promotion of regional Conferences: more effective witness by service, and service as witness.

We suggest:

1. Creation of a national diaconal structure, designed to coordinate the efforts of regional Conferences.

2. Delegation to the national governing board or committee of two members from each regional Conference.

3. Begun by the creation of a planning committee, formed out of two or more regional Conferences, assigned to prepare a constitution (see model in Appendix C to this chapter).

4. Under the constitution, an executive committee could be formed, and national meetings planned.

5. Purposes for a national diaconate:

a. To coordinate on a national level activities of regional Conferences where these could thus function most effectively.

b. To focus regional efforts just as Conferences focus local efforts.

c. To provide stimulation and information through a national diaconal newsletter.

d. To develop instruction manuals and plan training conferences.

e. To provide the nation's deacons with access to and influence on provincial, state, and national welfare agencies, programs, and legislative decisions.

f. To provide technological expertise out of the reach of local and regional diaconates.

g. To coordinate disaster relief extending beyond regional boundaries.

h. To lift the eyes of the local and regional diaconates to international needs, and provide instruction for cooperation with international relief agencies both public and private.

i. To provide organization and staff for national relief projects; to do the same for international programs.

6. Advantages of a national diaconal board:

a. The provision of information to regional and local diaconates.

b. Clearing center for solution of problems encountered in local and regional services.

c. Evaluation of organizations seeking financial support and gifts in kind for national and international service.

d. Creation and presentation of film and other programs on national and worldwide needs, and the best ways of coping with these.

e. Development of slide programs for use in the local congregation.

f. Provision of instructors and manuals for training regional diaconates.

g. Exerting influence on seminary education to include exploration of diaconal perspectives.

h. To assist the regional diaconates in projects beyond the resources of any one Conference.

i. To support representatives in federal, provincial, national, and state capitols to influence welfare legislation and secure funds for national or state-wide, or provincial, projects.

j. Develop programs designed to respond to medical, literacy, and other deprivation needs which extend across the nation in various forms.

k. Provide national diaconal response to refugees, making arrangements for local reception, sponsorship, housing, job hunting, adjustment.

l. Concern for undocumented aliens, migrant workers, major needs in large metropolitan areas.

m. Coordination of disaster relief plans in regional Conferences, and accumulation of a disaster relief fund to be allocated as needs arise.

6. In summary: creation of a national diaconate remains an aspiration. Local diaconates which succeed in developing active Conferences in their localities can raise their sights to this broader objective.

C. *INTERNATIONAL DIAKONIA*

Local congregations, national denominations, and regional Conferences can all aspire to international service. The challenges and the needs are real. But they must be carefully analyzed and studied before action is proposed. Problems must not be underestimated, and no programs should be proposed without contact with agencies already in the field. Involved are opportunities like these:

1. Agricultural development to provide more and better nourishment for a community and nation.

2. Sanitary improvements.

3. Health care, and development of sound hygiene.

4. Community leadership training.

5. Educational improvements, training of skills, schooling in modern techniques and use of new technologies.

6. All with due respect to the culture of the native region.

D. *AND THE GREAT COMMISSION*

There always is on-going dispute between those who advocate a "word" ministry of missions, and a "deed" ministry of missions. We do not enter directly upon that dispute here, except to note that efforts to combine "word" and "deed" ministries seem to result in an uneasy alliance, with advocates of one or the other seeking priority. Because— the separation of "word" from "deed" is artificial.

We have already argued that there is an inseparable unity between faith and love. That to believe *is* to love. That to love *is* to do the deeds required by the Lord through His Word; and, therefore, to love—that is obey—*is* to believe. All separation of "word" from "deed" is artificial, and becomes useful only for purposes of discussion.

In short, the mission sent out only to "say" cannot be an authentic mission; for if the "saying" be truly believed by those who are sent, "doing" will be the inevitable concomitant. Missionaries who simply "say" the Word, without "doing" the Word, are not bearing the authentic Gospel, and the Lord's blessing upon their labors is by way of exception.

This becomes clear, as noted before, upon closer examination of the Great Commission laid upon the Church by her Lord and Head shortly before His ascension: "All authority in heaven and on earth has been given to me. Go therefore and make disciples of all nations, baptizing them in the name of the Father and of the Son and of the Holy Spirit, teaching them to observe all that I have commanded you; and lo, I am with you always, to the close of the age" (Matt. 28:18-20).

The purpose of mission, according to the Lord's Commission, is the making of disciples.

Who is a disciple?

A follower. One who obeys a Master. One who listens for, and does, the Master's word. To make a disciple, it is necessary, then, to be "teaching them to observe all that I have commanded you...." Only those thus taught, and thus obedient, can be and are, disciples. Or, again: the believing do, and the doers believe! This is the heart of the Great Commission, the charter of mission.

But that Commission moves on a crucial assumption: it is spoken to the Lord's Disciples, and through them to the Church they founded upon the Old Testament structure. That is to say, the Commission itself assumes that those who carry it out are already *disciples*! That is, are already doers of the Word, if they be disciples indeed: "But be doers of the word, and not hearers only, deceiving yourselves" (Jas. 1:22).

It is futile to ask, or to argue, therefore, whether or not mission involves *both* "word" and "deed". If it is authentic mission, done by true disciples in obedience to the Great Commission, it will be at one and the same time "word-deed". The Word will be the Lord's, and the deeds will be in obedience to that Word. And the recipients of mission will *hear* and *see, at one and the same time* and *in one and the same missionary*, the Word and its fruits: preaching-and-diakonia!

Striking confirmation of the alliance of "word" and "deed" in the Great Commission is supplied by a recent study by Piero Gheddo, entitled *Why Is The Third World Poor?* (Orbis Books, 1973). Father Gheddo, both missionary and journalist, carefully develops the thesis that Third World poverty inheres in mistaken conceptions of both man and his world, rooted in primitive and pagan religions which govern Third World poor nations. Man, as seen in primitive religions is the victim of the fates and evil spirits. He requires liberation in Christ to free him for planning his own future and accepting responsibility for his own society. The world, as seen in primitive religions is the private haunt of spirits who forbid change. It must be perceived as the creation of a loving God who intends it for man's use and development. Christian mission, Gheddo insists, is indispensable as a foundation upon which liberated efforts to move the poor world toward prosperity can be built, and will thrive. Word liberates in-deed!

Mission is the means to diakonia among converts who themselves come to believe and thus to socio-economic progress.

We conclude, therefore, that those in pagan lands who truly hear the "peace of Jesus Christ" (Acts 19:36) preached, will at one and the same time behold His Body going "about and doing good" (Acts 10:38); and that they, liberated in Christ, will themselves become "word-deed" witnesses in their homelands, breaking the chains of superstition which have so long held them in physical bondage to poverty and need. All this in the spirit and intent of the greatest of missionaries, who declares before King Agrippa, "I was not disobedient to the heavenly vision, but declared first to those at Damascus, then at Jerusalem and throughout all the country of Judea, and also to the Gentiles, that they should repent and turn to God and perform deeds worthy of their repentance" (Acts 26:19-20).

The Bible knows no separation of "word" and "deed" ministries, and neither should the Church. There is simply a division of office: the pulpit preaching, the deacons serving, the elders overseeing—but each exhibiting in themselves the unity of belief and love, of faith and obedience, of teaching and serving.

International mission *is* international diakonia; and international diakonia *is* international mission; and the Church should distinguish between them only for purposes of discussion.

APPENDIX A - CONSTITUTION FOR A DIACONAL CONFERENCE

ARTICLE 1: NAME
The name of this organization is ....

ARTICLE 2: BASIS
The basis of the Conference is Scripture and Formula of Subscription for the office bearers of....

ARTICLE 3: MEMBERSHIP

Past and present deacons in the .... Churches in .... are automatically members of the Conference. All other members of the .... Churches of .... qualify for membership by making known their interest and by participating in the activities of the Conference.

ARTICLE 4: PURPOSE

a. The .... Diaconal Conference exists for charitable and religious purposes: to promote the basic task of the deacons, the administration of Christian mercy, and to present and discuss the responsibilities and opportunities of deacons so that they can be challenged to administer the love of Christ.

b. To establish close contact and fellowship among the diaconates.

c. To inform the deacons regarding the needs of various institutions and organizations of mercy.

d. To assist the deacons and other Church members in meeting diaconal needs in the Church and community in the name of Jesus Christ.

ARTICLE 5: CONFERENCE BOARD

a. The Conference Board shall consist of the elected officers, two Ministerial Delegates, and one representative of each diaconate or steering committee in .....

b. The Conference Board shall take care of all matters of business and administration of the Conference, nominate its officers, and make arrangements for Conference meetings as required by the constitution.

c. Each diaconate shall have the right to present proposals to the Conference Board. Such proposals shall be submitted to the Board Secretary in writing and signed by the secretary of the diaconate presenting the proposal. The Board Secretary shall present these proposals at the next regular Board meeting.

ARTICLE 6: EXECUTIVE BOARD

a. The Executive Board shall consist of the elected officers and two Ministerial Delegates.

b. The Conference Board authorizes the Executive Board to administer all of the business of the Conference when the Conference Board is not in session.

ARTICLE 7: OFFICERS

a. The officers of the Conference Board shall consist of President, Vice President, Secretary, Assistant Secretary, Treasurer, and Assistant Treasurer.

b. The officers shall serve for two years with half of the officers retiring each year. The Vice-President shall succeed the President, the Assistant Secretary shall succeed the Secretary, and the Assistant Treasurer shall succeed the Treasurer, so that each year a new Vice-President, Assistant Secretary and Assistant Treasurer shall be elected.

c. Election of officers shall be at the last Conference meeting of each calendar year from nominations submitted by the Executive Board. The terms of officers shall begin with the January Board meeting following election and shall be for two full years. Officers shall be elected from the membership of the Conference.

d. The President shall preside at all Conference Board meetings, Conference meetings and special meetings. He shall select members to serve on such committees as the Board shall deem necessary.

e. The Secretary shall record the minutes of each Conference Board meeting, Conference meeting and special meetings. He shall notify the Board members of Board meetings and the diaconates and churches of Conference meetings. He shall send minutes of meetings to Board members and handle correspondence for the Board and Conference.

f. The Treasurer shall receive, record, and disburse funds in behalf of the Conference. He shall render a financial report at each Conference Board meeting and each Conference meeting. His books shall be audited at the end of his term of office.

g. The Vice-President, Assistant Secretary and Assistant Treasurer shall function in the absence of the President, Secretary, and Treasurer respectively and shall aid them whenever possible.

h. All officers shall serve the Conference without remuneration.

ARTICLE 8: MINISTERIAL DELEGATES

a. Two Ministerial Delegates shall be elected by....to serve on the Conference Board. The Conference shall suggest possible nominees to.....

b. Each Ministerial Delegate shall serve for 2 full years. One new Delegate shall be elected each year.

ARTICLE 9: DIACONAL CONSULTANT
a. The Conference shall employ a full-time Diaconal Consultant.
b. The Conference Board shall be responsible for hiring and supervising the Diaconal Consultant.

ARTICLE 10: MEETINGS
a. Regular meetings of the entire Conference shall be held at least twice a year. The Conference Board may call additional meetings when necessary.
b. The Conference Board shall meet four times each year or additionally as determined by the President.
c. The Executive Board shall meet monthly or additionally as determined by the President.
d. A quorum for any Board meeting will consist of 6 or more members.

ARITCLE 11: FUNDING
Each church represented in the Conference shall be challenged by the Board and the diaconates to contribute financially toward the cost of the programs of the Conference.

ARTICLE 12: DISSOLUTION
Those assets of the Conference remaining after all debts have been paid at the time of dissolution of the Conference shall be donated to.....

ARTICLE 13: AMENDMENTS
Amendments to the constitution may be made with a two-thirds majority vote of the Conference Board. A notice of such amendments must be sent to each diaconate at least four weeks before the Conference Board meeting so that each diaconate may be given the opportunity to discuss such amendments before the meeting.

(Adapted from form in use by the Diaconal Conference of Classis Kalamazoo, Michigan, Christian Reformed Church)

APPENDIX B - PROFILE OF DIACONAL CONSULTANT

PRIMARY RESPONSIBILITY:
The primary responsibility of the diaconal consultant will be to assist local diaconates in the....Conference, and to give guidance concerning opportunities and priorities for Christian diaconal action in response to human need.

SECONDARY RESPONSIBILITY:
To correlate and integrate the program of Christian mercy with mission outreach for a combination of word and deed ministry.

OVERSIGHT:
The work of the consultant will be supervised by the Conference Board or by committee appointed by the....Diaconal Conference.

SPECIFIC TASKS:
1. To become familiar with all available resources for meeting human needs in the Conference area: diaconates, Churches, governmental and private agencies and resources, and the like. To encourage and school the development of expertise groups and talent pools in allied congregations.

2. To serve as Christian advocate before boards, agencies, and courts for needy families as appropriate, especially as concerns: housing problems, medical and dental care, employment and welfare services, problems of the aged, youth counseling, etc.

3. To be available to diaconates and pastors for counsel, and to advise or refer those persons recommended for professional counseling by them.

4. To engage in all other activities consonant with the scope of this office and designed to highlight the diaconal concern of this Conference for the needs within its region.

(Drawn from the "job description" for diaconal consultant drafted by the Diaconal Conference, Classis Kalamazoo, Michigan, Christian Reformed Church)

APPENDIX C - MODEL CONSTITUTION FOR NATIONAL/INTERNATIONAL DIACONAL AGENCY

Following is the constitution of the Christian Reformed World Relief Committee (CRWRC), which we reproduce here as a typical model for organizing such outreach.

The Constitution of the Christian Reformed World Relief Committee
Preamble
Whereas our Savior and Lord entrusted his people with the care of the poor of the world when He said, "the poor ye have always with you,"

And whereas we live in a sin-distorted world in which severe misery and distress frequently occur,

And whereas the sacrifice of Christ was made for the redemption of the whole man, body and soul,

And whereas Christ has ordained that His Church must be engaged in a ministry of mercy in deed, as well as in word,

The Christian Reformed Church in humility and gratitude to God hereby establishes this Christian Reformed World Relief Committee to minister in the name of our Lord to man distressed by reason of the violence of nature, the carnage of war or other calamities of life, and to relieve the sufferings of the needy of the world that man may be restored as the image-bearer of God and live to praise God as the Creator, to trust him as Redeemer and to obey him as Lord.

To this end we set forth the following rules of order:

Name: The name of this organization shall be the

Christian Reformed World Relief Committee
Article 1
Membership

The board of directors of the CRWRC shall be composed of one member from each classis and six members-at-large. Whenever possible the classical delegates shall be deacons. Nominations for these members shall be solicited by each classis from the area deacons' conference and after election by the classis, one name shall be presented to synod for approval together with an alternate. These members shall serve for a period of three years and shall be subject to re-election for a second term according to the rules of synod. One-third of the board members shall be elected each year. The members-at-large shall include a medical doctor, a sociologist, an attorney, a business-man, an accountant and a minister. These shall be elected according to the rules of synod. This board of directors shall have its office in Grand Rapids and shall be incorporated according to the law of the State of Michigan.

Article 2
Executive committee

A. Its personnel — There shall be an executive committee composed of the members-at-large and 12 delegate members as elected by the board.

B. Its meetings — The executive committee shall meet regularly four times a year; when necessary, additional meetings may be called.

C. Its authority — The board of directors of the CRWRC authorizes its executive committee:

1. To administer the affairs of the CRWRC during the period when the board of directors is not in session, with the understanding that:

a. it shall regularly consult the president, director and/or general secretary of the CRWRC.

b. no action with respect to any important matter is to be taken, if it can possibly be deferred until the annual meeting of the board of directors of the CRWRC.

2. To take care of all matters that the board of directors may have overlooked at its annual meeting which require action.

Article 3
Meetings

A. The board of directors shall meet annually at the time and place designated by the executive committee.

B. A majority of the board of directors shall constitute a quorum.

Article 4
The work of the CRWRC

A. To receive and administer the offerings and contributions of the church for the work of relief and rehabilitation of the needy of the world.

B. To collect and store items that may be used for emergency relief such as food, clothing, medical supplies, etc.

C. To supervise and control all domestic and global emergency relief in such areas where the local church is unable to meet the need.

D. To supervise and control such permanent benevolent activities as are designated by synod.

E. To appoint and designate area deacons' conferences for the management of special benevolent projects.

Article 5
Administration of relief

A. In areas where the Christian Reformed Church is represented both at home or abroad.

1. It will be the responsibility of the CRWRC to administer the work of emergency relief.

a. The CRWRC shall specify what constitutes relief or service to be given in each case.

b. The CRWRC shall determine the amount of relief to be distributed in any given disaster area.

c. The CRWRC shall seek the services of neighboring diaconates and/or deacons' conferences and missionaries to carry out the work of relief in all domestic disaster areas.

d. The CRWRC shall seek the services of the general conferences of missionaries to carry out the work of relief in all foreign disaster areas.

e. Those who are authorized to administer relief in disaster areas shall render detailed reports to the CRWRC for their approval.

f. All funds not utilized by the area deacons, missionaries or conferences shall be returned to the general fund of CRWRC.

g. No emergency relief program shall extend beyond a year without the approval of synod.

2. The CRWRC shall work in co-operation with the mission boards in regard to the management of such permanent benevolent causes which are requested by the mission boards and endorsed by synod (e.g. medical, educational, sociological programs, etc.).

a. The CRWRC shall specify and define each permanent benevolent cause and shall seek approval of such from synod.

b. The CRWRC shall determine the yearly appropriations for each permanent benevolent cause.

c. The CRWRC shall, whenever possible, designate local diaconates and/or deacons' conferences, and missionaries and missionary conferences, to administer these permanent benevolent activities.

d. Those who are authorized to administer these permanent benevolent activities shall render monthly reports to the CRWRC.

B. In areas where the Christian Reformed Church is not represented:

1. The CRWRC shall determine whether or not emergency relief shall be given in disaster areas where the Christian Reformed Church is not officially represented. Priority shall be given to those areas which meet the following conditions:

a. Where CRWRC is able to send its own personnel to the field.

b. Where follow-up missionary activity can be anticipated.

c. Where a Christian witness can be achieved by this ministry.

2. The administration of emergency relief shall be conducted along the following line of procedure:

a. Co-operation with other relief agencies will be sought whenever this does not endanger the identity of the CRWRC.

b. The committee shall at all times attempt to assure the proper use of funds and materials.

Article 6
Relationship with other relief agencies

A. Relationship with relief agencies of sister churches.

Wherever possible co-operation with relief agencies of our sister churches shall be established.

B. Relationship with other Christian or secular relief agencies.

Aid will be given as indicated under administration of relief, B, 2.

C. Relationship with governmental relief agencies.

Relationship with these governmental relief agencies should be encouraged, provided there is no compromise of the basic principles of CRWRC.

Article 7
Relationship to synod

A. Synod shall appoint the members of the CRWRC according to regulations for membership.

B. Synod shall elect from nominations to be presented by the CRWRC for the following position or positions: the general director of the CRWRC and/or the general secretary of the same.

C. The CRWRC shall present its annual report to synod for approval and/or action.

Article 8
Duties of the director and/or the general secretary of the CRWRC

A. He shall be responsible to the CRWRC and its executive committee.

B. He shall keep complete records of all transactions at the meetings of the CRWRC and its executive committee.

C. He shall conduct all correspondence and maintain files relating to the work of the CRWRC.

D. He shall arrange and present all business and documents requiring the attention of the CRWRC and its committees, and prepare an agenda for all meetings of the CRWRC and its committees.

E. He shall submit to the CRWRC and its executive committee all reports required by synod, and attend meetings of synod and its advisory committees as representative of the CRWRC and as adviser on the matters of the committee.

F. He shall maintain proper contact with the diaconates, conferences, boards and other agencies of the Church.

G. He shall visit the congregations, classes and diaconal conferences as occasion may require and as the CRWRC or its executive committee may direct, for the purpose of information, liaison, consultation and the promotion of the work of the committee.

H. He shall report to each meeting of the executive committee of the CRWRC.

I. He shall bring the work of the CRWRC as closely as possible to the heart of the church.

J. He shall implement the decisions of the CRWRC and its executive committee as assigned to him.

Chapter 23.

SEVENTH CIRCLE

POSITIVE DIAKONIA

"...by works is faith made perfect" (Jas. 2:22).

"...that the man of God may be perfect, equipped for every good work" (II Tim. 3:17).

"You, therefore, must be perfect, as your heavenly Father is perfect" (Matt. 5:48).

The Seventh Circle of Service holds an ideal before the diaconate.

That ideal is the entire congregation united with their deacons in the service of human need, within the Body and within the parish, and extending outward to embrace, with others, the world.

SCOPE

Perfection has no scope. It is an all-embracing aspiration, an obligation laid upon the Church by her Lord and Head.

We discuss, then, some facets of this ideal and aspiration as they challenge the diaconate to challenge the congregation.

A. *THE ROUTE*

The ideal is not within the reach of human grasp. The deacons know this. The congregation, elders, and ministry all know it, too. But this knowledge does not relieve any Christian of obligation: "You, therefore, must be perfect...." So the Lord commands.

The gulf between obligation and ability drives us to the Word and the Spirit to ignite the desire for perfection and to illumine the way toward it. The Lord who demands a perfection we will not attain this side of heaven does not leave His Church ignorant of the way, nor bereft of all power to seek it. He sends the Spirit who will illumine the Word: "But the Counselor, the Holy Spirit, whom the Father will send in my name, he will teach you all things, and bring to your remembrance all that I have said to you" (John 14:26). By inspiration the Words of the Lord were inscribed for our instruction. Through the Spirit the Word becomes clear and powerful: "When the Spirit of truth comes, he will guide you into all truth; for he will not speak on his own authority, but whatever he hears he will speak, and he will declare to you the things that are to come. He will glorify me, for he will take what is mine and declare it to you" (John 15:13-14).

The Lord's promise of the Spirit must not be confused with charismatic revelations. The Spirit does not create special revelations. He takes the Word of the Lord and applies it with power to the willing heart. The congregation, therefore, caught up in the desire for perfection will reach out for it through a pulpit powerfully preaching the Scriptures. This is the key to truly positive diakonia.

The goal is summarized by John Calvin as follows: "We are the stewards of everything God has conferred on us by which we are able to help our neighbor, and are required to render account of our stewardship. Moreover, the only right stewardship is that which is tested by the rule of love. Thus it will come about that we shall not only join zeal for another's benefit with care for our own advantage, but shall subordinate our interests to those of our neighbor" (*Institutes of the Christian Religion*, III.7.5).

B. *WAY STATIONS ON THE ROAD TOWARD PERFECTION*

1. *Cooperation:*
Full cooperation among the offices of the Church is indispensable. The chain is only as strong as its weakest link. Unless the ministry is courageously preaching the Word, and unless the eldership supports such preaching, disciplines disobedience, and stimulates diaconal activity, the deacons cannot hope to reach out toward perfection.

2. *Eagerness to serve:*
The fruit of such cooperation as suggested above will be a growing willingness to serve through the diaconate on the part of the whole congregation. From youth onward, the Christian must be schooled by the Church in the duties of stewardship, and their rewards.

Members nominated to office should stand with joy and if elected should serve with all their might.

3. *Using talent:*
We rarely use more than ten percent of all our innate talent, said the distinguished Harvard University psychologist-philosopher William

James. A congregation also has a far greater wealth of skills and talent than are put to the service of the neighbor, both within and without the Body. Aware of this, an alert diaconate is always busily matching skill and talent to need. The young have their gifts to bring; the elderly theirs; and all in between these age brackets must be stimulated to share goods, influence, enthusiasm, skills, talents.

4. *Escaping the apprenticeship syndrome:*

Deacons are not fledgling elders. Theirs is a crucial office, fully capable of challenging all the abilities either the younger or the older member brings to it. That congregation is guilty of tragic mistake which perceives of diaconal office as a holding pattern in preparation for the eldership. Nomination to one office or to the other should depend solely upon aptitude for the tasks required of each.

5. *Unified responsibility:*

The tendency to depreciate "counting pennies" applies to the diaconal office only when that is about all the deacons do. It is wise, however, to center all financial responsibility in the congregation in its diaconate. Decentralization of financial functions among a variety of committees is not efficient administration, and deprives the deacons of valuable information and contacts.

6. *Communication:*

We have made suggestions regarding the diaconal newsletter and other means of open communication between the deacons and those they serve as Body of Christ. The road toward perfection is paved with openness, and closed by undue secrecy—while, of course, confidentiality is always respected. Get the story out! Get reactions in!

7. *All deliberate speed:*

There will always be a gap between aspiration and achievement. There will be lagging behind in one or another of the Circles of Service we have sketched. Do not despair. Do not attempt too much at once. Plan carefully, learn from both successes and mistakes. Be alert to who you are and what you are doing, and ought to be doing. Pray. And trust the Lord. He will bless willing hearts and eager hands.

PART VI

BLUEPRINTS AND PROJECTIONS

Chapter 24.

BLUEPRINTS: PARABLES FOR DEACONS

Certain parables seem written in the Scriptures to inspire the diaconate. Parables like these:

A. THE GOOD SAMARITAN: AWARE, CARE, SHARE

The parable of the Good Samaritan is familiar. A man was traveling from Jerusalem to Jericho. He is fallen upon by thieves who stripped and beat him and left him lying at the roadside half dead. A priest passed by, saw the victim, and crossed over to avoid him. So did a Levite. But a Samaritan, stranger to the victim by race and religion, saw him and had compassion on him. He bound up the man's wounds, put him on his beast, took him to an inn, and paid in advance for his care and keeping.

"Which of these three, do you think," the Lord asks, "proved neighbor to the man who fell among the robbers?" On hearing the answer, "The one who showed mercy on him," Jesus said, "Go and do likewise" (Luke 10:25-37).

First, one of the perpetual problems which deacons face is illumined here. Between the Samaritan and the victim there was no kinship of religion or community. Yet Jesus clearly commands just this kind of mercy. The Church, through her deacons, is obliged to reach out in care and concern and practical assistance to all those about her who are in need.

Second, this parable highlights three attitudes which deacons must cultivate for themselves and seek to spread in the congregation. They are:

1. Are you aware?

Three people passed by the man lying beaten along the roadside. No doubt all three saw him there. But two of them were not aware, somehow, that here was human need crying out for their help. Perhaps they were too busy with their own affairs, or with those of formal service to God. Whatever the explanation, they were not aware.

It is a question which deacons must persistently put to themselves, both individually and in their meetings together: are we aware of the needs about us? Do we see with the eye of love what cries out for our attention? In fact, do we want to see need and hear cries of distress?

And does the congregation want to be aware? Does it want to know who needs what the congregation through its collective giving or individual talents could provide?

Part of the service of the diaconate to the Body is a series of lessons in awareness—after being sure that the diaconate has learned from them itself.

2. Do you care?

Two of those who passed by the man at the roadside may have been aware, but did not care. They felt no compulsion to assist. They heard no mandate of conscience. They declined to be neighbors.

From becoming aware to starting to care can be a difficult step. All kinds of reasons might be advanced among the deacons, or in the congregation, why needs of which they have reluctantly become aware cannot really be met.

The parable passes no judgment on the two who either were not aware, or did not care. It only pronounces blessing on the one who did. The inference is unmistakable, and the command reinforces it: God requires caring, a caring that overcomes whatever obstacles may be posed against service.

3. Will you share?

The Lord has only one answer to this question: "Go and do likewise!"

This is the burden of the diaconate, and that of the congregation. Those who are of God must be neighbors to any who is in need of whatever God has given them to share with others.

The parable of the Good Samaritan was told, as it were, for deacons.

B. THE VINEYARD: FOR THOSE WHO DO NOT CARE

The prophet Isaiah tells of a vineyard planted on a very fertile hill. Its owner did all that one can do to prepare that vineyard to produce choice grapes. But it produced only wild grapes. And in his disappointment, the owner declares that he will destroy that vineyard and make it a wasteland where only briers and thorns will grow ever after (Is. 5:1-6).

The same theme is taken up by our Lord, and reported in three of the Gospels (Matt. 21:33-46; Mark 12:1-12; Luke 20:9-19).

In each instance, it is clear that by the vineyard is meant the Church. For her the Lord has done all that can be done to insure the fruits of obedience and service. He has planted. He has preserved. He has sent prophets and teachers to instruct in His ways. He has given His Son that the guilt of the Church might be washed away. And what then does He ask of us? The obedience summed up in the love of God and neighbor.

The role of the deacons is to distribute the fruit of the vineyard to those in need. The role of the vineyard is to provide the fruit for such distribution. And the absence of such fruit is no little thing. The terrible punishment foretold by Isaiah did fall upon fruitless Israel, and does fall upon fruitless congregations throughout history: "Do not be deceived; God is not mocked, for whatever a man sows, that he will also reap. For he who sows to his own flesh will from the flesh reap corruption; but he who sows to the Spirit will from the Spirit reap eternal life" (Gal. 6:7-8).

Hear then the conclusion of the matter, an admonition to the congregation and mandate to the diaconate: "Let us not grow weary in well-doing, for in due season we shall reap, if we do not lose heart. So then, as we have opportunity, let us do good to all men, and especially to those who are of the household of faith" (Gal. 6:9-10). "For He will render to every man according to his works: to those who by patience in well-doing seek for glory and honor and immortality, He will give eternal life; but for those who are factious and do not obey the truth, but obey wickedness, there will be wrath and fury" (Rom. 2:6-8).

C. THE GOOD SAMARITAN: ANOTHER LOOK

A man traveling from Jerusalem to Jericho falls among thieves.
They rob and beat him, leaving him half-dead at the roadside.

A priest hurries by, perhaps late for the time of sacrifice. He ignores the bloody figure in the ditch. So does a Levite who next comes by. Two religious professionals neglect the love of neighbor which they profess.

But a stranger, a Samaritan, one of a people alien to the beaten man, pauses, bends to dress the man's wounds, hoists him on his donkey, takes him to an inn, and pays in advance for his care.

All this is a story told 'round the world: the parable of the Good Samaritan (Luke 10:25-37).

But has it become so familiar that you do not notice that the question which provoked the parable is not the question which our Lord answers?

The discussion began over eternal life. How shall we inherit that most desirable of all blessings? A lawyer wants to know: "And behold, a lawyer stood up to put him to the test, saying, 'Teacher, what shall I do to inherit eternal life?' "

Jesus asks him what the Law requires, and the lawyer knows: to love God above all and our neighbor as ourselves.

Jesus commends his answer and adds, "Do this and you will live."

"But he, desiring to justify himself, said to Jesus, 'And who is my neighbor?' "

This is strange language. How "justify himself"? For what?

We know from our own experience. What we mean to justify by complicating the definition of "neighbor" is our own behavior in doing what the priest and the Levite did. We mean to leave the definition of "neighbor" so vague as to justify passing by many who lie beaten on life's roadsides. And we mean to substitute the delight of talk for the difficulties of obedience. The lawyer indeed means to "justify" himself—and us.

This then is the question shrewdly posed for the afternoon's leisurely exploration with the "Teacher": just who is my neighbor? That is, who is the one I must love as I do myself? Not everyone, surely? Least of all a stranger or alien? By what marks shall I know him? Puzzles enough for an endless delay in actualizing love.

But the Lord brushes such speculation aside. He is a Teacher who aims at action: "*Do* this...and you will live"!!

After telling the immortal story, Jesus quietly rephrases the lawyer's question. He does not say, "There, now you see who your neighbor is—not the priest, not the Levite, but the beaten stranger..."

No, He rephrases the question in a way which can no longer be endlessly refined, disputed, and thus evaded: "Which of these three, do you think, proved neighbor to the man who fell among the robbers?"

What was to be a long afternoon's idle talk ended abruptly. The lawyer was obliged to say: "The one who showed mercy on him."

And the clever would-be disputant was then dismissed with a curt,

"Go and do likewise"! Why waste time discussing how we will know who our neighbor is? Just go and *be* "neighbor" to someone, to anyone, in need. Let the needy find his neighbor in you.

Drop the talk. Cut the chatter. Take God's gifts of time, money, goods, talents, counsel, a listening ear, a helping hand...out there where someone can use them.

To love a neighbor as yourself means simply to *be* a neighbor whenever and wherever you can.

Who is the neighbor?

Each of us is—or ought to be!

D. *GIVE AND FORGIVE*

"Give us this day our daily bread, And forgive us our debts, as we forgive our debtors" (Matt. 6:11-12).

A parable may be drawn from these familiar lines, taken from the prayer which the Lord instructs all Christians to use: "Pray then like this..." (Matt. 6:9).

Notice the play on words: "give" but "forgive".

The prefix "for" has the force of "not" here, of negation, of blotting out. We are asking God to "give" us all that we need for daily life, but "not" to give us the debit against our account which such giving lays upon us. *Give* us the bread, we pray, but *not* the debt which taking it should put upon us: give and forgive.

We need from God all that sustains daily life, all that makes it comfortable and enables us to do our work and enjoy our play. The Lord invites us to ask "Our Father" for all this. And He commonly gives far more than we know how to ask. This is why the prayer is made very simple: "daily bread" covers the needs we know and countless others of which we are completely unaware.

But this we do know, or should: we are far from using all His gifts in His required service, namely in the loving of the neighbor as ourselves. The debt we incur by accepting His gifts must needs be forgiven, and at once: we pray "give" and "forgive" in the same breath. Too much of what we are asking for will end up on the altar of self—or even of Satan.

The words flow easily enough...give...forgive. Who knows how often we have mouthed them?

But the Lord, whose prayer this is, obliges us to take upon ourselves a pledge: "as we forgive our debtors".

215

And who are they?

They must be those who bear the same relation to us that we bear to God: recipients of "daily bread" at our hand.

We acquire "debtors" just as God acquires them, by doing good. We put others in debt to us by doing for them what we ask God to do for us: give us what we need! as we give others what they need!!

The command to love the neighbor as ourselves means to make debtors. How else shall we be able to keep our part of the prayer's pledge, "as we forgive our debtors"?

Two obligations are implied by the pledge we say so readily:

1. That we make debtors through our generosity, and

2. That we exact no compensation from them in return, not even thanks or appreciation.

Then we can pray, "Forgive us our debts, as we forgive our debtors."

The Lord stresses this relationship: "forgive, and you will be forgiven" (Luke 6:37).

The Lord emphasizes this solemn truth in another familiar story— which follows.

E. *SIMON'S SURPRISE*

Simon the Pharisee invited the "Teacher" to dinner. Whatever he may have expected in the way of good talk, he certainly did not anticipate what he was going to hear about himself. (Luke 7:36-50).

The Lord came to dinner.

While He was sitting at the table, "a woman of the city, who was a sinner" slipped in among the guests. Saying nothing, the woman "began to wet his feet with her tears, and kissed his feet, and anointed them with the ointment" which she had brought with her.

The Pharisee was disappointed. He thought that he had invited a "prophet" to be his guest, but this "Teacher" was apparently quite unaware of how unsavory was the character of her who was touching Him. A wasted evening after all, Simon was probably thinking, for, "If this man were a prophet, he would have known who and what sort of woman this is who is touching him, for she is a sinner."

Thus will men prescribe how God ought to behave—if only He were as "wise" as we, in our own sight, are!

But the Teacher was more of a prophet than Simon could possibly have surmised, and He breaks into Simon's reverie with what will become a scathing rebuke: "Simon, I have something to say to you...."

Unaware of what lies ahead, Simon asks, "What is it, Teacher?"

And the Lord begins to talk of debts and debtors—the theme we have just considered in the Lord's Prayer.

"A certain creditor had two debtors: one owed five hundred denarii, and the other fifty. When they could not pay, he forgave them both. Now which of them will love him more?"

Like the lawyer asking "Who then is my neighbor?" Simon walks into the trap from which there will be no escape. He says, "The one, I suppose, to whom he forgave more."

Whereupon Jesus lists the ways in which the woman had served Him in courtesies which Simon had callously neglected: Simon had not given Him, as custom required, water to wash His feet before dinner—the woman had supplied the lack with her tears. Simon had greeted Him with no kiss, as courtesy required—the woman had kissed His feet. Simon had provided no oil with which He might groom His hair and beard—the woman had anointed His feet with ointment.

She had, in short, shown Him much love; Simon very little.

But the love we show reflects the love we have received. The debts we create by giving, and then forgive, measure our debts against God which He has graciously forgiven: "Therefore, I tell you, her sins, which are many, are forgiven, for she loved much; but he who is forgiven little, loves little."

Those who create few debtors by acts of love are, in fact, forgiven few of the immense range of debts we owe the Father. An absence of love for the neighbor betrays an absence of entrance upon the forgiving love of God.

The deacon has a dual concern in all of his efforts to persuade believers to share:

1. That, as God commands, the needy shall be satisfied with the gifts which He has entrusted to the stewardship of others for this purpose, and

2. That a generous heart testifies to a forgiven sinner, while a stingy heart betrays its own hardness.

F. *APPRENTICESHIP CHRISTIANITY*

"I am the way, and the truth, and the life..." (John 14:6).

Deacons are concerned with the way in which Christians live.

There is something to be learned about that from this remarkable saying of Jesus.

Have you ever wondered why the Lord puts this order—way, truth, life—on His answer to Thomas' question?

The Lord had said to His disciples that He was going away. Thomas speaks for them all in asking: "Lord, we do not know where you are going; how can we know the way?"

Thomas thought that knowing comes first, and then going the right way follows. So, often, do we. A few years ago a book based upon this text was issued by several authors who tried to improve upon the Lord's teaching method by revising His order: they made it into, "the truth, the way, and the life". But that is not what the Lord says, and it is not, therefore, what He means. Jesus is talking about apprenticeship Christianity, where doing precedes understanding. And to deacons this makes all the difference in the world—and beyond it.

Our Lord's heavenly Father destined Him to be raised in a carpenter's family. So, at least, is the tradition regarding Joseph. And carpentry, like most skills, can be talked about endlessly, but is really learned only by doing. Oh yes, the master carpenter tells the apprentice what to do, but the apprentice comes to knowing carpentry only by doing it. That makes all the difference between a sagging door hung by a novice and a neatly fitted one hung by a craftsman. The novice knows *about* carpentry; the master *knows* carpentry! This is true about most of living. First the doing, under guidance, and then the understanding. First the way; then the truth!

This, we say, is of great importance to deacons, because your business in the Church is not so much with talking as with doing—not so much *about* the way as *on* the way. Not with theoretical Christianity but with apprenticeship Christianity.

Remember that our Lord was not predestined by His Father to birth where we might have expected Him, say into Herod's palace or a Scribe's scholarly abode. He was born, by divine design, into a laboring man's dwelling. He draws, in all His teaching, upon examples taken from Everyman's daily life.

It is entirely in keeping with His upbringing by Joseph and Mary, according to God's predestined intent, that our Lord precedes understanding with doing. He sets the *way* before the truth! His hermeneutic (that is, His method of interpretation and understanding) is an apprenticeship hermeneutic. And it is an Everyman's hermeneutic. Open to all who believe. Not reserved for the learned, or the wealthy, or the powerful, or the famous. Quite the opposite, really: "And

218

the common people heard Him gladly" (Mark 12:37). To all who, like Jesus' own disciples, learned their work by doing it, He quite naturally would say: first the way, then the truth of understanding, and in these the true life. Apprenticeship Christianity. Just the kind which deacons teach themselves, by doing, and encourage others to learn, by giving.

Oh yes, like the master craftsman, the Lord offers guidance for finding the right way. The Psalmist pointed that out centuries ago: "Thy word is a lamp to my feet and a light to my path" (Ps. 119:105). Peter said it, too: "Lord, to whom shall we go? You have the words of eternal life" (John 6:68).

The Lord's word-order is fundamental: first the way; then the truth grasped by our understanding; and, in these, the discovery of new life: I am the way, and the truth, and the life.

One more thing deacons must observe: Jesus says, "I am...."

We never seek, or walk, the way alone. He is the very Word that sheds light upon the path: "In the beginning was the Word, and the Word was with God, and the Word was God...In him was life, and the life was the light of men" (John 1:1, 4). Those who come to understand the Word by doing it on the way of, and to, life, find that He has been joined with them on the way: "If a man loves me, he will keep my word, and my Father will love him, and we will come and make our home with him" (John 14:23). This blessed discovery of the presence of Jesus and His Father in the Word which guides our feet along the way is no doubt what "understanding" the truth really means. That is, we understand the Word by standing-under the Word as it illumines our path. And in such standing-under we have Jesus as companion, for He too came to walk the way set by His Father's will: "I seek not my own will but the will of him who sent me" (John 5:30).

Those who walk the way of obedience, that is the way of love to God and for neighbor made manifest in deeds, discover that Jesus Christ is, indeed, the way, the truth, and the life: "I have been crucified with Christ; it is no longer I who live, but Christ who lives in me; and the life I now live in the flesh I live by faith in the Son of God, who loved me and gave himself for me" (Gal. 2:20).

The challenge to every diaconate is to serve the congregation by opening to each member opportunities to walk the way of obedient love through sharing in deacons' services to the needy. The diaconate should think of itself as one of the open doors upon the way that leads to truth and life. Your hand, extended to the Body *for* gifts and to the needy *with* these gifts guides believers along the Lord's true way.

Chapter 25.

PROJECTIONS

Progress follows vision.

Deacons who aspire to participate in the Lord's designs for His Church must dream a little, must extend their reach beyond their grasp. Look up! Look around! Look ahead! Your office is an active function of a Body which is in league with the most progressive force in history, the power of the risen Lord: "having the eyes of your hearts enlightened, that you may know what is the hope to which he has called you, what are the riches of his glorious inheritance in the saints, and what is the immeasurable greatness of his power in us who believe..." (Eph. 1:18-19).

Vision taps that power, when it is vision bent upon obedience to the Head of the Church, whom God raised from the dead, "and made him sit at his right hand in the heavenly places, far above all rule and authority and power and dominion, and above every name that is named, not only in this age but also in that which is to come; and he has put all things under his feet and has made him head over all things for the church, which is his body, the fulness of him who fills all in all" (Eph. 1:20-23).

You cannot hope too much, envision too grandly, anticipate beyond His competence to bless. Therefore, in this chapter, we urge you to think big about diakonia! In so doing, you are simply forging practical dreams for the extension of His hands, His eyes and ears, and His willing feet into greater and greater ranges of service.

Think on things like these:

A. THE CHURCH AND THE WELFARE STATE

We live in the era of the welfare state.

The Church is largely responsible for the coming of the modern wel-

221

fare community. The Church could be largely responsible for purging welfare of its faults and problems. IF enough deacons caught the vision!

The Church brought about the welfare state in two ways:

1. As we have seen, the Word which the Church proclaims demands charity and justice for the poor. As this Word has permeated at least the Western world, an alerted public conscience has demanded public welfare. The Church is the parent of the welfare community.

2. But the Church did not, and perhaps in some respects could not, measure up to her own ideals. Not all the starving were fed, not all of the homeless given shelter, not all of the oppressed and exploited relieved. The cries of the needy ascended to heaven. The Lord answered with the welfare state. The government undertakes to do what the Church demands and then fails to achieve by herself.

Thus the Church is, both by commission and by omission, author of the welfare state. Deacons start from here. Government has undertaken to do what conscience, tutored out of the Scriptures, demands but fails, through the Church, entirely to achieve.

It is futile, now, to argue long over the rights and wrongs of the welfare state. History will not reverse itself.

What is important, with an eye on tomorrow, is to discern what constructive relations may be developed between alert diaconates and public welfare. And it is immediately obvious that diaconates are uniquely qualified to amend what are commonly perceived as defects in the welfare system. Consider items like these:

1. The deacon knows that all goods come from the hand of God. How stimulating for the needy welfaree to know that! How sobering for the chiseler! To know that God in heaven, looking down upon distress and responding to its cry, gives! This is exactly what welfare *is*! God's giving! You know that, but are you saying it? Are you teaching critics of the welfare system that God alone provides? That He is basic to welfare, and that without His Fatherly care neither birds of the air nor man nor beast would eat at all: "Look at the birds of the air: they neither sow nor reap nor gather into barns, and yet your heavenly Father feeds them. Are you not of more value than they?" (Matt. 6:26). God alone makes welfare possible. And this must always be known and said, even though under normal circumstances both He and we prefer that bread be given from above by way of our work here below: "Let the thief no longer steal, but rather let him labor, doing honest work with his hands," says St. Paul, though we must not

neglect what follows: "so that he may be able to give to those in need" (Eph. 4:28). The needy, whom the Lord supplies through the work of others, will ever be with us (John 12:8). Public welfare is one of the Lord's vehicles of provision for the needy as He also provides for the birds of the air. The needy should know this! So should the rest of us!

2. The state, however, appears in welfare as a neutral agent. Welfare workers may, or may not, take an interest in pointing recipients to the original Giver. This fact should burden the heart of the deacon, and of the Church. And becomes a driving incentive for deacons to get involved in the welfare system. Let God be properly honored, and thanked, for checks which come from the state but bear the return address of heaven! This is the basis for your interest in infiltrating the welfare process.

3. The state has no incentive to involve deacons as witnesses to the largesse of their Lord. But the state has an interest in efficiency, and economy, and getting the most out of every welfare dollar. And here the diaconate finds its lever! Welfare is notoriously the victim of what must be generalized regulations, made to apply to everyone and therefore applicable precisely to almost no one. Justice in the abstract, which is the only way that justice can be sought through legislation, comes in practice to be injustice, often, in the concrete. Some recipients get more, or other, than they need; some get less, even much less; while others are constantly tempted to "beat" the system in every way they can. Overburdened and usually unappreciated case workers struggle between bureaucracy and reality, frustrated by both. Many do heroic work against sometimes crushing odds. How much they could use the steady hand, firm faith, and constructive vision of the diaconate! Is such a combination impossible? Forbidden by the separation of Church and state? All depends upon how big you are willing to dream, and to work, and to hope, and to pray! Who holds "all authority in heaven and on earth" (Matt. 28:18)? Your Lord, or the state? What have you asked Him, and trusted Him, to do about welfare lately? He has given you every incentive to break, somehow, into the system!

4. Welfare, now, is commonly impersonal. Instead of creating community, it tends to destroy it. The case worker can rarely provide the personal touch which the love of Christ incites the deacon to radiate. How much more the welfare system, just as it is, could do for uniting the needy with the rest of society if the money and the assistance were given in the name of our common God and Father! You could see to

223

that, if welfare were somehow administered with your help! Even if you only went along with the case worker, and stayed behind to round out what he or she does in the neutral name of government. Have you ever thought of that? It will be probably your best chance of worming your way into an otherwise crumbling public diakonia.

Yes, we think of deliberate strategies. Your goal is to restore charity to the Church, which alone is fully capable of administering genuine diakonia! Perhaps you begin by tagging along, and staying to add in goods, or dollars, or teaching, or listening whatever love senses is lacking in the welfare program as it applies to this particular person or family. Perhaps, if you do that well, some deacons can join other Christians already serving the Lord as professional case workers. And, if the Lord wills, in due season much of the welfare relief done in your parish or community is finally largely funneled through your hands. Separation of Church and state? Leave that to the Lord. If your church building catches fire, the tax-supported fire department will put it out. Why? For the common good. It is the common good which bridges the gap so artificially created by—we think—a misunderstanding of the First Amendment of the U.S. Constitution. And it will be the common good which chooses the efficiency of diaconal administration of welfare funds once you have demonstrated that only be individual handling of cases can welfare dollars do the most good. Try it! And with the Lord be the rest!

Try it? Yes, in ways like these:

1. Get to know all you can—all there is to know—about public welfare in your community. If yours is a rural congregation, or one in a small community where welfare is unknown, be prepared to offer assistance to diaconates serving in urban areas where for some families welfare is by now a way of life.

2. Get to know welfare case workers. Some may be members of your own congregation. Some, perhaps many, will be servants of the same Lord you seek to honor. Find out how you might supplement their case work, both personally and with assistance in goods and funds.

3. You will no doubt discover that while welfare basically consists in "throwing money" at problems, there remains much left over for deacons to do. There might be cooperation with case workers in teaching right use of money, better ways of heating, of preparing food, of caring for household goods, and making clothes go a longer way. Deacons' wives and deaconesses might, with prudent care for personal safety, participate in such training, either in the home or at the

Church. Cooperation between welfare workers and collections of used clothing and staple foods maintained by volunteer workers at the Church opens doors.

4. Venture further by proposing pilot projects, in which the diaconate undertakes to assume the welfare load for selected families for a period of time. Do this under public scrutiny, with open books, and preconceived measures of efficiency. Let the figures speak. Let the families testify to what the touch of love adds to the welfare dollar. And thus undertake to convince the public mind that welfare need not be a "mess," if done in His name and through His—that is, your—hands! Do you know of a better gleam of hope to shed into a system of public charity no one likes but no ones know how to amend?

5. Do a study of what is so readily called "the separation of Church and state". Note that the First Amendment not only rejects public "establishment" (that is tax-support) of religion, but equally prohibits the state from interference with "the free exercise thereof". Some day that second clause will re-open the doors of public education to Christianity. But for now let the deacon observe that the so-called "wall of separation" is breached, as we have already observed, by the common good. Not only in the case of fire, but also when snow clogs the city streets leading to the Church—public vehicles plow them. Taxes are not collected from religious institutions. Police protect them, as does the military in time of war or riot. The common good binds Church and state together. And what greater contribution, now, to the common good than setting the welfare system back on its feet? Try it, and see!

6. Aim at the time when a certain share of welfare funds coming into your community are gratefully funneled through your hands. That this may, in the long run, oblige your congregation to join others in hiring a professional deacon or deaconess is all the more thrilling challenge!

Dream, deacon!

Your vision will never outreach God's grasp!

B. *SOCIAL STRUCTURE AND HUMAN NEED: MARXISM AND LIBERATION THEOLOGY*

There are those who believe that some social structures do impose poverty upon the many in the interests of the few. And they then conclude that the way to combat poverty is by way of revolutionary change of prevailing structures. This is the approach of Marxism. It is an approach more recently advocated by "liberation" theologians, who were once called "theologians of revolution". Many of these theologians speak out of the context of South America. They are quite willing to use Marxist analyses of social evil, and to suggest violent revolution as a way to eliminate human need.

The profile we have been developing in this *Handbook*, drawn we believe from the Bible, bears upon revolution as a means of structural change. Indeed, we think of universal diakonia as antidote to violent revolution.

We do believe that one crucial change in social structures contributes to human welfare at all levels of life, and that is the change from dictatorship and tyranny to the democratic state. But the violent, Marxist-oriented revolutions of this century have invariably been followed by extreme totalitarianism. The Communist state arising out of Marxist-inspired revolution is the ultimate in modern tyranny. Such structural change can never receive Christian endorsement.

Revolutions inspired by a Christian desire for liberty of worship have given birth to democratic institutions in the Netherlands, in France, in England, and in colonial America. Such structural change the Christian can endorse. It provides a political atmosphere in which the Church can breathe, preach, and freely witness in diakonia.

How, then, is diakonia an antidote to Marxist revolution?

Recall, first, your own history. Your office as deacon emerged in the Jerusalem Church in antithesis to a primitive communism, as we have already suggested in Chapter 9. The Church began with an attempt to "hold all things in common" (Acts 2:44, and 4:32). Very soon a whole class of members was neglected: "the Hellenists murmured against the Hebrews because their widows were neglected in the daily distribution" (Acts 6:1). The matter must have been serious, and the need extensive, because to meet it the Apostles recommended the appointment, not of one or two deacons, but of seven (Acts 6:3)!

Is this simply a passing matter only of historical interest to us?

We think not.

At issue is a very fundamental principle: the communal sharing of goods puts everyone at the mercy of the administrators. This is the basic defect of Communism. Where everyone theoretically "owns" everything, in practice no one can be assured of enjoying anything! And if this occurred within the Church, in the very flush of renewal after Christ's resurrection, how much more likely in the secular, totalitarian state! Indeed, how true of the Communist state, as the *Gulag* (prison system) of the Soviet union, and the refugees from Marxist states testify. Communism is not a viable alternative to ...

To what?

To diakonia, in a free society, done by a Church inspired to serve!

What the Lord said to His people Israel on the lips of Moses, the Church now proclaims to the world: "But there will be no poor among you...if only you will obey the voice of the Lord your God, being careful to do all his commandments which I command you this day" (Deut. 15:4-5).

Revolution to achieve the political freedom which permits full obedience to the Lord's commandments? Yes, by all means!

Revolution to achieve elimination of the poor through the installation of a Marxist, or any other, tyranny? Not at all! This is the lesson taught by the experience of the Jerusalem Church, and exhibited unmistakably among those who now suffer under Communist dictatorship. Let the deacon, and the young, and the liberation theologian take note!

Let it be conceded, in good faith, that the objective of liberation theology is humane. That the inspiration of such theology is the gross oppression of the weak and the poor by the rich and the powerful, often with the connivance of the Church. But the Word is sure: "But there will be no poor among you..." when? When the voice of the Lord is heard—from faithful, and in South America courageous, pulpits. And when the commandments of the Lord are obeyed. And such obedience, so far as the Body is corporately concerned, occurs in the work of the deacons!

In short, the deacon stands on the firing line in the on-going struggle between using structures of freedom for the witness of service, and perverting social structures into Marxist totalitarianism through violent revolution.

By pursuit of Marxist rather than democratic political goals, liberation theologians neglect a fundamental Biblical truth. At issue in all political struggle is freedom to proclaim and obey the Word, not control of production and distribution of goods. The Word freely spoken, and heard unto obedience, focuses on the distribution of goods—that, in a sense, is what this whole *Handbook* is about. But to put goods ahead of freedom for the Word is to lose both. So the Lord says to Satan: "Man shall not live by bread alone, but by every word that proceeds from the mouth of God" (Matt. 4:4, quoting Deut. 8:3).

And that is why the Communist states may provide more food, better housing, warmer clothing, and improved health care than what preceded them, only to find that all of these together do not satisfy man's hunger for freedom, that is, for opportunity to live in obedience to divine law.

The answer to Marxist structural change through violent revolution aimed at "dictatorship of the proletariat" was spoken by the Apostle Peter when Jesus asked His disciples if they, like the fickle crowd, would also desert Him. Peter replies, "Lord, to whom shall we go? You have the words of eternal life" (John 6:68). Revolution mounted to ensure the free preaching of these words is blessed. Revolution mounted to substitute another power for the creative force of His words only imposes the darkness of tyranny upon the soul.

But the deacon must remember that Marxism appealed to a world in which the Church did more speaking than obeying of the inspired Word. And some of those whom the Church never spoke for, and never served, turned in frustration to the "gospel according to Marx"—and still do! And they create powerful states which threaten the freedoms hard won for the West in Christian self-sacrifice.

Can human need be met while political freedom is preserved?

Yes, wherever diakonia perceives itself as crucial alternative to Marxism!

Do your part, wherever you as deacon are led.

What you do, in obedience to the words of eternal life, opens up an alternative to liberation theology and Marxist revolution.

Remember that your office was re-instated in the tradition of the Levites just because the Church does have a workable alternative to the failures of Communism! Make yourself and your calling just such a visible, witnessing alternative!

C. THE CHURCH AND INTERNATIONAL COMMUNITY

The Church of Jesus Christ is one!

One Head implies one Body: "There is one body and one Spirit, just as you were called to the one hope that belongs to your call, one Lord, one faith, one baptism, one God and Father of us all, who is above all and through all and in all" (Eph. 4:4-6).

The Church has for centuries confessed her unity: "I believe one, holy, catholic Church...." So goes the Apostles Creed.

Notice that the Church universal is the object of belief, not of sight:

"Now faith is the assurance of things hoped for, the conviction of things not seen" (Heb. 11:1). "I believe one, holy, catholic Church"— so millions of Christians have confessed across hundreds of years. So we join them today.

We know, however, that the Church universal does become visible in the local congregation. But the visible unity of the entire Church has never been achieved, and since the Reformation seems further removed than ever from accomplishment. Denominational divisions are not eclipsed by various national and international councils of churches. Nor has the breach between Protestantism and Rome ever been healed.

The visible institutional unity of the Church may never be achieved. Certainly in this era it remains an object of faith.

But while the institutional unity of the Church lags far behind our confession, a united diaconal witness opens a fruitful avenue to visible oneness.

The Church has but one Savior, Head, Master, Lord. And because this is so, the Church is, in His holy sight, one Body. And therefore diaconal hands are always His hands, no matter from which congregation they extend mercy. Diaconal eyes are always His eyes, no matter where opened to need. Diaconal ears are always His ears, whatever and wherever the cries they discern. Diaconal feet bent upon His errands are ever His feet no matter from where and to whom they hasten.

Remember this, deacons!

Yours is the overt and visible testimony to the unity of the Body of Christ. When your work is joined with that of other diaconates, you make still more visible the oneness of the Church. Deacons who lift their eyes to regional, national, and even international diakonia aspire to ever more visible witness to the one, holy, catholic Church! Diakonia pursued cooperatively becomes visible sinew binding the universal Church into objective unity.

Take inspiration from reflecting that the Church is the most enduring and most comprehensive of all institutions. No institution has lived longer and broken through more barriers of language, culture, and geography than has the Church. How better, then, to manifest this univeral and enduring Body than in united diakonia?

Consider your role in the Church of Jesus Christ as the true ecumenicity! Serve each circle of your responsibility (see Part V) in the light of contribution to making the whole Body visible before men!

Move progressively from narrower to broader Circles to expand the range of your witness to the unity of the Church.

On the one hand, do each duty, meet each challenge, seek out each opportunity to be truly a deacon as if the Lord had but your hand, eyes, ears, feet, and willing heart to serve Him. Knowing, on the other hand, that you are engaged with countless other deacons in making visible to a needy and desperate world the Church universal in which resides the only hope that the world has for both temporal and eternal felicity!

EPILOG

"Let me sing for my beloved a love song concerning his vineyard:
My beloved had a vineyard on a very fertile hill.
He digged it and cleared it of stones, and planted it with choice vines;
He built a watchtower in the midst of it,
And hewed out a wine vat in it:
And he looked for it to yield grapes...." (Is. 5:1-2).

He is still looking;
To the Church,
And to you, Deacon or Deaconess, whoever and wherever you are!

APPENDIX I - THE DEACON AS TRUSTEE

The function of trustee will involve at least some of the responsibilities discussed below.

A. *INCORPORATION*

Usually, incorporation takes place when a congregation is organized, and usually it is perpetual in nature. Proper incorporation, under relevant law, is important for claiming ownership to property, to qualify for tax exemptions (real estate and sales), to employ persons and withhold social security (FICA) taxes, and the like.

Deacons should know that there are two common methods of Church incorporation:

1. Trustee incorporation: trustees are elected or appointed from out of the congregation (often elders or deacons) who hold the Church's property in the name of the congregation.

2. Membership incorporation: the entire membership are trustees in

the eyes of the law, but will then be represented by an executive board chosen by the congregation.

The form of congregational incorporation may long ago have been forgotten. Routines proceed without any reference to it until, unhappily, differences develop within the Body which threaten a division. Then the questions of legal ownership of property, of endowments, etc. become acute and can end up in court. Trustees do well to know what their articles of incorporation are. This becomes urgent, also, when denominational tensions threaten a split, as too frequently occurs. What claim, if any, does the denomination have on the local congregation's property? Better these things are known under clear skies than when storms have arisen.

B. *THE TRUSTEE: REQUIREMENTS FOR*

The trustee may be defined as one who "manages for others," or as one who "holds title on behalf of others." To perform the tasks flowing from these definitions, the trustee should have some ability to manage affairs, to work well as member of a team, and knowledge and skills in property and financial matters. These qualifications must be kept in mind in the nomination and election, or appointment, of the trustee.

Discussion, below, of the tasks of the trustee will indicate the range of aptitudes which nominees or appointees should display.

C. *THE BOARD OF TRUSTEES: ORGANIZATION*

The board (or committee) of trustees should hold regularly scheduled meetings, probably not less than once a month.

A chairman should be chosen who has the ability to lead without domination, and who can conduct meetings sc as to draw all members into creative interaction. The chairman must prepare an agenda for each meeting, and a recording secretary must be appointed to keep minutes and records. The temptation to neglect proper minutes or bypass proper procedures will in the long run compromise the work of the trustees. The chairman or secretary must ensure that all necessary documents are safely stored and readily to hand, like: insurance policies, warranties, inspection reports, permits, etc.

At the first meeting of the new (or fiscal) year, sub-committees should be appointed or re-appointed, standing instructions and procedures reviewed or instituted, and various individual assignments made.

Division of labor within the board of trustees can be structured in terms of the two major functions the board performs. We outline these here, and will then discuss each in deatil.

1. Management functions: planning future developments, forseeing needs

preparing the annual budget, and its control

purchasing procedures, procurement, insurance

coordination of building use

liaison with Pastor(s), employees, governing body, congregation, outside agencies, etc.

2. Maintenance functions: maintenance control and inspection of building(s)

safety and fire inspection

energy conservation

boiler inspection

work detail

organ maintenance, piano tuning

A third planning committee function emerges if the congregation contemplates expansion of facilities or acquisition of additional ones. Important here is careful financial planning.

A clear profile of trustee obligations enables the chairman and the board to allocate responsibilities among those best equipped to do them well.

D. MANAGEMENT FUNCTIONS

1. Planning future developments, foreseeing needs:

We consider here the normal foresight required for constructive growth. If, as noted above, the congregation contemplates a major building program, or substantial acquisitions of, say, adjacent properties, this should be the province of a special committee probably involving others besides the trustees.

Prudent foresight involves:

a. Estimation of needs for space and facilities

b. Planned replacement or repair of existing facilities and equipment

c. Most effective use of facilities, especially in view of energy requirements

d. Painting, decorating, updating of facilities, equipment

e. Replacements of Bibles, hymnals, textbooks, play equipment

f. Adjustment of insurance coverage

g. Reckoning with inflation

The board of trustees may wish to distinguish between long range and short range planning, with perhaps a sub-committee for each or a program for each.

Planning is an on-going process. It is enriched and modified by inspection reports, new information, and first-hand observation. Let your program be your guide and aspiration but not your straitjacket.

2. Preparing the annual budget, and its control:

a. Point of departure is last year's budget: consider how well you were able to adhere to it; shortages, surpluses, weaknesses, etc.

b. Require that all budget requests be in on time, or early, with sufficient (but not unnecessary) justification.

c. Give special consideration to proposals of the salary committee, ensuring that all needs are considered and that inflation is allowed for.

d. Discuss all proposals in full board (or committee) meeting, taking care to avoid, if possible, future complaints of inequities.

e. After full discussion, appoint a special sub-committee to survey the whole, to make obvious adjustments, and to submit final proposal.

f. Submit final proposal to careful scrutiny, and be prepared to explain all items.

g. Agree in advance who will answer questions when the budget is presented for adoption.

h. Submit the budget to the governing board or congregation for discussion and acceptance.

Once adopted, the budget returns to the board of trustees or one of its sub-committees for on-going control. The following are involved:

a. The timing of disbursements to accord with income.

b. Balancing off of, say, energy bills in the winter with maintenance expenditures over the summer.

c. An agreed-upon order of priorities: what *must* be purchased, and what can, if necessary, wait?

d. The timing and letting of contracts must be viewed in the light of budget and cash flow.

e. Quarterly statements must be prepared so that the board can monitor expenditures against income and require general obedience to budgetary limits.

f. Certain prudent procedures should be mandatory, like:

1) Whoever signs the purchase order should not be same person who signs the check, so far as feasible.

2) Invoices should always be properly approved, and loose funds carefully accounted for.

3) Discount for prompt payment must not be neglected, and extra discount to churches pursued.

g. It is highly desirable that financial statements be shared with the congregation on a regular basis.

In all these matters it should be remembered that public scrutiny of non-profit and charitable organizations is becoming (and properly so) more intense. The Church must admit of neither scandal nor even hint of scandal in its handling of money and other material possessions.

3. Purchasing procedures, procurement, insurance:

a. Have purchases made, so far as possible, centrally and by one person, and select that person as having a knack for getting the best value.

b. If the purchase involves substantial funds (set a minimum amount), make it a practice to solicit several bids.

c. Check the possibility of ordering in bulk, through denominational or area cooperation.

d. Keep track of suppliers offering special discounts to churches.

e. If the Church has open accounts, for example in the purchase of janitorial supplies or choir music, place a limit on such accounts.

f. Except for minor routine purchases, require the use of order forms with one copy attached to the invoice before it is forwarded to the treasurer for payment.

g. Be sure that invoices are approved for payment only after quality and quantity have been carefully verified.

h. Be tactfully, but firmly, sure that purchases made from members of the congregation are fully competitive with those which might be made elsewhere; and avoid approving under the guise of a donation what is in fact simply a regular discount obtainable anywhere.

i. Insurance requires careful attention, especially in times of inflation, in matters like:

1) Keep policies current, with special attention to expiration

dates and extent of coverage and addenda received during the policy lifetime.

2) Get professional advice, if need be, as to the adequacy of the building and furnishings coverage in time of inflation.

3) Take special note of policies which are effective only if inspection is current, for example boiler insurance, elevator insurance, etc.

4) Consider special insurance coverage for staff and employees as various group plans become available.

5) From time to time let insurance coverages out for bid; not all rates are alike.

4. Coordination of building use:

On the one hand, a vast deal of capital investment in church property may often stand largely unused; on the other hand, at certain hours and on certain days there can be real competition for space. Use of the kitchen can become an issue, as can use of the sanctuary or auditorium, and the right of pupils to practice on the organ or piano, or of outside groups to use church facilities.

We recommend:

a. The adoption of a written policy, unless there already be one, governing the use of building and facilities, subject to amendment in the light of hitherto unforeseen difficulties; including:

1) Use of the sanctuary: for what purposes beyond those of the congregation itself? Rental? Sponsorship of outside groups from within the congregation? Use of the organ? At what fee?

2) Use of the kitchen: by whom, at what cost, etc.?

3) Use of other facilties, and by whom and on what terms?

b. When facilities are specially used, be sure that:

1) The rate is agreed upon, and someone sends the bill.

2) An arrangement is made for the use of keys, final closing, etc.

3) The custodian is remunerated for extra work (and by whom).

4) That the custodian has a written schedule of projected use well in advance and the extent of his obligations in each case.

c. One trustee or other appointee, or a small committee, should be obliged to carry out the policies governing use of building and facilities, and should serve as contact point for the user, for the custodian, and for any others who become involved.

A Church can make itself known and appreciated in the community if it is prudently generous with the public use of its facilities. But such use can become a source of friction within, and source of disappointment without, the congregation unless handled with care and precision developed out of careful, foresightful planning by the board of trustees or its representatives.

5. Liaison or communications:

The management of church property and activities becomes an involved business, complicated by the fact that so many people need to cooperate together, most of them on a part-time basis. The board of trustees must be sensitive, therefore, to the flow of information, the willingness of cooperation, and the achievement of results in all facets of management. Pastors and governing board must be kept informed, as must the congregation, on all matters affecting them.

E. *MAINTENANCE FUNCTIONS*

1. Maintenance control and inspection of building(s):

These inspections should be made regularly, preferably once a month. They should cover the work of the custodian(s), general wear and tear on the building and contents, with special attention to working elements in the plant like boilers, pumps, etc. Problems should be corrected immediately.

A check list for such inspections appears at the end of this Appendix.

2. Safety and fire inspection:

These inspections should be made quarterly. Watch for potential sources of danger. City and state agencies will furnish guides to such inspection. Catalogs of safety products offer valuable hints. Fires can be prevented by regular inspections by a certified electrician, and all electrical systems in the building should have an annual check. Correct deficiencies at once.

3. Energy conservation:

Most church buildings were erected before conservation of energy held high priority. Expert advice can make for savings through insulation and adjustment of heating facilities. Careful planning of activities, selected use of certain sections of the building, etc., can save fuel. Some recommendations for building alteration will require budgeting over several years. Begin with those promising most immediate results.

A check list of energy conserving measures can be obtained from governmental agencies and from public utility offices.

4. Boiler inspection:

Most insurance policies will require annual boiler or furnace inspection. Certificates of inspection should be posted in the boiler room, with another copy filed with the insurance policy. There should be no storage of any kind in furnace or boiler room. The room should be neat and clean, with door always closed and sufficient ventilation available (and used).

5. Work detail:

Many jobs required to maintain building and grounds can be done by volunteers from within the congregation, especially by retirees. Trustees should maintain a list of those who have skills they can be urged to share with the Church in this way. Call upon these persons directly rather than issuing a blanket call for volunteers. The work will be done on time, and usually most skillfully in this manner. Include congregational youth in these forms of service.

6. Organ maintenance, piano tuning:

A regular inspection by qualified professionals can save the congregation money in the long run and avoid much frustration besides. Skimping on such services becomes doubly costly. Keep a record of such inspections so that time does not slip unnoticed away since the last one.

F. *SUMMARY*

In the light of the variety of management and maintenance functions required to provide the congregation with the best in facilities and equipment, the board of trustees should allocate its time and efforts systematically. Assignments and responsibilities can best be made in terms of trustees' skills and interests, with everyone taking a broad interest in the integration of each part of the board's work.

G. *SUMMER MAINTENANCE CHECK LIST*

1. Exterior building repair
   a. Roof
   b. Painting
   c. Storm window/door removal and storage
2. Parking lot repair and re-striping
3. Lawn mower tune-up and sharpening - other tools

    4. Oiling of blowers and fans
    5. General cleanliness
    6. Boiler inspection - heating system
    7. Care of lawn/plantings/fertilizer/watering

H. *WINTER MAINTENANCE CHECK LIST*

    1. Clean or replace furnace filters
    2. Oil furnace motors and blowers
    3. Snow removal equipment in good order
    4. Ice removal supplies like salt and sand on hand
    5. Storm windows installed
    6. Snow plowing contracted or assigned
    7. Church vehicles winterized
    8. Exterior lighting for building and parking lot in order
    9. Protection for plants/bushes
   10. Mats in place for snow, mud, dirt
   11. General cleanliness and polish

I. *SAFETY AND FIRE INSPECTION CHECK LIST*

    1. Fire exit signs working
    2. Fire exits clear
    3. Fire routes clearly indicated
    4. Sprinkler valves open and pressure gauge checked
    5. Electrical cords in good condition
    6. Coat racks safely fastened
    7. Projection screens and wall maps properly secured
    8. Clear marking on steps
    9. Non-skid mats and safety treads where applicable

J. *BUILDING ENERGY AUDIT*

    1. Furnace vents and filters always clean
    2. Set-back thermostats checked periodically - proper settings and timing
    3. Check controller clocks after power outages: parking lots, hot water heaters, set-back thermostats, etc.
    4. Steam traps checked for proper operation, where steam heat is used

5. Door closers checked for proper operation
6. Weather stripping sound and effective
7. Add storm windows wherever possible
8. Light shut-off regulations posted and obeyed
9. Time clocks installed on water heaters, and working
10. Toilet and urinal check for flush valve leakage
11. Consider separate thermostats for different parts of building
12. Install or add insulation where possible
13. Consider low ceiling fans to circulate rising warm air

These check lists are suggestive only and can be adapted to each situation as required.

CATALOG OF USEFUL TEXTS

THE AGED

Ps. 71:9, 18 - Do not cast me off in the time of old age; forsake me not when my strength is spent.

So even to old age and gray hairs, O God, do not forsake me, till I proclaim thy might to all the generations to come.

Ps. 90:10 - The years of our life are threescore and ten, or even by reason of strength fourscore; yet their span is but toil and trouble; they are soon gone, and we fly away.

Ps. 92:14 - They still bring forth fruit in old age, they are ever full of sap and green.

Ps. 148:12-13 - Young men and maidens together, old men and children! Let them praise the name of the Lord, for his name alone is exalted; his glory is above earth and heaven.

Prov. 16:31 - Grey hair is a crown of glory; it is gained in a righteous life.

Is. 46:4 - Even to your old age I am he, and to gray hairs will I carry you. I have made, and I will bear; I will carry and I will save.

Luke 2:37 - And as a widow till she was eighty-four. She did not depart from the temple, worshipping with fasting and praying day and night.

Tit. 2:2-3 - Bid the older men be temperate, serious, sensible, sound in faith, in love, and in steadfastness. Bid the older women likewise to be reverent in behavior, not to be slanderers or slaves to drink.

TO BELIEVE IS TO SERVE

Ps. 37:3 - Trust in the Lord, and do good.

Matt. 3:8 - Bear fruit that befits your repentance.

Matt. 5:16 - Let your light so shine before men, that they may see your good works and give glory to your Father who is in heaven.

Matt. 10:42 - And whoever gives to one of these little ones even a cup of cold water because he is a disciple, truly, I say to you, he shall not lose his reward.

Matt. 25:45 - Then he will answer them, "Truly, I say to you, as you did it not to one of the least of these, you did it not to me".

John 3:21 - But he who does what is true comes to the light, that it may be clearly seen that his deeds have been wrought in God.

John 15:2, 14 - Every branch of mine that bears no fruit, he takes away, and every branch that does bear fruit he prunes, that it may bear more fruit. You are my friends if you do what I command you.

II Cor. 9:8 - And God is able to provide you with every blessing in abundance so that you may always have enough of everything and may provide in abundance for every good work.

Eph. 2:10 - For we are his workmanship, created in Christ Jesus for good works, which God prepared beforehand, that we should walk in them.

Phil. 1:11 - Be filled with the fruits of righteousness which come through Jesus Christ, to the glory and praise of God.

Col. 1:10 - Lead a life worthy of the Lord, fully pleasing to him, bearing fruit in every good work and increasing in the knowledge of God.

II Tim. 3:17 - That the man of God may be complete, equipped for every good work.

THE BLESSINGS AND BURDENS OF THE RICH

Genesis 13:2 - Now Abraham was very rich in cattle, in silver and in gold.

Deut. 8:8 - You shall remember the Lord your God, for it is he who gives you power to get wealth.

I Sam. 2:7 - The Lord makes poor and makes rich; he brings low, he also exalts.

Job 31:24-25, 28 - If I have made gold my trust, or called fine gold my confidence; if I have rejoiced because my wealth was great, or because my hand had gotten much; I should have been false to God above.

Ps. 49:16-17 - Be not afraid when one becomes rich, when the glory of his house increases. For when he dies he will carry nothing away, his glory will not go down after him.

Prov. 10:2, 22 - Treasures gained by wickedness do not profit, but righteousness delivers from death.

The blessing of the Lord makes rich, and he adds no sorrow with it.

Prov. 11:4, 28 - Riches do not profit in the day of wrath, but righteousness delivers from death.

He who trusts in his riches will wither, but the righteous will flourish like a green leaf.

Prov. 30:7-9 - Two things I ask of thee: deny them not to me before I die. Remove far from me falsehood and lying; give me neither poverty nor riches; feed me with the food that is needful for me, lest I be full, and deny thee, and say, "Who is the Lord" or lest I be poor, and steal, and profane the name of my God.

Eccl. 5:13-14 - There is a grievous evil which I have seen under the sun: riches were kept by their owner to his hurt, and those riches were lost in a bad venture; and he is father of a son, but he had nothing in his hand.

Eccl. 5:19 - Every man also to whom God has given wealth, and possessions and power to enjoy them,...this is the gift of God.

Eccl. 6:1-2 - There is an evil that I have seen under the sun, and it lies heavy upon men: a man to whom God gives wealth, possessions and honor, so that he lacks nothing of all that he desires, yet God does not give him power to enjoy them, but a stranger enjoys them; this is vanity; it is a sore affliction.

Jer. 9:23-24 - Thus says the Lord: "Let not the wise man glory in his wisdom, let not the mighty man glory in his might, let not the rich man glory in his riches; but let him who glories glory in this, that he understands and knows me, that I am the Lord who practice steadfast love, justice and righteousness in the earth, for in these things do I delight, says the Lord."

Matt. 6:19-21 - Do not lay up for yourselves treasures on earth, where moth and rust consume and where thieves break in and steal, but lay up for yourselves treasures in heaven, where neither moth nor rust consumes and where thieves do not break in and steal. For where your treasure is, there will your heart be also.

Matt. 6:24 - No one can serve two masters; for either he will hate the one and love the other, or he will be devoted to the one and despise the other. You cannot serve God and mammon.

Matt. 13:22 - As for that what was sown among thorns, this is he who hears the word, but the cares of the world and the delight in riches choke the word, and it proves unfruitful.

Luke 6:24 - Woe to you that are rich, for you have received your consolation.

Luke 12:15 - And he said to them, "Take heed, and beware of all covetousness; for a man's life does not consist in the abundance of his possessions."

I Tim. 6:10 - For the love of money is the root of all evils; it is through this craving that some have wandered away from the faith and pierced their hearts with many pangs.

I Tim. 6:17-19 - As for the rich in this world, charge them not to be haughty, nor to set their hopes on uncertain riches but on God who richly furnishes us with everything to enjoy. They are to do good, to be rich in good deeds, liberal and generous, thus laying up for themselves a good foundation for the future, so that they may take hold of the life which is life indeed.

Jas. 5:1 - Come now, you rich, weep and howl for the miseries that are coming upon you.

I John 2:15 - Do not love the world or the things in the world. If any one loves the world, love for the Father is not in him.

I John 3:17-18 - But if any one has the world's goods and sees his brother in need, yet closes his heart against him, how does God's love abide in him? Little children, let us not love in word or speech but in deed and in truth.

CARE FOR THE POOR

Ex. 22:25 - If you lend money to any of my people with you who is poor, you shall not be to him as a creditor, and you shall not exact interest from him.

Deut. 15:7-8 - If there is among you a poor man, one of your brothers, in any of your towns within your land which the Lord your God gives you, you shall not harden your heart or shut your hand against your poor brother, but you shall open your hand, and lend him sufficient for his need, whatever it may be.

Job 29:12 - I delivered the poor who cried, and the fatherless who had none to help him.

Ps. 82:4 - Rescue the weak and the needy; deliver them from the hand of the wicked.

Prov. 22:9 - He who has a bountiful eye will be blessed, for he shares his bread with the poor.

Isa. 58:7-8 - Is it not to share your bread with the hungry, and bring the homeless poor into your house; when you see the naked to cover him, and not to hide yourself from your own flesh? Then shall your light break forth like the dawn, and your healing shall spring up speedily; your righteousness shall go before you, the glory of the Lord shall be your rear guard.

Matt. 25:35 - For I was hungry and you gave me food, I was thirsty and you gave me drink, I was a stranger and you welcomed me.

Rom. 12:13 - Contribute to the needs of the saints, practice hospitality.

II Cor. 9:6, 9 - The point is this: he who sows sparingly will also reap sparingly, and he who sows bountifully will also reap bountifully. As it is written, "He scatters abroad, he gives to the poor; his righteousness endures for ever."

CHRIST AND THE DIACONATE

Mark 10:43-44; Matt. 20:27-28 - It shall not be so among you; but whoever would be great among you must be your servant, and whoever would be first among you must be your slave.

Matt. 23:11 - He who is the greatest among you shall be your servant.

Mark. 9:35 - If any one would be first, he must be last of all and servant of all.

Luke 12:37 - Blessed are those servants whom the master finds awake when he comes; truly I say to you, he will gird himself and have them sit at the table, and he will come and serve them.

Luke 22:26-27 - But not so among you; rather let the greatest among you become as the youngest, and the leader as one who serves. For which is the greatest, one who sits at table, or one who serves? Is it not the one who sits at table? But I am among you as one who serves. (I am as a deacon among you).

Matt. 25:40 - And the King will answer them, "Truly, I say to you, as you did to one of the least of these my brethren, you did it to me".

Matt. 25:41ff - Then he will say to those at his left hand.....

John 13:15-17 - For I have given you an example, that you also should do as I have done to you. Truly, truly, I say to you, a servant is not greater than his master, nor is he who is sent greater than he who sent him. If you know these things, blessed are you if you do them.

John. 13:34-35 - A new commandment I give to you, that you love one another; even as I have loved you, that you also love one another. By this all men will know that you are my disciples, if you have love for one another.

John 15:8 - By this my Father is glorified, that you bear much fruit, and so prove to be my disciples.

DILIGENCE AND MOTIVATION

Deut. 6:17 - You shall diligently keep the commandments of the Lord your God, and his testimonies, and his statutes, which he has commanded you.

Prov. 10:4 - A slack hand causes poverty, but the hand of the diligent makes rich.

Prov. 27:23 - Know well the condition of your flocks, and give attention to your herds.

Eccl. 9:10 - Whatever your hand finds to do, do it with your might....

Mark 1:35 - And in the morning, a great while before day, he rose and went out to a lonely place, and there he prayed.

Rom. 12:13 - Contribute to the needs of the saints, practice hospitality.

I Cor. 3:9 - For we are fellow workers for God; you are God's field, God's building.

II Cor. 8:7 - Now as you excel in everything, see that you excel in this gracious work also (liberality).

Eph. 4:28 - Let the thief no longer steal, but rather let him labor, doing honest work with his hands, so that he may give to those in need.

II. Thess. 3:10-11 - For even when we were with you, we gave you this command: If any one will not work, let him not eat. For we hear that some of you are living in idleness, mere busybodies, not doing any work.

Heb. 12:12-14 - Therefore lift your drooping hands, and strengthen your weak knees, and make straight paths for your feet, so that what is lame may not be put out of joint but rather be healed. Strive for peace with all men, and for the holiness without which no one will see the Lord.

GENEROSITY TOWARD FELLOW BELIEVERS

Rom. 12:13 - Contribute to the needs of the saints, practice hospitality.

Gal. 6:9-10 - And let us not grow weary in well-doing, for in due season we shall reap, if we do not lose heart. So then, as we have opportunity, let us do good to all men, and especially to those who are of the household of faith.

GOD'S USE OF THE RICH

Gen. 14:19-20 - And Melchizedek king of Salem brought out meat and wine; he was priest of God Most High. And he blessed him and said, "Blessed be Abram by God Most High, maker of heaven and earth; and blessed be God Most High, who has delivered your enemies into your hand!" And Abram gave him a tenth of everything.

Gen 45:11 - And there I (Joseph) will provide for you, for there are yet five years of famine to come; lest you and your household, and all that you have, come to poverty.

Ruth 2:1, 8-9 - Now Naomi had a kinsman of her husband's, a man of wealth whose name was Boaz. Then Boaz said to Ruth, "Now, listen my daughter, do not go to glean in another field or leave this one, but keep close to my maidens. Let your eye be upon the field which they are reaping, and go after them. Have I not charged the young men not to molest you? And when you are thirsty, go to the vessels and drink what the young men have drawn.''

II Sam. 19:32 - Barzillai was a very aged man, eighty years old; and he had provided the king with food while he stayed at Mahanaim; for he was a very wealthy man.

II Ki. 4:8 - One day Elisha went on to Shunem, where a wealthy woman lived, who urged him to eat some food. So whenever he passed that way, he would turn in there to eat food.

I Chr. 29:2 - So I (David) have provided for the house of my God, so far as I was able, the gold for the things of gold, the silver for the things of silver, and bronze for the things of bronze....

II Chr. 17:5, 7-9 - Therefore the Lord established the kingdom in his hand; and all Judah brought tribute to Jehoshaphat; and he had great riches and honor. In the third year of his reign he sent his princes,....to teach in the cities of Judah, and with them the Levites, ...and with these Levites, the priests....And they taught in Judah, having the book of the law of the Lord with them; they went through all the cities of Judah and taught among the people.

II Chr. 32:27, 30 - And Hezekiah had very great riches and honor...for God had given him very great possessions. This same Hezekiah closed the upper outlet of the waters of Gihon and directed them down to the west side of the city of David.

Job. 1:3; 29:12-17 - This man was the greatest of all the people of the East. I delivered the poor who cried, and the fatherless who had none to help him. The blessing of him who was about to perish came upon me, and I caused the widow's heart to sing for joy. I put on righteousness, and it clothed me; my justice was like a robe and a turban. I was eyes to the blind, and feet to the lame. I was a father to the poor, and I searched out the cause of him whom I did not know. I broke the fangs of the unrighteous, and made him drop his prey from his teeth.

Matt. 27:57-58 - When it was evening, there came a rich man from Arimathea, named Joseph, who also was a disciple of Jesus. He went to Pilate and asked for the body of Jesus. Then Pilate ordered it to be given to him.

Luke 19:8 - And Zachaeus stood and said to the Lord, "Behold, Lord, the half of my goods I give to the poor; and if I have defrauded any one of anything, I restore it fourfold."

Acts 9:36 - Now there was at Joppa a disciple named Tabitha, which means Dorcas or Gazelle. She was full of good works and acts of charity.

JUSTICE

Deut. 16:20 - Justice, and only justice, you shall follow, that you may live and inherit the land which the Lord your God gives you.

Ps. 82:3-4 - Give justice to the weak and the fatherless; maintain the right of the afflicted and the destitute. Rescue the weak and the needy; deliver them from the hand of the wicked.

Prov. 14:31 - He who oppresses a poor man insults his Maker, but he who is kind to the needy honors him.

Isa. 1:17 - Learn to do good; seek justice, correct oppression; defend the fatherless, plead for the widow.

Isa. 56:1 - Thus says the Lord: "Keep justice, and do righteousness, for soon my salvation will come, and my deliverance be revealed."

Amos 5:7, 11-12 - O you who turn justice to wormwood, and cast down righteousness to the earth! Therefore because you trample upon the poor and take from him exactions of wheat, you who afflict the righteous, who take a bribe, and turn aside the needy in the gate ....

Micah 6:8 - He has showed you, O man, what is good; and what does the Lord require of you but to do justice, and to love kindness, and to walk humbly with your God?

John 7:24 - Do not judge by appearances, but judge with right judgment.

I Cor. 13:6 - Love does not rejoice at wrong, but rejoices in the right.

LIBERALITY

Ex. 35:21 - And they came, every one whose heart stirred him, and every one whose spirit moved him, and brought the Lord's offering to be used for the tent of meeting, and for all its service, and for the holy garments.

Deut. 16:10, 17 - Then you shall keep the feast of weeks to the Lord your God with the tribute of a freewill offering from your hand, which you shall give as the Lord your God blesses you.

Every man shall give as he is able, according to the blessing of the Lord your God which he has given you.

Ps. 41:1 - Blessed is he who considers the poor!

Ps. 112:9 - He has distributed freely, he has given to the poor; his righteousness endures for ever, his horn is exalted in honor.

Prov. 11:25 - A liberal man will be enriched, and one who waters will himself be watered.

Prov. 22:9 - He who has a bountiful eye will be blessed, for he shares his bread with the poor.

Eccl. 11:1 - Cast your bread upon the waters, for you will find it after many days.

Isa. 58:10 - If you pour yourself out for the hungry and satisfy the desire of the afflicted, then shall your light rise in the darkness and your gloom be as the noonday.

Matt. 5:42 - Give to him who begs from you, and do not refuse him who would borrow from you.

Matt. 6:3-4 - But when you give alms, do not let your left hand know what your right hand is doing, so that your alms may be in secret, and your Father who sees in secret will reward you.

Luke 3:11 - And he answered them, "He who has two coats, let him share with him who has none; and he who has food, let him do likewise."

Luke 12:33 - Sell your possessions, and give alms; provide yourselves with purses that do not grow old, with a treasure in the heavens that does not fail, where no thief approaches and no moth destroys.

Act. 20:35 - In all things I have shown you that by so toiling one must help the weak, remembering the words of the Lord Jesus, how he said, "It is more blessed to give than to receive."

I Cor. 16:1 - Now concerning the contribution for the saints: as I directed the churches of Galatia, so you also are to do.

II Cor. 9:11-13 - You will be enriched in every way for great generosity, which through us will produce thanksgiving to God; for the rendering of this service not only supplies the wants of the saints but also overflows in many thanksgivings to God. Under the test of this service, you will glorify God by your obedience in acknowledging the gospel of Christ, and by the generosity of your contribution for them and for all others.

Hebr. 13:16 - Do not neglect to do good and to share what you have, for such sacrifices are pleasing to God.

I John 3:17-18 - But is any one has the world's goods and sees his brother in need, yet closes his heart against him, how does God's love abide in him? Little children, let us not love in word or speech but in deed and truth.

PREVENTION OF POVERTY IN ISRAEL

Ex. 21:2 - When you buy a Hebrew slave, he shall serve six years, and in the seventh he shall go out free, for nothing.

Ex. 22:25 - If you lend money to any of my people with you who is poor, you shall not be to him as a creditor, and you shall not exact interest from him.

Lev. 25:35-37 - And if your brother becomes poor, and cannot maintain himself with you, you shall maintain him; as a stranger and a sojourner he shall live with you. Take no interest from him or increase, but fear your God; that your brother may live beside you. You shall not lend him your money at interest nor give him your food for profit. I am the Lord your God...

(Also see the laws on the Sabbath year. Ex. 23:10-11, and Deut. 15:7-11; and the law on the year of jublilee, Lev. 25:10).

REWARDS FOR SERVICE

Deut. 4:40 - Therefore you shall keep his statutes and his commandments, which I command you this day, that it may go well with you, and with your children after you, and that you may prolong your days in the land which the Lord your God gives you forever.

Isa. 3:10 - Tell the righteous that it shall be well with them, for they shall eat the fruit of their deeds.

Matt. 16:27 - For the Son of man is to come with his angels in the glory of his Father, and then he will repay every man for what he has done.

Rom. 2:10 - But glory and honor and peace for every one who does good, the Jew first and also the Greek.

I Cor. 3:8 - He who plants and he who waters are equal, and each shall receive his wages according to his labor.

Tit. 2:7, 14 - Show yourself in all respects a model of good deeds. Who gave himself for us to redeem us from all iniquity and to purify for himself a people of his own who are zealous for good deeds.

Tit. 3:14 - And let our people learn to apply themselves to good deeds.

Heb. 10:23-24 - Let us hold fast the confession of our hope without wavering, for he who promised is faithful; and let us consider how to stir up one another to love and good works.

Heb. 10:36 - For you have need of endurance, so that you may do the will of God, and receive what is promised.

Jas. 1:22, 27 - But be doers of the word, and not hearers only, deceiving yourselves.

Religion that is pure and undefiled before God and the Father is this: to visit orphans and widows in their affliction, and to keep oneself unstained from the world.

Jas. 2:17, 20 - So faith by itself, if it has no works, is dead.

Do you want to be shown, you foolish fellow, that faith apart from works is barren?

Jas. 3:13 - Who is wise and understanding among you? By his good life let him show his works in the meekness of wisdom.

I Pet. 2:12 - Maintain good conduct among the Gentiles, so that in case they speak against you as wrongdoers, they may see your good deeds and glorify God on the day of visitation.

II Pet. 1:10-11 - Therefore, brethren, be the more zealous to confirm your call and election, for if you do this you shall never fall; so there will be richly provided for you an entrance into the eternal kingdom of our Lord and Savior Jesus Christ.

Rev. 2:10 - Be faithful unto death, and I will give you the crown of life.

Rev. 14:13 - And I heard a voice from heaven saying, "Write this: Blessed are the dead who die in the Lord henceforth."

"Blessed indeed," says the Spirit, "that they may rest from their labors, for their deeds follow them!"

Rev. 22:12 - Behold, I am coming soon, bringing my recompense, to repay every one for what he has done.

INDEX OF SCRIPTURAL REFERENCES

GENERAL INDEX

F

G.

M

P

S

T

U

V

W

Y